LONDON'S
RIVERSIDE

New London Bridge engraved by Edward William Cooke, 1833

ERIC de MARÉ

London's Riverside

PAST, PRESENT AND FUTURE

———

That which flows continually by some
sympathy is acceptable to the mind, as if thereby it
realised its own existence without end.

Richard Jefferies

MAX REINHARDT
LONDON

Printed and bound in Great Britain for
MAX REINHARDT LTD
10 Earlham Street, London w.c.2
by Richard Clay and Company, Ltd,
Bungay, Suffolk
Set in Monotype Plantin
First published 1958

CONTENTS

A carved keystone on the river front
of Somerset House

ILLUSTRATIONS

A map of 1827 on pages 184–5 from Chelsea to Greenwich will give the reader his general bearings in all periods.

*All the photographs, except that on page
213, were taken by the author*

INTRODUCTION

'In which respect an Alderman of London reasonably (as me thought) affirmed, that although London
received great nourishment by the residence of the
Prince, the repaire of the Parliament, and Courtes of
Justice, yet it stoode principally by the advantage of
the scituation upon the River.'

John Stow, 1603

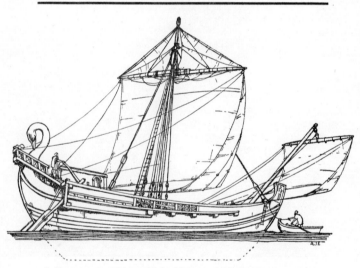

A Roman merchant ship which could have been seen on
London's riverside in the second century A.D. (Crown
Copyright, Science Museum, London)

Chelsea Reach from Battersea Bridge looking towards the Albert Bridge; far off on the right are the four chimneys of Battersea Power Station.

INTRODUCTION

THIS IS A guide for Everyman through Time and Place to the longest street of the largest port and of the most crowded city in the world—London's inexhaustible river.

Let's face it from the start: London is a mess—provisional, illogical and largely unplanned. Though the fabric of the riverside has changed time and again through the centuries and has often achieved great charm, that which we see today rarely reveals either charm, wholeness, dignity or beauty. It is as Nathaniel Hawthorne described it a century ago, 'the backside of the town bordered with the shabbiest, blackest, ugliest, meanest buildings I ever saw'.

But London's riverside is fascinating in spite of its seedy squalor, provided we explore it with some knowledge and with an open, tolerant eye. As Lautrec observed when he was painting the Moulin Rouge: 'Everywhere and always ugliness has its beautiful aspects; it is thrilling to discover them where nobody else has noticed them.'

So we shall feel for the firm structural skeleton beneath the grey skin and the adipose flesh. We shall look not only for the familiar landmarks but also for the incidental beauties of the riverside to be discovered in the small detail, in the chance vista, in some lyrical mood of the weather, or in some old and evocative association.

London is the Scattered City as opposed to the Concentrated City of the Continent—Rasmussen's tolerant, undespotic city. In this character lie both its faults and its virtues. Its lack of grand, open and premeditated vistas is summed up in the Cockney song:

> *Wiv a ladder and some glasses*
> *You could see to 'Ackney marshes*
> *If it wasn't for the 'ouses in between.*

Along the river perhaps only three scenes approach nobility—Battersea Power Station floodlit on a misty night, the view from Hungerford Bridge towards the east where the King's Reach makes its majestic sweep towards the City, and Greenwich Hospital seen from the Isle of Dogs at any time when the tide is in. Except at Chelsea, Georgian and domestic, to the west, the rest is mostly confusion.

13

Battersea Power Station at night.

⟨ RIVER DEPICTIONS

Yet confusion can, by chance and thanks mainly to the water, often produce its own kind of beauty. That riverside dweller, Henry James, for one, saw the riverside with more affection than his compatriot Hawthorne: 'I like the Thames best when it is all dyed and disfigured with the town and you look from bridge to bridge—they seem wonderfully big and dim—over the brown, greasy current, the barges and the penny steamers, the black, sordid, heterogeneous shores. This prospect, of which so many elements are ignoble, etches itself to the eye of the lover of "bits" with a power that is perhaps worthy of a better cause.'

A young Chinese artist, Tseng Yu, also saw the river in the same kind of way not long ago on a visit to London: 'The beauty of London lies not on her bright flower and tender trees but on her dirt, filth, rust, smog and the magnificent slum and swamp along the bank of Thames.'

Many other foreign artists have depicted the river with a kind of ecstasy, especially men like Monet and the nocturnal Whistler. How different are their vague, impressionistic and romantic views from the sharp and detailed eighteenth-century visions of Canaletto and Samuel Scott, so sunny, classical and sparkling. Theirs was another London. To-day it is in the twilit monochrome of a November evening when a great black hulk of a lighter floats solemnly upstream on the tide, the water-man still as a statue at his sweep, when the lights begin to flicker across the oily water, when only the masses of the buildings are bold and all the dull details have been erased by darkness, that the river looks its best. And no urban ugliness can dominate for ever where water is shimmering, and dignified boats are afloat—least of all in that low light of dusk or dawn or fog by which the writers and artists of later years have evoked the *genius loci* of the river. This is Whistler's river when 'the evening mist clothes the riverside with poetry as with a veil, and the poor buildings lose themselves in the dim sky, and the tall chimneys become campanili, and the warehouses are palaces in the night'.

Perhaps every land is more exciting to the foreign eye than home, but the river can also stimulate the imagination of the Londoner himself with its rich historical associations, its half-hidden cosmopolitan life among the docks, its odd and suggestive medley of names—Mermaid Causeway, Cherry Garden Pier, Golden Anchor Stairs, Galleons Reach, 'Limey-Housey Causeway'—and its ancient maritime links with every far-off corner of the world. Richard Jefferies wisely observed that until it is painted, or sung by poets and described by writers, nothing is human; among many other descriptive writers, he has helped to human-ise London's riverside in that special way of his which seems to sense all things with the vivid percipience of fever. Hear him, not coughing in the fog now, but meditating on a hot, sunny day above the Pool:

'The bright morning sun of summer heated the eastern parapet of London Bridge; I stayed in the recess to acknowledge it. The smooth water was a broad sheen of light, the built-up river flowed calm and silent by a thousand doors, rippling only where the stream chafed against a chain. Red pennants drooped, gilded vanes gleamed on polished masts, black-pitched hulls glistened like a black rook's feathers in sun-light; the clear air cut out the forward angles of the warehouses, the shadowed wharves were quiet in the shadows that carried light; far down the ships that were hauling out moved in repose, and with the stream floated away into the summer mist. There was a faint blue colour in the air hovering between the built-up banks, against the lit walls, in the hollows of the houses. The swallows wheeled and climbed, twittered

'The tall chimneys become campanili, and the warehouses are palaces in the night.' A view from Wapping River-Police Station towards Rotherhithe; on the left is the tower of St. Mary's Church.

and glided downwards. Burning on, the great sun stood in the sky, heating the parapet, glowing steadfastly upon me as when I rested in the narrow valley grooved out in prehistoric times. Burning on steadfast, and ever present as my thought. Lighting the broad river, the broad walls; lighting the least speck of dust; lighting the great heaven; gleaming on my finger-nail. The fixed point of day—the sun.'

Or try that river lover and champion of waterway revival, Sir Alan Herbert, recalling a dark voyage up river sometime in the 'thirties:

'And in the evening, a little after sunset, you may enjoy what I judge to be the most lovely experience in London—the journey through the dusk from Wapping to Westminster. There are not many lights in the Pool; the warehouses are dark, become dignified and mysterious palaces, fortresses, or temples . . . the Tower Bridge is a colourless outline, a children's toy, against the faint rose of the western sky, and St. Paul's dome, beyond, is only the ghost of a dome. . . . The bridges come thick and fast—Cannon Street and Southwark, and St. Paul's and Blackfriars. It is dark and alarming under the cavernous arches where the tide rushes fiercely round the piers, gleaming like swift snakes in the dim light. . . . And you come out through Blackfriars Bridge at last into a fairyland of light and shadow, water tumbling and sparkling, water ebony and smooth. . . . You have come back from the rough haunts of commerce to the elegant heart of London; and it is as if the city had been illumin- ated this night for your particular benefit. But London hangs out the same lights every night for all of us; only a few of us see them, for we travel by omnibus and tram and motor-car.'

⟦ LONDON IS THE RIVER

That is the trouble with the river today—we turn our backs on it. It is too inaccessible to the pedestrian and no longer seems to belong to the town. All its great dockyards—seventy miles of wharf and quay—are hidden from us behind immense walls, and a life, mysterious and apart, is lived upon it by the select few. We cross the river as fast as we can, never pausing to enjoy the breezy views to left and right as we roar across a bridge. When we come down to its side we tear along the embank- ments with their heavy and interminable granite walls which cut us off too firmly from the river's alien world—rarely pausing to enjoy its visual and historic offerings.

Yet through all London's history of two thousand years, right up to the nineteenth century, the river was woven into the texture of the Lon- doner's daily life as his busy high street, broad and noble, where going and coming was easier, more rapid and more pleasant than in the built- up hinterland of congealed houses. Along and beside the river, when the docks formed part of the waterfront and broad quays stood beside the river, the whole population toiled and revelled and loafed. The river was London then, and London was the river. So it is today, but in a much less direct and less colourful way.

Indeed, London owes its very birth, its size and strength and its whole long life to its river, and so to explore the river is to explore London it- self. London may, in fact, be said to have spread inland from the Thames, and most of the City's great architectural monuments lie along its banks: Chelsea Hospital, Greenwich Hospital, the Hall and Abbey of Westminster, Lambeth Palace, Somerset House, the Customs House, Southwark Cathedral, the Tower. Even the City's greatest monument, St. Paul's Cathedral, rises near the river and its dome dominates every

B

'London hangs out the same lights every night for all of us.' Westminster from the roof of the Royal Festival Hall.

river scene towards the east. Many small but notable buildings, like the old parish churches, stand on or near the riverside too, and many pleasant oases of green, among them Battersea Park and its new Pleasure Gardens, carrying on the old traditions of Vauxhall, Ranelagh and Cremorne. There are the riverside pubs, the oddities, the Georgian houses with their trim classic doorways (including, of course, those of the most delightful of all London streets, Chelsea's Cheyne Walk). And the smells: the special muddy smell when the tide is low, others more exotic and spicy down in Wapping, and that mysterious feminine perfume which eternally haunts the masculine gloom of French Ordinary Court.

PAST, PRESENT AND FUTURE

The story of London's riverside is a long and confused one, and this book attempts to unravel its tangled skeins and to weave from them clear, articulate and formalised patterns.

I have tried here to penetrate the personality of London's riverside: in a way, to psycho-analyse it. That has a peculiar fascination. The biographer, Hesketh Pearson, has recorded a talk he once had with H. G. Wells:

'Then we had a slight breeze. I had manifested a biographical interest in some of the people who had lived in Hanover Terrace, such as Dickens and Wilkie Collins, and he irritably exclaimed: "Why do people live in the past?" "Because the past, which we know, is more interesting than the future, which we don't know," I replied. "Isn't the present good enough for you?" "Yes, quite. But one of its principal charms is that it enshrines the past." '

That was a good riposte and gives the reason why both past and past-in-present will chiefly interest us here. We shall sail through twenty centuries in the first part of the book, helped greatly in our explorations by the old delineators and map-makers, from Wyngaerde to Havell, from Agas to Mogg. Then we shall make a landfall at the present day and explore the riverside on foot. Finally we shall sail off again, this time into the future, for creating the future as we would like it to be has its charms too. Like my *Time on the Thames*, which, though mainly a guide to the tideless river of the pleasure-boat, includes proposals for maintaining the river style as a unique National (Strip) Park, this work also tries to provide a final, constructive bias. That the riverside squalor may possess its negative, residual and incidental attractions gives no excuse for accepting that squalor indefinitely, and it is essential, if only for the sake of urbanity and pleasure, to bring the river back once more into our daily life.

【 HOW LONDON WAS BORN

Meanwhile let us at once take a preliminary trip back in time in order to discover why London was born and why it is true to say that London *is* the river.

Rivers, more than other geographical elements, have made human history, not least in these watery islands. London has made history, and the Thames has made London. No other town in Europe has been so completely dependent upon its river as London. A river has many advantages to men: it provides an easy means of travel where the going on land is difficult, and, on account of the low friction of movement in water, it affords an economical means of transport. It also forms a defensive barrier. It may supply an important food in its fish and it always provides that first need—drinking-water. It was as a means of travel, as a highway, that the Thames became and remained of greatest importance in human affairs, chiefly because it ran east towards the Continent; it was also served well by the tides, and it ran fairly slowly, so that it was easily navigable in either direction. Moreover, its non-tidal, but still navigable, length ran across the greater part of the island through its most fertile, and for centuries its most productive, region.

But why was London born and why did it survive and grow just where it did along the river? As well as being an advantage, a river is a nuisance, because it forms a barrier to communication. A river must therefore be bridged at the nearest possible point to its mouth, because in that way long detours inland to a crossing are avoided. Along the whole upper stretch of the tidal Thames there is one place only where two spurs of high, dry and gravelly land face each other fairly close to the river—on the south bank at Southwark and on the north bank at the foot of the eastern one of the two hills on which the City stands. Here, then, the most important crossing of the Thames was bound to be built.

In early times the river was probably fordable at Westminster, but only at low tide. The lowest point which was fordable *at any time* was miles upstream—at Wallingford in Berkshire. All the fords nearer London were comparatively unimportant because they were unreliable. That is why Wallingford has so long and vital a history. Today it is a small, sleepy town served only by a branch railway line, but centuries ago it was one of the most important centres in the country, settled in turn by Britons, Romans, Saxons and Danes, and there occurred one of the main events in our history—the crossing of the river by William the Conqueror on his march to occupy London. Significantly, only two towns of any size in the British Isles do not lie by, or near, an ancient ford or bridge-head; they are Malvern and Shaftesbury. In fact, as a glance at the map will show, our whole road system is based on the linking together of fords and bridges, and therefore of the settlements they generated.

Today London has many bridges, but right up to 1749, when the first Westminster Bridge was erected, it had only one. Once established, the Bridge inevitably developed into the centre on which converged the commerce not only of Southern England, but also of all that from the midlands and the north on its journey to the Continent. The chief highways of the country running from north and south (especially from the port

'The sharp and detailed eighteenth-century visions of Canaletto and Samuel Scott, so sunny, classical and sparkling.' An archway of old Westminster Bridge by Scott looking north. (Reproduced by courtesy of the Trustees of the Tate Gallery)

of Dover) would make straight for the Bridge, and at the same time, since the Bridge itself would form a barrier across the river, sea-going vessels would come to rest there by the quays, while the smaller boats coming down from the upper reaches would stop there to tranship their cargoes. So the Bridge would form, not only a crossing, but a terminus and a centre of transhipment between the maritime and the inland trade. And the Bridge would divide the river, creating in time two distinct riverside cultures on its either side.

Contributory factors helped to build the City. The tributary streams of the Thames furnished a natural position of defence, and along the river were the accommodating deep-water harbours of the Fleet River, Dowgate (at Walbrook's mouth, just to the west of Cannon Street Station), Billingsgate and Queenhithe. In Romano-British times the Lea provided a useful communication between London and Verulam (St. Albans), which was one of the chief centres of the country. Finally London was a convenient market for that considerable fishing industry of the river which flourished, even in salmon, before the water became thoroughly polluted only a century ago by the sewage of the capital.

So far as is known, the Romans were the first to build a bridge across the Thames at London, and they chose a spot for the Bridge which had the added attraction of being the point along the river conveniently nearest to the south coast and thence across the Channel to Gaul and to Rome. The first road the Romans built in these islands was probably Watling Street, which led straight from *Portus Dubris* (Dover) to *Verulam* and the North. This road has been traced as far north as Shooter's Hill at Blackheath on the south of the river, and down the Edgware Road as far as Hyde Park Corner on the north of the river. If these two points are joined on the map they will intersect the Thames round about Westminster Bridge, and this suggests that the first Roman crossing may not have been a bridge, but a ford at Westminster, and that later the road was diverted to cross the river by bridge close to where the present London Bridge now stands. An alternative conjecture is that, since the part of Watling Street running south of the river points directly, not to Westminster, but to Lambeth, and since, if it went there, it would have been provided with firm going, the first Roman crossing may have been by ferry. A ferry is known to have plied for centuries from the neighbourhood of Lambeth Palace across to Horseferry Road (a telling place-name).

⟨ THE GREAT MART

London has been, first, last and always, a market. Indeed, the first mention of London on record is a phrase by Tacitus which refers to the town specifically as such; though well defended, it was never a military station in Roman days. It is easy to see why London became a traders' settlement; it is less easy to understand why the City not only maintained its unique position through the centuries (quite naturally and never by a forced artificiality), but also expanded rapidly, first during the Roman occupation and later after the Dark Ages, until it has finally spread like moss on a rock into the great, crazy megalopolis we know today—so vast, uneconomical, disordered and, in the main, so drab and ugly a wilderness of brickwork, that many, no doubt in a wishful spirit, have prophesied its inevitable and catastrophic doom. Take, for example, Richard Jefferies's grim vision in his *After London*: 'Thus the low-lying parts of the mighty city of London became . . . a vast stagnant swamp, which no man dare enter, since death would be his inevitable fate. There exhales from this oozy mass so fatal a vapour that no animal can endure it. The black water bears a greenish-brown floating scum, which for ever bubbles up from the putrid mud of the bottom. . . . There are no fishes, neither can eels exist in the mud, nor even newts. It is dead.'

In spite of its sweet retreats and its many fascinations, London is now a consuming cancer, which has been allowed to grow without foresight ever since it burst out of its walls in the seventeenth century and began to devour, one after another, the rural village outposts. It still goes on growing, in spite of the remedial proposals of the planners—proposals which have been numerous, but mostly tepid, piecemeal and impotent. As that normally cheerful Londoner, Samuel Pepys, would sigh: 'What will be the end of it, God knows.'

As a market London has continually expanded because the economic strength of a place lies less in its productive power than in its spending and consuming power—its capacity for effective demand. As a rich centre of commerce and exchange, with a large population and a spirit of independence, London became the strategic focus of the land, the focus also of the machinery of finance, of shipping exchange and, to include Westminster and the Strand, of administration and the law, as well as of the Court and of the powerful and wealthy aristocracy; finally, therefore, it became a centre of culture, entertainment and the arts. For all its faults and its decadence, London remains, as it has always been, an organic, if tangled growth, grotesque, but tremendously alive.

Though it has always possessed its many small-sized industries, it is as a mart with an ever-increasing momentum that London has produced its vitality, until today its wharves and docks extend miles down-river as far as Tilbury, and the City of London is not only a great depository, but also a great counting-house.

Apart from the lure of the market-place, London's growth had other causes. For one thing, the City has always possessed local security based upon a large, and as a whole, wealthy, vigorous and independent burgher population using a well-protected, land-locked port. Thus London was not only a valuable recruiting centre in times of warfare or rebellion, but also provided a supply base which could be re-stocked by way of the river. As a result, throughout England's history, the side which had London as an ally was always the winner. Even the Conqueror found it inadvisable to attack London directly, and, after conquering, was careful to recognise the pride, power and military skill of its citizens —at least on the north bank, for he did destroy Southwark as a warning.

Secondly, in spite of its geographical eccentricity to the south and

east, London was, in fact, for centuries not merely the nexus of communications by land and water, but lay at the economic centre of gravity
of the country, the centre of the wide pasturage which, after the Agrarian
Revolution, produced the staple export of wool.

Thirdly, the river provided natural ease of approach for foreign ships
—a deep channel, no high obstacles to cut off the wind, no narrows or
islands, and a useful, swinging, double tide to help the square-rigged
ships along.

Fourthly, the City provided the foreign merchants with the certainty
that a market was waiting at the port for their goods—with the certainty,
too, that they could refill the holds for the return journey, not with
wasteful ballast, but with other goods for sale and profit.

Lastly, the port lay at a convenient position as a half-way house for
trading exchange between the lands of the North Sea and the Baltic on
the one hand, and those of the Channel, the Bay of Biscay and the Medi-

'The magnificent slum and swamp along the bank of Thames.'
St. Paul's Cathedral and the City sketched from Bankside by
Tseng Yu, a Chinese artist.

terranean on the other—that is, between two distinct cultural areas
called, very broadly, the Teutonic and the Latin.

❲ THE CENTRE STILL

London is not a natural centre for the export of manufactured goods and
coal, which replaced wool as our chief exports after the Industrial Revolution. Nor is the river approach near the City deep or wide enough
readily to accommodate large modern vessels. London has therefore become less a point of transhipment than it was once. Yet all through the
nineteenth century, and during the early part of the twentieth, enormous
new enclosed docks were being built in the sodden shores of London's
river, moving always away from the original port eastward towards the
wider estuary and the sea. And it is remarkable that, though the main

industrial activities of this country have moved northward, and though the canals did focus on Birmingham, the centre of gravity of the country has remained at London so firmly that every important railway line and every important trunk road now terminates there.

Through the city's hum the quiet river still runs, dark, grubby and now rather empty above the Bridge compared with the days gone by, when here it was crowded, fresh and full of fish. But it is still as stately in its flowing as it appeared so long ago to the Roman soldiers when they first gazed across its glittering marshes towards the two green and rounded hills of their future provincial town. It is to the river and its old life that the amorphous ant-heap of today owes whatever dignity and æsthetic and climactic meaning it still possesses.

We shall make a thorough exploration now. But who can ever really know London, even its river parts? I shall try here to evoke the realities of its riverside through the years, but in the end we shall see the truth of Elizabeth Bowen's comment: 'Probably the magic of a city, as of a person, resides in its incapacity to be known, and the necessity therefore that it should be imagined.'

PART I

PANORAMAS OF THE PAST

'To this City, Merchants bring in Wares by Ships from every Nation under Heaven. The Arabian sends his Gold, the Sabean his Frankincense and Spices, the Scythian Arms, Oil of Palms from the plentiful Wood: Babylon her fat Soil, and Nilus his precious Stone: the Seres send purple Garments: they and Norway and Russia Trouts, Furs and Sables: and the French their Wines.'

William Fitzstephen,
a twelfth-century monk

A detail from Wyngaerde's panorama showing Billingsgate harbour in 1550.

The Tower of London and the Bridge with its rebuilt central chapel at the end of the fifteenth century. This is the earliest known drawing of the Bridge. (From a print of a Flemish illumination in the British Museum)

1 | Where the Roman Roads Converged

No SETTLEMENT OF any importance existed on the site of London before the Legions arrived. The Elizabethan tailor and antiquary John Stow, on whose quaint writings all subsequent histories of London are based, mentions the prehistoric town of Troynovant as a possible precursor of London, but that is the legend of a legend. The river itself, however, is one of the oldest in the world and was flowing long before human records began, probably as a tributary of the Rhine when England was part of the Continent. Where London stands now it poured for long ages through a deep ravine.

As the Celtic place-names reveal, the banks of the Thames, where the beds of gravel held back the forests, were settled at a prehistoric period, and the river has served as a highway for foreign trade and immigration at least since the Stone Age. The name London, like the name Thames, may be Celtic in origin, although its first recorded mention is in the Latin form, *Londinium*. Various roots have been suggested: that it came from the Old Celtic word *londos*, meaning fierce; that it was a place occupied by a Celtic family called *Londinos*; that London is a corruption of the Welsh words *Llyn Din*, meaning the city or fortress on the lake (for the existence of which lake there is no evidence); that it is a Gaelic compound, *Lon* meaning a plain and *dun* a hill (Cornhill); that it was called after *Londinières* in Belgium by Belgic invaders.

The possible Celtic derivation is the only indication that a pre-Roman settlement existed on the site, and even that is weak evidence, because the Roman invaders often gave native names to the colonial towns and forts they founded. The existence at London of any settlement bigger than a small landing-station and an anchorage, where a few solid merchant vessels from Gaul might have floated now and then, round about the time Jesus was preaching rebellion in Palestine, is unlikely. We can thus say with confidence that as a port and a colony London began with the Roman colonisation.

(THE SITE

Let us now picture the site of London-to-be as it appeared at the time of the final Roman invasion by the army of Claudius in the year A.D. 43.

Today much of the south bank is below high-water level and is protected from floods by some seven miles of embankment. But at the time of London's foundation the river ran more than fifteen feet below its present level. Hence the selection by the Romans of Southwark as a bridgehead, for this lay at that time high and dry above the marshy land. Today the tidal limit of the river is at Teddington, though before the pound locks were built the tide could be felt at times as high up as Staines. In Roman days, however, the shallower, wider, lower river may have ceased its ebbing and flowing at or near the site of London, probably where Chelsea is now. That would have added another reason to the ones already given why the Romans, with their practised judgement, selected the place for their crossing and their port; the advantage to shipping of the tide would be retained, while the crossing, whether ford, bridge or ferry, would be little disturbed by the tidal movements.

The river flowed in its great curves as now, but at low tide none of that sticky black slime we see today would have been exposed: only clean broad banks of sand and gravel. At Westminster, along the Surrey shore, at the mouths of the little tributaries of the Fleet and the Walbrook, and at the estuary of the River Lea, there was marshy land and labyrinths of creeks running among osiers and reeds, the haunt of wading-birds and of wild-looking men fishing from coracles. Above the marshes rose land covered with scrub and an occasional clump of trees, while northwards in the distance stood the wooded heights (now Highgate and Hampstead) where the great Forest of Middlesex began. Not far from the river two flat-topped hills ran up fairly steeply to a height of about fifty feet above the river, and these were divided by a valley along which flowed a clear stream with its source only a mile from the river, a stream which was to become known as the Waelbroc or Walbrook.

On those twin breasts were to be built both the Roman town in its final form and the later intra-mural city of the Middle Ages. At the crown of the western hill today stands St. Paul's Cathedral, and on the crown of the eastern hill Leadenhall Market; now the Walbrook is hidden underground and runs below the Bank of England and the Mansion House, entering the Thames as a trickle just to the west of Cannon Street Station. The landscape where the Romans began to build their settlement was a wild one and only here and there would any signs of humanity be visible in the form of a primitive hut or two made of wattle and daub and roofed with rushes.

A Roman port with its wharves and warehouses was growing at London even before the defeat of Caractacus in the days of Vespasian, and by then a rough bridge of timber had no doubt been built, though no record of a bridge exists before that of A.D. 984, when it was written in Anglo-Saxon: 'And that district at Aegeleswyrthe had formerly condemned a widow and her son because they had driven iron pins into [a figure of] Aelsie, Wulfstane's father, and that became detected, and they drew that crime forth from the widow's chamber. Then they took that woman and drowned her at London Bridge and her son escaped and was outlawed.'

Though the Romans built no great aqueducts or bridges of stone in these islands whose fame has survived, and though only a few remains of their bridges have been found here, they must have built many bridges to serve their roads. Remains are probably few because they used timber, of which there was a plentiful supply ready to hand. We can therefore assume that the Romans hastened to erect a bridge of timber at the London crossing at an early date, and that such a bridge survived there at least until the Roman legions were recalled to Rome and the Dark Ages descended.

Evidence of a Roman bridge at London was discovered when the mediæval bridge was demolished during the early nineteenth century; many Roman coins were dredged up when the piers were removed, and they were brought up in chronological order in dates covering five centuries. These may, of course, have been driven there by the flow of the river, but it is possible on the other hand that they were thrown into the water through hundreds of years to appease the spirits who reside in rivers (a ceremony which persists to this day, as at the Forth Bridge, where, they say, a pound's worth of pennies is picked up every summer month at the foot of the Dalmeny pier). In 1834 a fine bronze head of the Emperor Hadrian, who visited London, was also dredged up from the river near the old bridge at the Southwark end, and this can be seen at the British Museum. Stout oak piles were also found at this time covered with shoes of a hard iron which only the Romans were then able to forge.

The Roman bridge was no doubt rebuilt a number of times of timber, though it may have come to possess stone abutments and piers, and also a drawbridge at its centre to allow vessels to pass upstream. The Southwark

(South Work) head was probably defended with a tower or pair of towers either of timber or stone. The bridge ran just east of the present London Bridge towards the more easterly of the two hills. Some say that a second bridge was erected in Hadrian's time, but no clear evidence of this exists.

Before the second decade of the final conquest the port was already thriving as an *oppidum* having considerable traffic in trading vessels, as we can gather from Tacitus, who was particularly interested in Britain because his father-in-law, Julius Agricola, was governor there. Round about A.D. 100 he described the London of his time as a town 'not dignified with the name of *colonia*, but celebrated for its concourse of merchants and abundance of goods'. Timber buildings covered the hill to the east and a town hall or basilica (the prototype of the early Christian Church) faced a forum or market-place at the town centre. Some defensive earthworks may at first have surrounded the settlement which huddled around the banks of the Walbrook and up Cornhill.

Here by the Walbrook in early years were a half-fortified Roman port of moderate size and unpretentious buildings of wood, plaster and thatch. Then in A.D. 61, in the time of Nero, London's first blow fell. Boudicca, the Queen of the East Anglian tribe of the Iceni, laid the town to waste—in the few but adequate words of Tacitus: by massacre, gibbets, fire and crucifixion. She and her people had become enraged by the abuses of the local Roman bureaucrats and there was strong feeling everywhere at that time against the Roman usurers, who were calling in their loans and so threatening the British landowners with ruin. For the first time the river turned red with the reflections of London in flames. As one piece of circumstantial evidence of that conflagration we have the ashes found some ten to twenty feet down during fairly recent excavating, as well as a heap of coins, now in the London Museum, all minted before A.D. 54 and partly fused together by heat; these were unearthed seventeen feet down near the approach to London Bridge.

The legate Suetonius reoccupied London, Boudicca committed suicide, but the rebellion simmered on until pacification was brought by the tactful administration of Petronius. London was rapidly rebuilt and began to enjoy the peace and prosperity which was to last for nearly four hundred years. London became one of the great trading cities of the Roman Empire and the nerve-centre of the whole province of Britain.

Between A.D. 70 and 80, as an outcome of Boudicca's raid, a fort covering eleven acres was built on the north-west of the town where Cripplegate is now; and fifty years or more later, probably in Hadrian's time, the whole city, now stretching over the western hill, was enclosed with a massive defensive wall, nine feet thick at its base and surrounded by a moat. This gave the City within, the Square Mile as it is now called, the same outline as it has retained to this day. To these walls bastions were added, possibly in the fourth century or before, as extra protection against the Picts, Scots and Saxon pirates, being constructed perhaps as bases for the big new catapults which were the latest artillery invention.

(BEHIND THE ROMAN WALLS

Let us now try to reconstruct, from the rather flimsy evidence available, the Roman *Londinium* as it appeared in its most developed form after the walls had been built—at a time, that is to say, when it had grown into one of the five largest Roman cities north of the Alps and a major Roman city of second rank to be honourably named, in the middle of the fourth century, *Augusta*. The walls, about twenty feet high and three miles in total length, ran right round the town and along the riverside as well, where Thames Street lies now, between Blackfriars and the Tower. At the centre of the river wall was the entrance to Walbrook, and nearly a quarter of a mile to the east lay the arched bridge-gate to the city. The wall was built with tactical needs in mind to enclose the two hills and to make use of the waters of the tributaries—including the Fleet River to the west—as defensive ditches. Parts of the Roman wall can still be seen today.

The walls enclosed about three hundred and thirty acres, and the total population may have been anything up to fifty thousand—a cosmopolitan crowd of civil servants, tradesmen, craftsmen, artists, labourers, slaves and merchants, all mingling with a considerable floating population of seamen and visitors from other towns. The streets were laid out on a fairly rigid rectangular grid around a forum. Facing the forum on the north stood the basilica where Leadenhall Market stands today—the most imposing building of the town, having a main hall over five hundred feet long, and serving, at one and the same time, as a town-hall, law court and mercantile exchange. Around the forum stood other public buildings, including, no doubt, the Governor's house, the more important shops, a temple or two and a number of statues. From the south side a broad avenue ran down to the bridge-gate and the river. But important buildings would also be found in other parts of the town. In later years there would have been at least one Mithraic temple in the

c

A reconstruction of Roman London in its most developed form drawn by A. Forestier. (Reproduced by courtesy of the Trustees of the London Museum)

town, for the new worship, remarkably like Christianity in many ways, was becoming increasingly popular with the Roman soldiers. Among the more impressive buildings would be the sumptuous villas of the wealthier citizens, to be found especially along the banks of the Walbrook; some would be several storeys high, built around spacious inner courtyards paved with coloured mosaics and containing pools with fountains to remind the inhabitants of home.

Down by the river outside the wall ran a sturdy timber-sheathed embankment and timber wharves. A number of subsidiary entrances may have given passage through the wall to the warehouses within. Queenhithe may have been used as a deep-water harbour indented into the bank and surrounded on three sides by the wall. Further east the mouth of the Walbrook, a hundred yards wide, provided additional moorings. By the wharves all along the riverside lay the triremes, argosies, galleys and other craft, mostly manned by Greeks. From the holds of some were unloaded olive oil in great Italian jars, wine, pottery, glassware, bronzes and domestic luxury goods like carpets, woven fabrics, silks, perfumes, ivory and eastern spices brought from Italy and Gaul. Into the holds of others would go wheat, hides, cloth, lead and silver or more lively cargoes of cattle, slaves or hunting dogs.

Many small boats floated there too, local fishing-boats and perhaps some decorated barge with a swan's-head prow ready to carry its owner home in the evening to his villa and his orchards, which flourished on the alluvial soil of the island where Westminster Abbey would one day rise.

Across the bridge close by, now a well-built structure of painted timber standing on stone piers and decorated with bronze ornaments, we may imagine a troop of soldiers marching in good order on their way north to deal with the barbarians. They pass a litter wherein a fat merchant reclines, carried by his slaves towards some delicious, if somewhat provincial, debauch in the transpontine suburb by the bridgehead at Southwark. There a settlement covering some fifteen acres had grown up around a large inn for the use of late travellers from the south—a forerunner of the Tabard of Chaucer's time.

From the bows of a vessel sailing up the river the apprentice sailor must have been excited and impressed by his first view of London. But the long river wall and the conglomeration of low roofs rising up the two hills behind would have been rather dull and featureless compared with the city which was to grow up after the Conquest, with its forest of spires and towers dominated and unified first by the great steeple, and much later by the bold dome, of the great cathedral. Roman London was a lively place, all the same, with plenty of flourishing shops, many social clubs and public baths and entertainments of all sorts, including gladiatorial shows.

To complete the picture, we must decide whether or not a large structure of defence stood at the Tower in Roman times. A tradition has survived that it did. In Shakespeare's *Richard III* Prince Edward speaks: 'I do not like the Tower of any place. Did Julius Caesar build that place, my lord?' Buckingham answers: 'Upon record, my gracious lord.' But the record is not known. Citadels were not built outside the walls in Roman times, as they were later on in the Dark and the Middle Ages. It is possible that the tradition of the Roman fort on the site of the Tower arose because a fortified knoll, perhaps no more than a stockade around an earthwork, was erected there towards the end of the Roman occupation to ward off the raids of the pirates who came sailing upriver with increasing frequency as the Roman power declined. Or the so-called fort may merely have been that bastion of the wall which was later to form part of the base of the Wardrobe Tower. In any case, Julius Cæsar could not have built it.

⟦ AFTER THE ROMANS

What happened to London after A.D. 423, when the legions began tramping back across the bridge to the south coast for embarkation on their way to defend the other frontiers of the threatened empire? Nothing is clearly known, but the unaided citizens and the Latinised Britons must often have been harassed by the Saxon invaders from the east and south.

No doubt the town, captured and recaptured, became increasingly ruinous, but struggled on somehow as a trading centre behind its defensive
wall; the half of the city lying to the west of the Walbrook may have become unoccupied. It was never completely destroyed or deserted, for
when the darkness lifted and England re-entered European civilisation
in the seventh century it was a town of some importance still.

In 670 the Cathedral of St. Paul's, begun by Ethelbert in 610, had
been re-sited on the western hill and the growing re-settlement proceeded in the reverse direction to the Roman—that is, from the western
hill around St. Paul's towards the eastern hill. The Venerable Bede in
his *Ecclesiastical History* stressed the value of London as a trading centre
early in the year 731, and referred to it as 'the mart of many nations resorting to it by sea and land'. The growing Christian cult and its
Church, serving as the repository of what remained of Roman civilisation, began to produce some order in these wrecked and depopulated
islands, and those great organisations of psychic and economic stability,
discipline and corporate power—the Benedictine monasteries—of which
no fewer than three grew up on the banks of the Thames (at Chertsey,
Abingdon and Westminster), spread their benign influence in the revival of agriculture, architecture and learning.

Then came the second series of invasions, those of the feral Danes and
Vikings, and more violence and devastation followed throughout the
eighth, ninth and tenth centuries. Westminster Abbey, on its damp
island of Thorney (distinguished by its thorn thickets), was devastated
and destroyed. But it arose again before the Conqueror arrived. During
the ninth century London in particular suffered from raids and was for
a time in the hands of the Danes until Alfred drove them out, repaired
the Wall and organised the City government. The attacks, now more
for conquest than piracy, continued during the ninth and tenth centuries, and the legendary story has come down to us of Canute's first
attempt to reduce the town by digging a canal round the Southwark
bridgehead in order to bring his warships above bridge. Canute finally
won the kingdom and, for a brief spell of fifty years until the Conquest,
London and the lower Thames enjoyed comparative peace.

How can we imagine London, then, through these six wild centuries
after the Romans left? Most of the old Roman street plan did not survive and the Roman buildings fell in ruins and were replaced by rougher
structures made either of wattle and daub or of the abundant stones and
rubble which lay around. Roofs all became thatched or shingled, for no

more tiles or bricks were made. Alfred, King of the West Saxons, re-built the walls in 885 and, according to Stow, 'having brought this whole realm, from many parts, into one monarchy, honourably repaired this city, and made it again habitable'. Tolls and wharfage fees were charged to shipping which came from Rouen, Hamburg, Bremen and other towns of the Continent, and there at the wharfs among the other craft would occasionally be seen a fine, slim Viking ship with brightly coloured square sails woven with decorative emblems.

⟦ THE ABBEY, THE BRIDGE AND SOUTHWARK

At Westminster the Abbey Church is known to have existed in 740. It may have been standing as a rough timber fane in 616, though Bede does not mention it. By tradition this was the church built by Sebert, King of the East Saxons, whose tomb can still be seen in the ambulatory of Westminster Abbey. According to an even earlier tradition a Temple of Apollo stood on the site of the Abbey in Roman times. A charter of King Offa of Mercia of 785 still exists and can be seen in Westminster's Chapter House; it grants lands and privileges to the Church of St. Peter 'at Thorney, in the terrible place'. In the late tenth century twelve Benedictine monks came here from Glastonbury, and here King Harold was buried in 1040. The pious Saxon King, Edward the Confessor (1042–66), rebuilt the Abbey in a grand way and restored the royal palace close by. He may be considered to be the true founder of West-minster Abbey, and with him began that association of Westminster with the royalty of England which has persisted to this day. According to the chronicler, Edward had decided to carry out his grand recon-structions at Westminster, 'for that it was near unto the famous and wealthy city of London and also had a pleasant situation among the fruitful fields and green grounds lying round about it, with the principal river running hard by, bringing in from all parts of the World, great variety of wares and merchandise of all sorts to the City adjoining; but chiefly for the love of the chief apostle, whom he reverenced with a special and singular affection'.

The Bridge, as we have already seen, was standing in 984 and prob-ably some sort of structure of wood had survived since Roman days. The Anglo-Saxon Chronicle, not a particularly trustworthy document, mentions the Bridge a number of times as standing between the years 1009 and 1014, while the Olaf Sagas record a battle by the Bridge be-tween Danes and Saxons, the latter being allied with Norsemen under

St. Olaf (from whose name Tooley Street in Southwark is derived). The Sagas record that: 'Between the castle and Suthvirki [Southwark] there was a bridge, so broad that two waggons could pass each other upon it. On the bridge were raised barricades, both towers and wooden parapets in the direction of the river, which were nearly breast high; and under the bridge were piles driven into the bottom of the river. . . . Now when the attack was made [by King Ethelred] the troops stood on the bridge everywhere and defended themselves. . . . King Olaf, and the Northmen's fleet with him, rowed quite up under the bridge, laid their cables around the piles which supported it, and then rowed off with all the ships as hard as they could down stream.' That move succeeded and London Bridge was broken down.

A number of contemporary references to the Bridge after that episode have survived, especially tales of disasters by flood and fire, but the Bridge seems to have been rebuilt each time, always in timber. All during the centuries of unrest the Bridge would have served not merely as a crossing but as a useful obstacle to the further progress of the plundering fleets.

At the north end of the Bridge at the time of the Conquest stood an Anglo-Saxon church which was unusual at that time in being of stone. A reference in a confirmation of a grant by William I to Westminster Abbey dated 1067 refers to the stone church of Magnus near the Bridge. Wren's church of St. Magnus the Martyr built in 1676 after the Great Fire stands on the site.

Southwark existed as a settlement on the south bank by virtue of its defensive position at the bridgehead and also as a terminus with hostelries for late travellers from the south along Ermyn Street and Watling Street. As the Olaf Sagas state: 'on the other side of the river is a great cheaping town called Southwarke'. This great cheaping town was never to become a rival in trade to the city and port across the river. It was instead to become, through the convenience of Sanctuary, the abode not only of prelates and divines but also of debtors, criminals, prostitutes and pimps.

In that vital year of 1066, then, London—in spite of the vicissitudes of the past grim centuries—was once more a proud and well-regulated city based on a flourishing port. Though the Treasury remained at Winchester until the reign of Henry II, when it moved to Westminster, London was now the capital of England.

2 | The Mediæval River

IN HIS REORGANISATION of the country William the Conqueror was taking no chances, so he rapidly built two castles, partly to defend the town but mainly to control any uprising of the citizens. These were Windsor Castle and the Tower of London. The Tower, like the Paris Louvre and in accordance with the strategy of the times, was built not in the centre of the town, but on its edge and by the river below bridge; in that way greater freedom of action and more opportunity of maintaining supplies to the castle were possible. Windsor Castle was the first to be built, as a point from which London could be controlled before the Tower was completed, and later it served as a support for the Tower, for it stood at striking distance only a day's march away along the Roman road through Staines.

Long before he had subdued the Saxon lords, and within four years of Hastings, Windsor Castle was so far constructed that William was able to hold his Court there. The new Tower on the south-east corner of the City took longer to build, and it was not even started until 1078; it cannot have been completed less than fifteen years after Hastings, and it was not until 1097 that the Conqueror's son, William Rufus, constructed its curtain wall.

The famous White Tower, *La Blaunche Tour*, embattled, square and turreted at each corner, *is* the Tower, and all the other structures around it are later accretions, some designed for defence, others for habitation, storage or Christian worship. It appears to have been built originally of a fine white freestone from Caen; and we learn from an order of 1241 that its first colour had been 'worn by the weather and by the long process of time', and that therefore it should be painted white. In that way the Tower served as a useful landmark for vessels sailing up the estuary.

The Tower was one of the four major riverside structures of mediæval London (the others being Baynard's Castle, on the south-west corner of the City, Westminster Abbey away to the west and, of course, the Bridge). As time passed, it became of less importance as a fortress and of more importance as a royal residence and a State prison. It has also in its time housed the Royal Mint, the Public Records and the Royal Observatory. Few of its memories are happy ones. Says Stow, London's Elizabethan chronicler: 'This Tower is a citadel to defend or command the city; a royal palace for assemblies or treaties; a prison of state

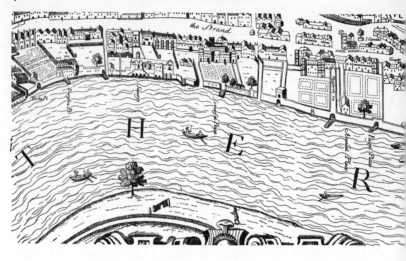

for the most dangerous offenders; the only place of coinage for all England at this time; the armoury for warlike provisions; the treasury of the ornaments and jewels of the crown; and general conserver of the most records of the king's courts of justice at Westminster.'

From early times right up to the nineteenth century it also held a menagerie. This was begun in 1256 by Henry III, who early that year gave the royal command: 'The King to the Sheriffs of London, greeting: We command you, that of the farm of our city ye cause, without delay, to be built at our Tower of London an house of forty feet long, and twenty feet deep, for our Elephant.'

The King also kept a white bear at the Tower; he ordered the sheriffs to provide the animal with a chain, a muzzle, a cord, and allowed fourpence a day for its maintenance.

The keep of the Tower as we see it today has not preserved its original appearance. It was repaired in the middle of the thirteenth century and again in 1532; then, according to Hatton (1708), 'it was almost new erected in 1637 and 1638, being built of boulder and square stone'. Except for four openings which remain on the south wall, all the original windows were obliterated in the time of William and Mary, when it became an arsenal, and larger windows were added. But its impressive original shape and character remain to remind us in its square, grim strength of the tough descendants of the Norsemen who first built it.

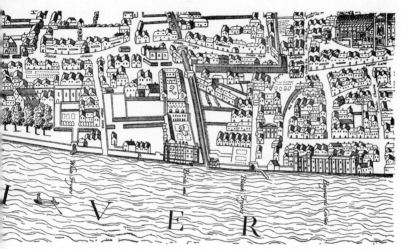

The riverside south of the Strand towards the end of the sixteenth century, when London was still largely mediæval in appearance. On the extreme right is Old St. Paul's and Baynards Castle; the Fleet enters the river to the west of the Castle beside Bridewell Palace built by Henry VIII on the site of the Whitefriars Monastery. On the left are the palaces and riverside gardens of the Strand and in the centre is the Temple. (A detail from the map of Agas)

The Normans were energetic builders, especially in stone, and the appearance of London was greatly changed in their time; it continued to change until well into the years of the Plantagenets. We have no clear visual record of the whole of London until the middle of the sixteenth century, when Antony van den Wyngaerde produced his panoramic drawing of Westminster, London and Southwark. But enough evidence does exist to give us a fairly vivid conception of how the town looked in the Middle Ages and of how people lived within it.

Let us try to see it now as it might have appeared from a ship gliding in with the tide to the harbour of Billingsgate, just below the Bridge in, say, the year 1377, when, according to the returns of the poll tax, the inhabitants of London numbered forty-five thousand. It was the year Richard II was crowned. The terrible times of the Black Death, and of the peasant revolt it helped to produce, were eighteen years past. The age of chivalry, religious ardour and full feudalism was dying.

The White Tower, gleaming in the sunlight, has been in sight for a long time across the marshes as we come sailing up river. Rising behind it lie the roofs and towers of the City, dominated by the great spire of Old St. Paul's. The Saxon church was destroyed by fire in 1066 and the new cathedral, started in 1078, is finished at last. It is the largest church in Christendom and the longest of any cathedral in England. Its spire of wood covered with lead rises to some five hundred feet, a good deal higher even than the spire of Salisbury, higher than the Great Pyramid of Egypt. At its apex gleams a great ball of copper-gilt, nine feet in diameter and surmounted by a cross fifteen feet high from which a proud eagle-cock surveys the City below.

That City is a maze of courtyards and crooked streets, some running right down to the river—a tight, picturesque jumble of buildings broken here and there by a green garden surrounding the great dwelling of a rich wool merchant. Among the larger buildings are the monastic houses, also with their gardens, the halls of the City Companies and many churches with their churchyards around. Some of the roofs are still thatched and the walls of the tenements below are of timber framing filled with wattle and whitewashed clay. But ever since 1189, when a law was passed in an effort to stop the frequent fires, more and more houses have been built of stone, at least up to the first storey, and the roofs of the better sort of buildings are now tiled, leaded or shingled. The churches and monasteries are of stone, decorated with carvings and traceried windows in the Gothic manner, and these religious buildings cover as much as a quarter of the City's whole area. A clump of trees can be glimpsed up the side streets here and there, standing in one of those many 'fair garden plots' mentioned by Stow, and frequently a spire or tower rises above the roofs to give the whole town the appearance from the river of a city of churches and bell-towers.

William Fitzstephen, the twelfth-century monk, and a Londoner by birth, who was present at the murder of Thomas à Beckett and later compiled his biography, tells us that there were in London in his time thirteen large conventual churches and one hundred and twenty-six parish churches; that number had probably increased by our year of 1377. Thus the average size of a London parish would have been three acres and three hundred people. Fitzstephen thought his London was a fine place, healthy, religious, well defended and inhabited by honourable citizens, handsome in dress and manner. The City matrons were 'true Sabine women' and the only pests of London were 'the immoderate drinking of foolish persons and the frequent fires'.

Though by the fourteenth century the City has spread beyond the

Mediæval London, 'a city of churches and bell-towers'. (From a wood-cut of 1497; reproduced by courtesy of the Trustees of the London Museum)

walls to some extent into the Liberties, whose bounds are marked by bars across the road like triumphal archways, the City itself is still clearly articulated by its walls and by the river to the south. But as we sail up in the year 1377 we see no wall along the riverside. That had decayed even by Fitzstephen's time, for he wrote: 'The wall is high and great, well towered on the north side, with due distances between the towers. On the south side also the city was walled and towered, but the fishful river of Thames, with his ebbing and flowing, hath long since subverted them.'

The memory of the wall remains today in the names of the gates such as Billingsgate. There was then, indeed, no great need of a complete river wall, for after the Danish invasions London suffered no attacks from the river—except for the bastard Falconbridge's abortive effort of 1471 and one or two piratical forays which were rapidly repulsed by the citizens.

⟦ THE BRIDGE

On our voyage, long before we have passed the Tower to starboard, we shall have been gazing ahead at the fabulous, world-famous Bridge with its overhanging houses, its rough and sturdy irregularity, its central chapel and its strange protective starlings like a row of long islands which so restrict the flow of the river that the whole structure is more like a weir than a bridge.

As we have said, we cannot be sure that during the nine centuries fol-lowing the Roman occupation London possessed a bridge, but it prob-ably did for much of that time, and this would always have been of timber. Stow wrote in his *Survey of London* (first published in 1598):

'Maister Fowle a learned manne, last Prior of Saynt Mary Overies Church in his life tyme, reported, that at the first, beeing no Bridge at London, but a ferrie, the ferryer and his wife deceasing, left the same ferrie to their daughter, a mayden named Marie, who with the goods left by her parents, and the profits which came by the sayde ferry, builded a house of Sisters, which is the uppermost ende of Saynt Maryes Church above the quier, where shee was buryed, unto the which house shee gave the oversight and profite of the same ferry: but afterwards the house of sisters was converted unto a College of priests, who builded the Bridge of timber, and from time to time kept the same in reparations, but con-sidering the great charges in repairing, lastly by the great ayde of the Cittizens of London, and others, they builded the same in stone.'

It is possible that Stow's ferry tale is true and that Overy may have evolved from 'Of the Ferry', though it is more likely that Over-ie means simply 'Over the water'. Reference to a bridge at the close of the tenth century comes in the laws of Ethelred in which the tolls of ships arriving '*ad pontem*' are fixed. Several contemporary references to the Bridge occur round about the beginning of the eleventh century, and we know that in 1163 a complete rebuilding took place in elm—probably the one to which Stow refers.

Anyway, the first stone bridge, which stood a little way to the west of the old elm bridge, was built to last. The City became its parasite. Since it concentrated trade, it became the great vested interest of the citizens, so that for centuries they successfully opposed the building of any other bridge further up-river, even though the town expanded outside the wall to the west and in the end became one with Westminster.

The Bridge was begun in 1176 as the first large stone bridge to be built in these islands, the work being under the control of Peter, chaplain of St. Mary's of Colechurch in the Poultry, usually called Peter Colechurch. There were twenty arches and the piers, 'of excellent free stone squared', were laid on oak planks supported by timber piles, mostly of elm. The pointed arches were irregular and one opening was not arched but contained a wooden drawbridge, the raising of which both protected the City from attacks across the Bridge and allowed tall ships to enter the river above-bridge. The drawbridge itself was protected on the City side by a strong gatehouse tower, horrifically decorated with the heads of traitors set on poles to discourage others.

The structure took thirty-three years to build, being completed in 1209, the eleventh year of King John. By then Colechurch had been dead four years and had been buried in the bridge chapel. The roadway was nine hundred and twenty-six feet long and the total width of the Bridge was only twenty feet, so that when the houses were erected upon it, the roadway between them was reduced to twelve feet in width. These houses, which contained shops on the ground floors with stalls facing the road and dwellings above, were all of timber framing supported by four feet of the Bridge's width and then by wooden arches and struts between the projecting piers. They grew in size at each rebuilding to three storeys high and more, and they were joined here and there across the road at the top storey; the road was therefore not only narrow but also rather dark in places. Right up to the period of their decay in the late eighteenth century, the houses were mostly inhabited by 'rich merchants and other wealthy citizens, mercers and haberdashers' (Stow). The houses were built there from the start primarily to produce revenue for the upkeep of the Bridge. Three major fires and at least four lesser ones occurred on the Bridge during its long life, and the houses were rebuilt many times. Thus the Bridge did not preserve the same appearance all through its six hundred years of life.

The noise along the Bridge must have been loud and ceaseless with the echoing sounds of the carts, horses, cattle and people passing by in the street, the fluttering and squawking of the numerous kites perching everywhere and the roar of the water below, which, as the tide turned, swirled down a height of five feet between the starlings. Shooting the Bridge was a common but dangerous practice throughout the centuries in spite of the proverb that arose: 'London Bridge was made for wise men to go over and fools to go under.' Among the many stories of shooting the Bridge is one to be found in the Harleian Manuscript: 'Also this same yere, the viij day of Nouember, the Duke of Norfolk, with many a gentil man, squyer, and yoman, tok his barge at Seynt Marye Ouerye be twen iij and v of ye belle a yens nygt, and proposyd to passe thorough London Bregge. Where of the forseid barge, thorugh mysgouvernance of stearyng, fell up on the pyles and ouerwhelmyd. The whyche was cause of spyllyng many a gentil man and othere; the more ruthe was!'

But the Bridge, in spite of the noise and the frequent troubles with drowning men, was a good place to live. Its street was comparatively clean because all soil and rubbish from the houses was thrown, not into a stinking midden in the street, as elsewhere in the town, but down trap-doors into the river. The outer windows admitted plenty of fresh air and sunshine into the houses and gave wonderful views up and down the river. Water could be pulled up in buckets straight from the river and fishing-lines could be suspended from the windows. The Bridge was a healthy place and even in the Great Plague only two of its inhabitants succumbed to the disease.

By holding back the ebb, the Bridge reduced the volume of tidal water passing it by about 25%, and so it brought a frequent freezing of the Thames to its west in cold winters, and permitted in later years those wonderful frost fairs of the river with their colourful streets of booths, roasting oxen and general bacchanalian festivity.

⟦ LONDON WATERS

Not far below the Bridge our ship of 1377 lowers sail and is manœuvred into the crowded harbour of Billingsgate, a square bay indented into the bank. A similar harbour lies above the Bridge, called Queenhithe, whose indentation will still be there in the twentieth century. These are the two most important harbours of London's mediæval port and there is rivalry between them. The considerable fishing industry of the time was first concentrated at Queenhithe, but later Billingsgate secured the trade—and the harbour fees. It had the advantage over Queenhithe that the larger ships coming up-river did not have to wait for the lifting of the drawbridge before docking.

Queenhithe, called Aetheredes Hyd in a charter of Alfred dated 899, may have acquired its present name when it came into the possession of the wife of Henry I; but the name may have come from the quern or mill for grinding the corn which was landed there. In some twelfth-century documents it is spelt Corn-hithe. It was still in royal possession in Henry III's time, for Stow says: 'King Henry III, in the ninth of his reign, commanded the constables of the Tower of London to arrest the ships of the Cinque Ports on the river of Thames and to compel them to bring their corn to no other place, but to the Queen's hithe only. In the eleventh of his reign, he charged the said constable to distrain all fish offered to be sold in any place of this city, but at the Queene hithe.'

Stow also refers to complaints made by the bailiff of Queenhithe that, in defiance of this royal order, fourteen foreign ships laden with fish arrived at the port of 'Belinge's Gate'. In Stow's time Queenhithe was still, in spite of its position above bridge, 'the very chief and principal watergate of the city'.

As early as 1279 all vessels were compelled by law to moor either at Queenhithe or Billingsgate, but as the size and number of ships increased other wharves were used and the larger ones dropped anchor in the river, their cargoes being unloaded into lighters and then landed.

At the mouth of the Walbrook was Dowgate, some two hundred and fifty feet wide, which gave facilities to shipping. 'Downgate', Stow says, 'so called of the sudden descending or down-going of that way from St. John's Church upon Walbrook unto the river of Thames.' Dowgate was less important than either Billingsgate or Queenhithe and by 1473 the watercourse of the Walbrook had been covered in, for Stow records that a mayor of the year 1440 gave two hundred marks towards vaulting over the tributary. On the east side of Dowgate stood the Steelyard, where Cannon Street Railway Station was one day to rear up. The Steelyard was a wharf and warehouses occupied by the Hanseatic League, called the Easterlings, from the year 1248. To quote Stow again: 'Next to this Lane [Cosin's Lane] on the East is the Stil-house or Stil-yard, as they term it, a place for Merchants of Almaine, that used to bring hither, as well Wheat, Rye, and other Grain, as Cables, Ropes, Masts, Pitch, Tar, Flax, Hemp, Linen Cloth, Wainscots, Wax, Steel, and other profitable Merchandises. . . . Their Hall is large, built of Stone, with three arched Gates towards the Street.'

The name Steelyard may derive from its association with the King's steelyard or beam which was set up here at one time for weighing imported goods. On the west side of Dowgate was the vintners' wharf where merchants of Bordeaux landed their wines. Further west still, on the outside of the city wall, the River Fleet ran into the Thames (also called at different times the Holbourne, Turnmill Brook or the River of Wells). Today it is hidden below New Bridge Street and Farringdon Street as a large sewer, but in the fourteenth century the Fleet offered docking facilities for quite a long distance, and coal was landed at a wharf there, a fact commemorated by the present Seacole Lane off Farringdon Street. Its name of Fleet, meaning a place where vessels can float, was usually given by Londoners to the lower part only of the Holebourne, and we learn from a petition of the time of Edward I that ten or twelve ships with merchandise 'were wont to come to Fleet Bridge, and some of them to Holeburne Bridge'.

Both the Walbrook and the Fleet became ever more silted up and polluted as the years passed, and the latter became known colloquially as the Fleet Ditch. This Fleet River, the Tybourne and the Westbourne were the three London rivers which lay outside the city walls and had their source in the Hampstead and Highgate 'massif'. Like the other tributaries, the Tybourne in 1377 ran open to the sky down towards what was one day to be Oxford Street, which it crossed near Stratford Place and then ran across Piccadilly and the Green Park to the front of the spot where Buckingham Palace now stands. (You can still see dips in the land on its course.) Then the Tybourne bifurcated (hence Twy, or double, and bourne, or brook); one branch ran *via* the future lake in St. James's Park into the river by the walls of the Westminster monastery (later New Scotland Yard); the other (now underground as the King's Scholars' Pond Sewer) swept the other way to form the old western boundary of Westminster, crossed the Vauxhall Bridge Road of today, ran down Tatchbrook Street and so into the river. These two streams formed the wild Thorney Island, on which Westminster Abbey was first built in Saxon times.

The Westbourne ran down through Paddington (eventually helping to create the Serpentine in Kensington Gardens and Hyde Park). From there it flowed to the point now occupied by Victoria Station and thence by two streams into the river near Ranelagh Gardens. Like the other streams, the Westbourne was eventually canalised as an underground sewer, and evidence of its existence can now be seen as a huge tube crossing the District line at Sloane Square Underground Station. (An intrepid adventurer might thus be able to paddle a canoe through the air unseen across a railway line in the very heart of London.)

⟦ SHIPS AND DOCKS

In our river journey of 1377 we shall find many other smaller harbours along the riverside apart from the Fleet, Dowgate, Queenhithe and Billingsgate, where the smaller boats and lighters can tie up and lie on the shingle at low tide. There is a wharf near the Tower, for instance, called Galley Quay, where the long Venetian galleys, each manned by one hundred and eighty oarsmen and protected by a company of archers, are moored during their annual visit to London.

What do we see around us as we step ashore on to the cobbles of Billingsgate? People are swarming there in bright clothes, some in long coats and thick turbans, others in coloured pantaloons and pointed hats. In architectural terms, perhaps the nearest equivalent scene to survive into the twentieth century is the Hanseatic Quarter in Bergen with its row of warehouses of painted timber—though the warehouses here in London are much less regular. As in Bergen, the smell of fish is pervasive and so is the din of unsprung carts, the shouts of street traders and the rowdy young apprentices. Many of the voices are exotic, for foreign merchants have built up London's trade and many have settled in the City. The German Hanseatic League occupies an important position at Dowgate, as we have seen, and to London merchants from all nations bring their wares by sea—Norwegians, Danes, Flemings, French, Italians from Venice, Florence and Genoa and Jews from Rouen among them.

Imports include fish and other foods, silk cloths of good quality, corn in times of shortage, wines from France, iron and timber from the Baltic and, at least since the days of Edward I, sea coal (to distinguish it from the charcoal which comes by land). The most important export is, of course, raw wool. In this fourteenth century 'by common opinion there were more than one hundred thousand sacks of wool yearly transported into foreign lands' (Stow). Fish is the most valuable of trades, for it is a common food, and the Fishmongers' Company has become the most powerful and wealthy of all the big City Companies.

Facing the quay stand the warehouses, dwellings, counting houses,

D

ships' chandlers, taverns, cook-houses, bakeries and breweries. 'On the north side, as well as on the south of this Thames Street, are many fair houses, large for storage, built for merchants,' says Stow. A number of breweries lie near the river, for they do well in London; as Howell (1657) was to remark: 'Thames water beer bears the price of Wine in many places beyond the seas.' And somewhere near Billingsgate there is at least one eating-house like that described by Fitzstephen: 'Besides there is, on the river bank, among the wines in ships and cellars sold according to the season, dishes of meat, roast, fried, and boiled, great and small fish, coarser meats for the poor, more delicate for the rich, of game, fowls and small birds. If there should come suddenly to any of the citizens friends weary from a journey and too hungry to like waiting till fresh food is bought and cooked, with water to their hands comes bread, while one runs to the river bank, and there is all that can be wanted. . . . For this is the public kitchen, very convenient to the city, and part of its civilisation.'

❪ LIVING CONDITIONS

Such comforts went hand in hand with the poverty, hunger and disease of the Middle Ages. Right up to the purging Great Fire of 1666 pestilence was always endemic and often pandemic. The wealthy merchant and the prelate lived in grand style, and their glazed windows looked out upon pleasant gardens and orchards, but the poor existed in cramped and squalid tenements facing on to dark yards or narrow, stinking alleys where oversailing upper storeys nearly closed out the sky above and drains ran as open sewers below. In the reign of Edward II an order was issued to stop the rearing of pigs, oxen and cows in the houses, but that was only a limited piece of legislation.

One potent cause of disease was the unhygienic use of rushes for covering floors. Another was the neglect of that sanitary precaution which the Greeks and Romans had always carefully observed—the burial of the dead outside the city walls. But the greatest danger lay in the water, which was obtained from the tributaries, wells, springs, from piped conduits, from the river itself, or from the water-bearers—tough and uncivil characters called cobs. The water, from wherever it came, was swimming with microbes gathered from the impure surface soil of the City, for most of the sewers ran straight down into the streams. As a result, the death rate was so high that deaths exceeded births and the City's population was maintained only by continual immigration from the provinces and from abroad. Plague was a constant menace, and the horrifying carts piled up with corpses on their way to the pits were seen too often. Even in normal years deaths were heavy from dysentery, typhus, malaria and smallpox. Serious plague came to London in 1094 and thereafter, up to and including the Great Plague of 1665, which killed nearly one hundred thousand inhabitants, there were twelve serious outbreaks. Therefore most Londoners who lived in the Middle Ages, and later, experienced at least one of these plagues during their lives, the most virulent being the *Sudor Anglicus*, or sweating sickness, mortal in three hours.

Medical knowledge was slight, but the hospitals attached to the religious houses did their best for the sick. One of them was at the Priory of St. Mary Overy near the bridgehead at Southwark, and this became the famous St. Thomas's Hospital.

⟦ FUN AND GAMES

In spite of, perhaps even because of, this ever-present danger of sudden sickness and death, life could be jolly enough in London, and there was plenty of entertainment for everyone—mystery plays and mummery, cock-fighting, bull- and bear-baiting, rowing, dancing, wrestling, shooting with bow and arrow, casting the stone and, in cold winters, skating on skates of bone. There were also periodic festivals and pageants, not least on the river, especially when the monarch travelled in state in the ornate royal barge from the Tower down to Westminster Palace, or when the Lord Mayor, who in the City ranked next to the King in status, was rowed to Westminster to receive the King's (nominal) approval of his election. In 1453 the Mayor began the custom of journeying to Westminster by water, and this went on until 1856, when the procession took to the land and became the annual Lord Mayor's Show.*

Almost always there was somewhere in progress 'a Fair where thousands meet but none can stay', or some procession would enliven the day and the Bridge would be decorated with pennants, tapestries, garlands and escutcheons to serve as a triumphal entrance to the City.

There was much sporting on the river. Fitzstephen, who stoutly maintained that 'a city should not only be commodious and serious, but also merry and sportful', described one river game: 'In Easter holidays they fight battles on the water; a shield is hung upon a pole, fixed in the

* Because the Show now increases traffic congestion in the City, there has been some talk recently of returning it to the river.

midst of the stream, a boat is prepared without oars, to be carried by violence of the water, and in the fore part thereof standeth a young man, ready to give charge upon the shield with his lance; if so be he breaketh his lance, he runneth strongly against the shield, down he falleth into the water, for the boat is violently forced with the tide; but on each side of the shield ride two boats, furnished with young men, which recover him that falleth as soon as they may. Upon the bridge,* wharfs, and houses by the river's side stand great numbers to see and laugh thereat.'

❲ ALONG THE RIVER BANKS

At the quay of Billingsgate in this year 1377 we can readily find a waterman to row us in his wherry up the Silent Highway. Once out in midstream below the Bridge, among the squat mediæval galleys with their high castles fore and aft, we see on our right just by the bridgehead the parish church of St. Magnus ad Pontem (of St. Magnus the Martyr, a Norwegian jarl of the twelfth century); it is a typical mediæval church with a square tower, a clerestory and pointed windows. (There Henry Yevele, the great Gothic architect-mason to Edward III, Richard II and Henry IV, was buried in 1400, and there at a much later time a famous incumbent was Miles Coverdale, translator of the Bible into English.)

Facing this building on the other side of the river is a similar Gothic church of stone with a square tower surmounted by a bell turret. This is St. Olave's in Tooley Street, which was dedicated to the sainted warrior king of Norway who, with Ethelred, in 1008 pulled down the wooden bridge of London in the way described. He was murdered at Drontheim in 1029, since when no less than four churches to his memory have been built in his name in London. A ruin by the eighteenth century, this church in Southwark was rebuilt in a handsome classical style in Portland stone in the year 1740 by the architect Henry Flitcroft. That church was pulled down in 1928 and the site sold to the Hay's Wharf Company, and there in its place the head office of that Company stands today. St. Olaf, however, was not forgotten, for a decorative linear design in black and gold mosaic of the King was incorporated in the wall of the new building.

We pass under the Bridge now close to the big central starling which supports the bridge chapel. It has been dedicated to Thomas à Beckett because it was in St. Mary Colechurch, of which Peter the Bridge's builder was priest, that Beckett was baptised. This is the Early English

* That must have been the old elm bridge.

chapel, to be rebuilt in the Perpendicular style. It is a fine large apsidal chapel having a crypt which can be entered from the starling and the nave above which can be entered from the road.

We float easily under a ribbed arch of the Bridge at the slack of the tide and see on the left, just west of the bridgehead, the church, hospital and attendant buildings of the Priory of St. Mary Overy. One day the church, after many changes, will become Southwark Cathedral.

Near the priory on the riverside lies Winchester House, the London palace of the Bishops of Winchester, built in 1107; it has its own stairs to the river. Beyond it is a smaller palace belonging to the Bishops of Rochester, and after it, up to a point where Blackfriars Bridge will one day lie, are a few scattered houses facing the bank of the river, or Bankside. Thereafter as far as the complex of Lambeth Palace is open land of marsh, orchards and polder fields drained by ditches running to the river.

We soon pass Dowgate on our right with its imposing block of buildings belonging to the Hansa merchants and then Queenhithe, sprouting a thicket of masts. Next the shallow inlet of Broken Wharf and after it Puddle Wharf, 'of one Puddle that kept a wharf on the west side thereof and now Puddle Water by means of many horses watered there' (Stow). Soon we come to the corner of the walled City marked strongly by a great stone fortress standing right on the water's edge. This is the

Baynards Castle, 'a rough, gloomy structure with a dozen towers.' (An engraving from Harrison's *History of London* c. 1780)

famous Baynards Castle, a rough, gloomy structure with a dozen towers and a central arched water-gate approached by river steps. Its name comes from a nobleman who landed with the Conqueror and built the place. Thereafter it was twice rebuilt—the last time in 1428 by Humphrey, Duke of Gloucester; Henry VII refurbished it in 1487 and most of it disappeared in the Great Fire. Its name survives into the twentieth century as a wharf and a City Ward. The fifteenth-century palace came into the hands of Henry VI after Gloucester's death and there the Crown was offered to Richard III, as correctly interpreted in Shakespeare's play.

Beside the Fleet River, beyond Baynards, stands another castle, also built by one of the Conqueror's men, Le Sir Montfichett, but this was destroyed about 1276, and on its site has arisen the monastery, church and precinct of the Black Friars, the Dominican monks who came to England in 1221; it is now in 1377 a fine, rich flourishing establishment, thanks to the initial favour of Edward I. The monastery and church were destroyed in the Great Fire, but remains have since been uncovered. For example, in 1872, when the offices of *The Times* were being built, part of a wall, probably of the frater, was found, and in 1890 an arcade was also discovered and was re-erected at Selsdon Park in Surrey.

Beyond the Black Friars' monastery the Fleet River runs into the Thames, and we can see boats moored all the way up the river to Fleet Bridge, which crosses the stream where Ludgate Circus will be one day. West of the Fleet's mouth rises the house of St. Bride's. This was a royal palace in the time of John, for that king summoned a parliament there, not surprisingly, for until the reign of Henry III parliament was held at no fixed place but wherever the king happened to be at the time; and the king lived in many places, for he travelled incessantly on State business, accompanied by a huge retinue and cartloads of documents. Later the western part of St. Bride's House was given to the Bishop of Salisbury and now in the fourteenth century that part is in a fair state, though the rest is a ruin, 'a laystall of filth and rubbish' (Stow). It was to remain a ruin until Henry VIII rebuilt it as a palace and renamed it Bridewell on account of the parish of St. Bride's and its well. Later it was partly destroyed in the Great Fire, then rebuilt and used as a house of correction, a kind of early Borstal, as we shall hear.

To the west of St. Bride's House, in the area south of modern Fleet Street, lies the monastery of the White Friars, or Carmelites, built on land given to them by Henry III; its garden extends to the river and its cloister, guest house, frater, prior's house and domestic quarters face us on the south of the complex. Behind these buildings rises the tall steeple of its church. In 1538 the order was dissolved; seven years later the church disappeared, and in time the area degenerated into a warren inhabited by outlaws and the scum of the City, that republic of squalor, vice and crime recalled by Otway, Shadwell and Scott as Alsatia. London, Southwark and Westminster all developed these warrens as a result of the privilege of Sanctuary permitted to religious properties.*

[LA STRAUNDE

As we continue our journey, we see beyond Whitefriars the buildings of the Knights Templars, who moved to this pleasant spot about 1160 from the old Temple in Chancery Lane. Here about 1180 they built their round Norman church, which was to survive into the twentieth century, be damaged in the Blitz and be well restored, together with the later square chancel, a Gothic addition of 1240. The order grew wealthy, became suspected of heresy, was suppressed by Edward I and was completely dissolved, with the Pope's sanction, in 1312. The consecrated part of their property here, to be called the Inner Temple, passed to the

* Sanctuary was a curious institution and became much abused. It survived after the Reformation, but thereafter it gradually weakened. At Westminster Abbey the privilege of sanctuary was first established by Sebert, king of the East Saxons, and it was later confirmed by Edward the Confessor, whose Charter reads:

'Edward, by the grace of God, king of Englishmen: I make it to be known to all generations of the world after me, that by speciall commandement of our holy father, Pope Leo, I have renewed and honoured the holy church of the blessed apostle St. Peter, of Westminster; and I order and establish for ever, that what person, of what condition or estate soever he be, from whence soever he come, or for what offence or cause it be, either for his refuge into the said holy place, he be assured of his life, liberty and limbs. And over this, I forbid under the paine of everlasting damnation, that no minister of mine, or of my successors, intermeddle them with any the goods, lands or possessions of the said persons taking the said sanctuary; for I have taken their goodes and livelode into my special protection, and therefore I grant to every each of them, in as much as my terrestriall power may suffice, all maner freedom of joyous libertie; and whosoever presumes or doth contrary to this my graunt, I will hee lose his name, worship, dignity, and power, and that with the great traytor Judas that betraied our Saviour, he be in the everlasting fire of hell; and I will and ordayne that this my graunt endure as long as there remayneth in England eyther love or dread of Christian name.'

A magnificient affirmation of the sanctity of the individual, and for the King probably good business too; it is the grant to every man of the right to go to hell in his own way—and with a sporting chance of earthly survival in joyous libertie.

Knights Hospitallers. Soon after that much of the property was leased
to a body of lawyers and this became known as the Middle Temple. In
the four Inns of Court—Middle Temple, Inner Temple, Lincoln's Inn
and Gray's Inn—'men of lawe expert and curious' (Chaucer) now live
and learn; their placing is significant, for it is 'half way between the
commercial capital at London and the political capital at Westminster, a
geographical position that helped the English lawyer to discover his true
political function as mediator between Crown and people' (Trevelyan,
History of England).

According to tradition, in the Temple gardens the red and white roses
were plucked by Richard Plantagenet and Warwick to start the brawl
which led to the Wars of the Roses.

Beyond the Temple grounds we shall be rowing along the side of the
Strand, a fairly steep bank rising up to a road which joins the City with
Westminster. Along the water-front here stand many fine houses where
magnates, bishops and abbots reside when they come to London to
attend councils or some great occasion of State or Church. The road
which serves them is now called the Strand, but at one time Whitehall,
the Strand and Fleet Street all came under the name of the King's Road,
for this was the monarch's way from his Westminster palace to the City
or to his palace by the Fleet. The Anglo-Saxon Chronicle tells of the
war between Godwin and Edward the Confessor in the year 1052 when
'the land-force meanwhile came above (the Bridge) and arrayed themselves by the strand'. In this context the strand no doubt means the
river's bank itself, but a road must have existed above the bank in Fitzstephen's time, for that scribe wrote: 'Also upwards to the west the
royal palace (of Westminster) is conspicuous above the same river, an
incomparable building with ramparts and bulwarks, two miles from the
city, joined to it by a populous suburb.'

The Strand was a street of palaces, facing open country to the north and
having beautiful gardens and lawns running down to the river to the
south. Already by the Conqueror's time at least one mansion stood on
La Straunde, for it is on record that Gilbert de Gant gave to Abingdon
Abbey a mansion which lay on the way to Westminster from London,
and as early as 1099 Ralph Flambard, Bishop of Durham, was living
there. Many palaces stand there now in 1377; greater and even more
stately mansions were to arise in Tudor times and later. The road itself
is now in a poor condition, like most of the roads in the Middle Ages,
and in parts it is overgrown with bushes. In Henry VII's time it was still

in bad shape, 'perilous and noisesome', in spite of attempts made by several monarchs to obtain improvements. A few streams cross the road and run down to the river, and these are spanned by small bridges.

Now as far as Charing Cross the Strand sweeps round to the south, and we shall pass mansion after mansion, varying in size and grandeur, some close to, others set back from, the riverside. These rambling, picturesque, embattled and richly textured houses, conveniently situated near to Westminster, are almost all the town residences or inns of the wealthy and powerful princes of the Church and their retinues—Exeter (later Essex) House, Bath (later Arundel) House, Lichfield and Coventry, Worcester and Llandaff, Carlisle (later Bedford) House, Durham, York. Another, right on the river, belongs to an aristocrat; this is the famous Palace of Savoy, first built for the Earl of Savoy in 1245 when his niece, Eleanor of Provence, was Queen of Henry III. Later it was to come into the hands of the Lancasters. In 1357, after Poitiers, John, King of France, was lodged there in luxurious captivity, and Geoffrey Chaucer, London's Comptroller of Customs, was housed there for a time. In 1381 the place was pillaged and burnt by Wat Tyler and his rebels, Duke John fled for his life, and thirty-two of the rebels found their way to the wine-cellar, where they became drunk and were mured in. For seven days and seven nights they yelled for help, but none came until they were dead. The Savoy remained thereafter a blackened ruin for a hundred years until Henry VII rebuilt it as a hospital for the destitute.

Also built by a non-churchman is York House, lying between the royal palace at Westminster and Charing Cross. It was first a 'fayre house' erected in 1240 for his own occupation by Hubert de Burgh, Lord Chief Justice of England, but he left it to the Black Friars, who sold it to the Archbishop of York. Wolsey acquired it, and then Henry VIII refurnished it and called it Whitehall Palace.

After the Dissolution in Henry VIII's time these properties mostly passed into the hands of the aristocracy, and Henry himself commandeered Durham House. They were rebuilt and other new mansions were added along the Strand, but by the twentieth century nothing remains of any except their memories kept alive in local place-names.

These big houses were for centuries one of the great riverside sights of London. As late as 1657 Howell wrote of them in his *Londinopolis*: 'The stately palaces that are built on both sides of her banks so thick, which made divers foreign ambassadors to affirm, that the most glorious

sight in the World (take water and land together) was to come upon a
high Tide from Gravesend, and shoot the Bridge to Westminster.'

Or to burst into song with Drayton:

> '*Then goes he on along by that more beauteous Strand*
> *Expressing both the wealth and bravery of the land,*
> *(So many sumptuous bowers, within so little space,*
> *The all-beholding Sun scarce sees in all his race).*'

The brightly coloured flowers and the gay figures sauntering with
feathers in their hats in the gardens receive a fine foil from the grey stone
walls of the palaces. Green lawns interpenetrate everywhere and across
them run wide pathways down to the carved water-gates and the steps
to the broad river, where many small craft pass by, some with sails set
and some moved by oars, some trading and piled high with fruit and
vegetables from the market-gardens up-river, others carrying passengers
of both high and low estate. A dignified game of swans floats by on the
fresh stream, and across the Lambeth marshes stretching away to the
south we can just glimpse, through a gap in the orchards, the roofs and
towers of Lambeth Palace. A cortège of State barges, gleaming with
gilded carvings and brilliant with coloured awnings and fluttering pennants rows by—perhaps bearing the King himself on his way down-river
to the Tower.

As we approach Westminster we see to our right Scotland Yard, a
palace where since Saxon times the Kings of Scotland 'and other estates
of that country' (Stow) resided when they came to London to pay
homage to the Kings of England. Being no longer required for that
purpose when the two crowns were united, the palace was converted
into lodgings and offices. Inigo Jones later resided there, and after him
Milton when he served as Cromwell's secretary. In 1829 a police office
was established there, and sixty years later this was removed a short way
to the south to New Scotland Yard.

(WESTMINSTER AND BEYOND

And here, making a great and confused mediæval complex, rise the stone
buildings of Westminster. Our waterman can rest on his oars while we
unravel the parts. But first let us consider the significance of Westminster. As we have seen, Edward the Confessor rebuilt the church and
made the place his royal residence. In the Abbey church all our monarchs since Harold—with the exception only of Edward v and Edward

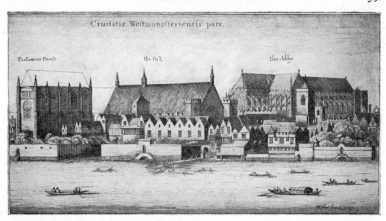

Westminster Palace engraved by Hollar. On the left is the Chapel of St. Stephen, the debating chamber of the House of Commons after 1547.

VIII—have been crowned. Westminster and its Abbey thus became symbols of the continuity of the Crown. But it was not merely tradition which made Westminster a Royal town and a centre of government and law since Saxon times; nor was it the glory and wealth which tended to concentrate there in its great Abbey and its royal palace. The citizens of London have always been jealous of their privileges and, being in a powerful position, they often acted in a truculent way against the pressures of King and national government. London was a free city and even the King had to demean himself so far as to seek the Lord Mayor's permission before he could enter it. Since the Conqueror's day therefore the King had not only maintained the Tower as a threat to the Londoners but had developed Westminster as a rival community. It is significant that kings rarely entered the City and never dared to live inside its walls. Kings and abbots not only tried to build up Westminster as a rival to the City in prestige and splendour, in which they succeeded, but as a rival also in trade, in which they failed.

For example, Henry III granted the Abbot of Westminster the right to hold a weekly market and an annual fair in Touthull (Tothill) to last three days, during which time the City would not be allowed to sell anything. Edward III extended the period to thirty-one days. This incensed the Londoners, who, in the end and with bad grace, paid the Abbot twelve thousand pounds of silver to regain their lost business. In 1352 Westminster obtained the privilege of being selected as a port for the Wool Staple in competition with the City. But nothing could alter the facts: the City possessed natural advantages over Westminster as a port; her Bridge funnelled traffic there and acted as a barrier to river traffic above the City; her population was far larger than that of Westminster, which even up to 1740 did not extend outside the Island of Thorney.

So in time Westminster ceased to serve as a port and achieved fame in other ways—that is, as the political and legal centre of the country. As the distinct purposes of the two towns developed, the old rivalries gradually died away, but that this rivalry was at times intense enough to produce mob violence is shown by some events of the year 1212. At a public wrestling match the men of Westminster, having armed themselves, fell treacherously upon the men of London, who fled behind the refuge of their walls. In revenge they pulled down the Abbot's house. Hubert de Burgh, the Chief Justice of England, proceeded to the Tower, and there called before him the Lord Mayor and Aldermen of London to demand the appearance of the ringleaders. They gave themselves up and were immediately executed in the straightforward manner of the times.

In 1225 the Law Courts had been fixed at Westminster, and there they remained until moved to the Strand in 1882. Because the King lived at Westminster with his Court, Parliament tended to meet there, and so Westminster became not only the King's headquarters but, as a result of that, both the administrative and judicial centre of the country. That is why the Houses of Parliament, standing on the site of an ancient royal palace, were, and still are, called the Palace of Westminster.

Now let us look at the edifices of Westminster as they appear in this year of the coronation of Richard II. Two main groups are evident—the royal palace by the riverside and behind it the Abbey, and its noble church which, since the days of Edward the Confessor's building, has been in a sense a huge Chapel Royal to the palace. The church has indeed been directly associated with government, for Parliament often met in its cloisters or in its chapter house, and for a long time one of its rooms contained the Treasury of England.

Around the Abbey lie well-tended gardens of which a fragment will survive into the twentieth century to form the College garden. In 1377 this is attached to the Infirmary of the Abbey, a fragrant place where healing herbs are grown for the making of simples and ointments.

Parts of the mediæval royal palace will still stand in the twentieth

Westminster Hall was reconstructed at the end of the fourteenth century, 'its roof supported by a superb hammer-beam roof'. (From an illustration in Ackerman's *Microcosm of London*, 1808)

century, notably the Great Hall, which will form a magnificent vestibule to the nineteenth-century Houses of Parliament and will come to be re-garded as one of the finest surviving Gothic rooms in the whole of

Europe. The hall was first built by William Rufus in 1097, when its windows were round-headed in the Norman manner, and its roof was supported by two rows of wooden columns. That is how we see it in 1377, but in 1398 it was to be reconstructed by Richard II; its windows became larger, with pointed arches and rich tracery, the room had a clear floor span of seventy-four feet wide and a length of two hundred and forty feet; its roof was supported by a superb hammer-beam roof of oak all carved with angels and other devices—the noblest roof in England, a country renowned for its masterly carpentry. The architect of the hall was the famed Henry Yevele, who co-operated on the roof design with Hugh Herland.

On its completion, the prodigal King, dressed in cloth of gold decorated with pearls and precious stones, kept 'a most royal Christmas there with daily joustings and runnings at tilt' (Stow)—a grand party at which three hundred servitors bore to the diners twenty-six roasted oxen and three hundred sheep beside fowls without number. A year later at a more sombre gathering in the same hall the King was deposed.

In this coronation year of 1377 around the old Norman hall cluster many buildings. Among them, to the south of the hall and almost rivalling it in size, is the Chapel of St. Stephen, an historic and imposing structure, tall and long; its eastern end with its great traceried window is facing us as we float on the river. First built by King Stephen in Norman style, it was reconstructed by Edward I after a fire in 1298 and was again rebuilt about 1347 by Edward III. Many of the great secular establishments of the Middle Ages contained a religious brotherhood, and so it was with the Palace of Westminster, in the form here of the College of St. Stephen, which was independent both of the King and the Abbot and possessed as well as this chapel, the chapel and crypt of St. Mary Undercroft, one of the other buildings in the great complex, completed in 1327 with a vaulted roof.

In 1547 these properties were confiscated by the Crown and the Chapel of St. Stephen was assigned for the House of Parliament. For nearly three centuries thereafter, until destroyed by the fire of 1834, the Commons debated there; thus it is from the plan of a mediæval chapel that the later debating chamber with its special lay-out evolved. The ritual of bowing which Members of Parliament still observe when passing in front of the Speaker's chair is attributed to the bowing either to the altar in St. Stephen's Chapel, or, going back further still, to the bowing to the image of the Virgin which stood in the Chapter House of the

Abbey wherein Parliament often met during these Middle Ages. Of course, St. Stephen's Chapel changed internally during the years and came to look more like a debating hall than a place of worship. It acquired a false ceiling beneath its high vault and in 1706 the walls were panelled by Wren.

The mediæval palace, then, is not a unified building but an accretion of halls and other structures of which St. Stephen's and the Great Hall are the two largest and most splendid. There is also the Painted Chamber which was the original nucleus of the whole palace. It was first built by Edward the Confessor as his abode, and that was the true origin of the Houses of Parliament to be. Here the Lords were to sit in later years. Its name comes from the mural paintings on its walls representing the Wars of the Maccabees and incidents in the life of Edward the Confessor which were executed in the time of Henry III. In this hall the death-warrant of Charles I was signed and here occurred that shocking incident when Cromwell and Marten threw ink in each other's faces. In the vaulted place below this chamber Guy Fawkes concealed his barrels of gunpowder.

Other accretions were added to the jumble, and we hear of the Queen's Hall, Marcolf's Chamber, the Antioch Chamber, the Prince's Chamber and the Little Hall, also called the White Hall, from which Whitehall Palace took its name; this became the Court of Requests and later, after 1801, the House of Lords. Finally there is the Star Chamber; its ceiling was decorated with stars, though its name came not from these but from the Jewish starrs, or bonds, which were stored here by the early Plantagenets. Here the Court of the Star Chamber met until abolished in 1641, and eventually the room was used to store the notched tally sticks for keeping the exchequer accounts, the over-zealous burning of which in the stove of the House of Lords one cold evening in 1834 caused the fire that destroyed most of the old palace.

Edward the Confessor's small abbey church was pulled down except for a few fragments and in its place Henry III began rebuilding it in the thirteenth century as a magnificent, airy, Gothic structure, with high vaulting held in by external flying buttresses. Leland, the sixteenth-century antiquarian, called it *orbis miraculum*, the wonder of the world. East of the choir lies a long Lady Chapel which was replaced in the time of Henry VII by the very late, ornate and fan-vaulted Gothic edifice. Begun in 1503 as a Lady Chapel, it was completed by Henry VIII about 1512 and was called Henry VII's Chantry Chapel. The exterior to the

east was particularly splendid with its five radiating chapels, and its
clerestory rising behind openwork buttresses.

The Victorian restorers did much harm to the exterior of the Abbey
church, but the interior retained its original character into the twentieth
century; and the circular Chapter House with its central column splay-
ing into a radiating roof like a tree, the cloisters and other parts have
also survived.

Around the Palace and the Abbey in 1377 sprawl many small
buildings, and here is much squalor, for Westminster has its Alsatian
sanctuary, like Whitefriars and Southwark, and in the shadows of the
glorious church lie pestilential slums which will not be finally cleared away
until Victoria Street is built in 1851. Its memory will persist in the
names of Thieving Lane and Broad and Little Sanctuary.

Let us continue upstream again, passing on our left another of those
divines' domains by the river. This is Lambeth Palace, belonging to the
Archbishops of Canterbury, towered and battlemented and more like a
castle than a palace, but very conveniently situated, for the Primate of
All England can reach Westminster from here in a few minutes merely
by taking a boat across the river. In 1490 the Palace received a grand
brick gatehouse with two sturdy towers, and this still stands in the
twentieth century. In Commonwealth days Parliament sold the place
and it grew ruinous; then, at the Restoration, Archbishop Juxon (the
priest who attended Charles I at his execution) rebuilt the Great Hall,
with its hammer-beam roof, which came to house the famous library.

South of the Abbey and Palace we see the Tyburn stream running
into the river, and on its bank stands the Abbot's Mill, which will give
the name Millbank to the future roadway here. Beyond the stream lies
open, marshy country called the Five Fields and the Neat House
market-gardens where the domestic districts of Belgravia and Pimlico
will one day arise. Here is a farm-house and there, far off, a windmill.
On the river banks grow the rushes and sedges where the wildfowl build
their nests. Chelsea is hardly a village yet, though a little church of the
thirteenth century stands there near the bank, surrounded by a few cottages, and by the river is a wharf, for the old name Cealchythe means
Chalk Wharf.

❰ THE TWO TOWNS

Now we can begin to see how twentieth-century London was formed.
The body has grown obese and the articulations are barely visible, but

the original skeleton can still be felt today beneath the fumed skin. There was the Bridge which formed the City; the merchants' city itself behind its protective walls and its busy port; the Tower on the south-east as the royal gesture of power; Westminster, the centre of government and law two miles to the south-west of the City but linked to the Tower by the river; Southwark as the south gateway to the Bridge, an ecclesiastical centre, a resting-place for travellers and a sanctuary for miscreants; between the City and Westminster the road of palaces and, spread everywhere, the properties of the religious houses. Around the walls of the City the suburbs ran into the Liberties up to the Bars and beyond and all around lay the fertile country sprinkled with manor-houses and villages, all of which were to be devoured by the voracious town. The port tended to move down-river and the residential suburbs to move the other way towards Westminster and to the north-west. So began the social and functional divisions of London into the City, the East End and the West End.

As for the river itself, its conservancy was handed over in a vague way to the City Corporation by Richard I in 1197, and in its hands it remained jealously guarded until 1857. This City jurisdiction extended all the way from the mouth of the Medway up to Staines, where, just beyond the town, may be seen to this day an aged stone on the north bank inscribed 'God Preserve ye City of London'. For centuries the legal position was never very clear and frequent disputes arose, especially concerning fishing rights. Then in 1613, in the reign of James I, a trial decided that the City and its Lord Mayor were in fact the legal conservators of the Thames.

In this river journey in the Middle Ages we have seen London in its most picturesque if unhygienic phase, with its silhouette of spires and towers, its wonderful Bridge of houses and its strand of grand palaces. The City's pride was summed up in the poem of Dunbar in praise of this 'flower of Cities all':

> *'Fresh is thy ryver with his lusty strandis;*
> *Blith be thy chirches, wele sownyng be thy bellis . . .*
> *Upon thy lusty Brigge of pylers white*
> *Been merchauntis full royall to behold;*
> *Upon thy stretis goeth many a semely knyght*
> *All clad in velvet gownes and in cheynes of gold.'*

LONDON WAS TO retain much of its mediæval appearance right up to the Great Fire of 1666, that dramatic nodal event in the City's history. Changes to London in Tudor times were gradual and piecemeal.

During the Wars of the Roses and after, London was growing ever more prosperous and her trade was increasing steadily. The middle classes were beginning to feel their power and the English merchants in London were at last successfully competing with the foreigners. Ship building became established along the banks of the Thames below the City. At Deptford Henry VIII created a shipyard as the cradle of the new Navy and in 1599, in Elizabeth's time, London's first dry dock was built at Rotherhithe. Then great adventures were on foot in England's name; there was privateering against Spain and the Merchant Adventurers company was formed for the discovery of lands not known. At Deptford, Drake's *Golden Hind* was moored for a time for the admiration and excitation of Londoners; the anonymous author of *An Apology of the City* (*c.* 1575) wrote proudly: 'It spreadeth the honour of our country abroad by her long navigations and maketh our power feared even of barbarous princes.'

Such things affected the look of the riverside, and the City under the Tudors gradually gained that half-Gothic, half-Renaissance look, with its untutored Italianate classicism, which we call Jacobethan. A new and prosperous atmosphere existed which, in such forms as the new Nonesuch House on the Bridge, must have seemed weird and glamorous to people even in those lusty and adventurous days.

⟦ THE CITY SPREADS

The expansion of London had been checked to some extent in the Middle Ages by the large amount of land owned by the monasteries, which formed a kind of Green Belt around the City; but when these were confiscated in 1538 after the Dissolution (which some have called the Great Pillage), buildings began to spread over these lands because the population was growing, partly as a result of the influx of Protestant refugees.

The wealthier merchants and the new rich took over most of the large houses within the City, and they built imposing new domains in the suburbs, of stone and brick elaborately decorated and with large win-

dows glazed with leaded lights. Hall, in his *Chronicle* of 1548, disapproved of them, for 'like Midsummer pageants, with towers, turrets
and chimney-tops', they seemed to him to have been erected not so
much 'for use of profit' as 'for show and pleasure, betraying the vanity
of men's minds, much unlike to the disposition of the ancient citizens,
who delighted in the building of hospitals and almshouses for the poor,
and therein both employed their wits and spent their wealth in prefer-
ment of the common commodity of this our city'.

The roads running towards the City gates, the area around the Tower,
and the north side of the Strand became increasingly built up, though
St. Giles was still literally in the fields and the country began west of
Charing Cross. As the number of ships arriving and departing grew,
the port extended below the Tower, and on the south bank shipyards
and timber-stacks sprang up. At Deptford the sound of hammering
never ceased on the grand new ships with their high poops and
their fat-cheeked prows eagerly facing the river. On the north
bank, houses spread as far as Blackwall, and there was ribbon development along the approach roads, mainly housing for shipwrights and
sailors.

Stow, writing at the close of the sixteenth century, tells us that:

'By the Tower of London is the Hospital of St. Katherine, founded
by Matilda, the queen, wife to King Stephen.* From this precinct of
St. Katherine to Wapping in the west, the usual place of execution for
hanging of pirates and sea-rovers, at the low-water mark, and there to
remain till three tides had overflowed them, was never a house standing
within these forty years; but since the gallows being after removed
farther off, a continual street, or filthy straight passage with alleys of small
tenements, or cottages, built, inhabited by sailors victuallers, along by
the river of Thames, almost to Ratcliffe, a good mile from the Tower . . .
and Ratcliffe itself hath been also increasing in building eastward, in
place where I have known a large highway, with fair elm-trees on both
the sides, that the same hath now taken hold of Lime Hurst, or Lime
Host, corruptly called Lime House, sometime distant a mile from Ratcliffe.'

In 1565 hackney coaches were introduced to add to the crowd, the
dangers and the din of the town. The watermen complained bitterly
of this threat to their livelihood and to the breaking of their virtual

* The site was later to be occupied by Telford's Katherine Docks.

monopoly in the carrying of passengers, but the coaches did not, in fact, greatly reduce their river trade.

Because of the difficulty of negotiating the Bridge and the increased size of vessels, the port between Billingsgate and the Tower was particularly busy. There ships arrived with fine clothes, silks, cottons, linens, spices, oils, wine, jewels and bullion; they departed with woven cloths, raw wool, tin, skins and the finished products of the fellmongers. Queenhithe, above bridge, was still active enough, however, and was now largely concerned with sugar imports. For a while at the end of the sixteenth century a curious apparatus could be seen by Queenhithe —a corn-mill worked by the tide and fixed between two barges moored in the river.

Smuggling was rife along the river and reached a point when Queen Elizabeth enacted a law to compel all ships to discharge under supervision only at certain legal quays.

(BIRD'S-EYE VIEWS

The general effect of the City seen from the river in the latter half of the sixteenth century was now warmer in colour than it had been, on account of the increasing use of red brick. Elaborate detailing appeared on the houses and much wood carving of unscholarly details of adapted classical orders, keystone gargoyles and heavy strapwork ornament. Few churches were built during this century, and work was concentrated on the new large mansions, especially those for Henry VIII along the riverside: at Whitehall, Greenwich, Bridewell and Chelsea. In the latter part of the century, behind the roofs of the City, stood the depressing sight of Old St. Paul's, now in decay and missing its splendid spire, which, with the roof, was burned down in 1561.

Almost nothing remains in the twentieth century of mediæval or Tudor London except the Tower, Westminster Abbey, parts of the Temple Church, parts of Lambeth Palace, the gatehouse of St. James's Palace, a few churches and that famous block of half-timbered houses in Holborn. But we can gain a very clear picture of Tudor London and Westminster with its riverside and Bridge from the maps and panoramas made in the latter half of the sixteenth century. The great bird's-eye view, ten feet long, attributed to Antony van den Wyngaerde, drawn between 1543 and 1550 and now at the Bodleian Library, is the earliest realistic representation of London. The *Civitas Londinum*, six feet long, attributed to Ralph Agas, a land surveyor and engraver, is more of a true map than Wyngaerde's drawing, though still a pictorial bird's-eye view. Its date is uncertain, but it seems to have been made between 1570 and 1600, in the latter part of Elizabeth's reign. One of the two earliest known copies is at the Guildhall, the other at Magdalen College, Oxford.

A third map is *Londinum Feracissimi Angliae Regni Metropolis* by Hofnagel, probably made in 1561 and therefore more or less contemporary with Agas's work. It is much smaller than the other two and is more of a true street map than the others, though still pictorial, in the fashion of the time; it forms an illustration to Braun and Hogenburg's work, *Civitates Orbis Terrarum*, of 1572. Finally we have the small-scale but beautiful maps of Westminster and London by John Norden which appear in his *Speculum Britanniae* of 1593.

Because all these 'maps' are pictorial, especially Wyngaerde's, which is particularly naturalistic, we can see exactly how Elizabethan London looked—right down to small and fascinating details such as doors and windows, ships, clothes, gardens and so on. In Agas's, for example, we can see how a man leads two horses to the riverside to fill the barrels on their backs with water, while up in Moorfields, just north of the wall, housewives are laying out their washing and some youths are practising the long bow.

[PLEASING PALACES

Wyngaerde's grand view takes us from Westminster right down to Greenwich, where the splendid Palace of Placentia, symmetrical and embellished with a dozen spires, has been refurbished. The Green Village goes back to the little Saxon settlement of Grenewic, and there two manors have stood by the river since Norman days, for Edward I is known to have stayed there. The two estates belonged for many years to the Abbey of St. Peter in Ghent; but Henry V, suppressing foreign religious houses, granted the land to the Carthusians at Sheen, who sold it about 1433 to Humphrey, Duke of Gloucester, a nobleman of culture who gave Oxford its first library. This being a strategic spot between the river and the Dover Road, the Duke fortified and embattled the manor and, forming a park around it, he called it Bellacourt. He also built a look-out tower on the hillside above the house, from the top of which a magnificent view of the estuary and of its shipping and of the Epping woods to the north could be enjoyed. In that tower Elizabeth was to imprison Leicester, and in a new building on the same spot

Old Greenwich Palace, or the Palace of Placentia; here reconstructed in a drawing of 1767 in the Guildhall Library.

Charles II installed Flamsteed as Astronomer Royal to solve the pressing maritime problem of longitude. Here later was to run the meridian from which all longitudes are now calculated, but the Royal Observatory was moved from there in 1950 to the clearer air of Hurstmonceux in Sussex.

When the Duke fell from power, Queen Margaret of Anjou took over the place, enlarged it and called it Placentia or her Manor of Pleasaunce. The Tudors used it frequently as a retreat, for it was conveniently near the Dover Road and the new naval dockyards of Deptford and Woolwich. Henry VII softened the military aspect of the façade with red brickwork pierced with mullioned windows. His son, to become Henry VIII, was born there and always had a strong affection for the place. He too altered the building, adding a tilt yard, towers, oriels, gables and twisted chimneys, and in the chapel he married three of his wives. Queen Mary II and Elizabeth were both born there, and there Edward VI died. Elizabeth delighted in her Greenwich Palace as much as had her father, for she declared: 'Sure the house, garden and walks may compare with any delicat place in Italy.' The Tudors held many court revels there, and when they were in residence the royal standard flew above the roofs and every armed ship that passed in the river fired a salute. The German traveller Hentzner described a typical Court of Queen Elizabeth's time held here in all its magnificence, the centre of it being the wonderful old virago herself in her brilliant red wig, her black teeth set in her thin, white face above a fantastic, billowing dress all laced and bejewelled. A century later, a grand new edifice took the place of the palace, and to that we shall return.

Some way west of Greenwich lies Deptford Village and Says Court. Wyngaerde's foreground then shows a near view of Bermondsey Abbey, now confiscated by Henry VIII, but apparently still in good order with a wide enclosed garden. In the foreground we also see the buildings of Southwark; the square tower of St. Mary Overy (now St. Saviour's) and the Palaces of Winchester and Rochester lie west of the bridgehead; the high street running south from the Bridge and built up with houses, inns and the church of St. George; and, opposite the church, Suffolk House belonging to Charles, Duke of Suffolk, who married the King's sister. That large and sumptuous mansion, unlike the unseemly entry east of the City, impresses travellers approaching London as the first sign of the City's reputed glory; its seven towers are surmounted with ornate cupolas, stepped gables and many courtyards, and it is ensconced in orchards and gardens.

Wyngaerde has drawn some figures in his foreground, including a man on horseback, and the clothes they wear help us to fix the date of the drawing fairly accurately. The houses spreading from Southwark High Street show clearly the vernacular dream-cottage style of the times with their roofs, some tiled and some thatched, walls half-timbered, and gables overhanging.

⟦ LONDON PLEASURES

Agas and Norden both show Bankside built up with a row of houses as far as the pleasure resort of Paris Garden; and its landing-stage lies on the edge of those fields and marshes of Lambeth where races and open-air games and dances are held. But Wyngaerde shows only a few buildings west of the Bridge and these include a huddle of houses called the Stews.

Behind Agas's houses stand two curious round structures open to the sky at their centres. They are used for bull- and bear-baiting and for cock-fighting, and dogs are shown chained up before a row of kennels in front of them. The bear ring stands on the ground which in the twentieth century is covered by the street called Bear Gardens near Rose Alley.

That this part of London may have been a pleasure resort since the foundation of the City, has been suggested by the discovery in the

district of a Roman gladiator's trident which may have been used in some local circus. But in these Tudor times there is no doubt about it— Bankside, with its bear gardens, playhouses, taverns and stews, is London's riverside resort of pleasure. A proclamation of 1545 refers to 'the Bank and such-like naughty places'. In spite of the Puritan phase,

London's riverside west of the Bridge in mid-sixteenth century. (Part of a nineteenth-century reproduction of Wyngaerde's great panorama, ten feet long, at the Bodleian Library). On the left is the Fleet River and Old St. Paul's Cathedral. In the foreground on the approach to the Bridge stands Suffolk House and by the bridgehead is the church with its tall square tower of St. Saviour's (now Southwark Cathedral). At the north bridgehead can be seen the old church of St. Magnus Martyr. The chapel, above its great starling, in the centre of the Bridge can be clearly seen and also the heads of traitors set on poles above the Bridgegate tower. Queenhithe dock lies on the north bank above the tower of St. Saviour's.

Bankside was to survive as a pleasure place until the eighteenth century, and then its vicious but virile glory faded away.

The round houses of Bankside, these Wooden Os, of which a whole series came to be erected, were used for various entertainments, for plays as well as animal baiting. The builder of the Swan Theatre, for instance, was instructed to make it suitable 'for players to play in, and for the game of bears and bulls'. Some were built purely as playhouses by the impresarios of the day like Henslowe and Alleyn, and while animal baiting was an old entertainment, the lay theatre was only just awakening.

Let us first see the animal sport. All classes, men and women, from the Sovereign downwards, regarded the baiting of animals as a fine and legitimate pastime. Elizabeth enjoyed it immensely and animals were kept for the royal pleasure under the management of a Master of the Royal Game of Bears, Bulls and Mastiff Dogs. The sport was stopped in 1642 by Act of Parliament, but it was revived at the Restoration and continued until 1835, when it was finally made illegal. The civic authorities disapproved of it, not on humanitarian grounds, but because, like any other public entertainment, it created mobs. Paul Hentzner, visiting England in 1598, described the game in his travel diary: 'The Bulls and Bears . . . are fastened behind, and then worried by great English bull-dogs; but not without great risk to the dogs, from the horns of the one, and the teeth of the other; and it sometimes happens they are killed upon the spot; fresh ones are immediately supplied in the places of those that are wounded, or tired. To this entertainment there often follows that of whipping a blinded Bear, which is performed by five or six men, standing circularly with whips, which they exercise on him without mercy, as he cannot escape from them because of his chain; he defends himself with all his force and skill, throwing down all who come within his reach, and are not active enough to get out of it, and tearing the whips out of their hands and breaking them.'

There were other animal shows in those days; dancing bears, for instance. At the Tower the royal menagerie was still maintained, including lions, which were sometimes persuaded to fight each other. By the Tower on any day during the reign of Henry VII might have been seen a polar bear attached to a chain, being led out for a swim in the river to fish for salmon. Just to the north-west of the Tower an open space is shown on all the maps which has a stage erected in the middle. Here another popular entertainment could be enjoyed from time to time when a public execution took place.

There were less cruel entertainments, especially dancing, for we were known abroad as the Dancing English. There were the annual fairs, which by Tudor times had become pleasure fairs and revelries as much as markets, and there could be seen conjurors, tumblers, jugglers and fire-eaters. Along the river, Greenwich, Southwark and Westminster had their annual fairs, and a special horse fair was held at Horseley Down, to the east of Southwark, opposite the Tower, where Agas shows right on the riverside a great 'Bare House' nestling in a wooded garden. Southwark Fair became—with Bartholomew Fair in London and Sturbridge Fair in Cambridge—one of the three biggest annual fairs in the country. It grew more and more hectic, and reached its most riotous tempo in the eighteenth century, when Hogarth depicted it with its waxworks, its giant, its tumbler, conjuror, tight-rope walker, bag-piper, prize-fighter, puppet show and theatre. All classes enjoyed these frolics, including the scum of the town, and by 1743 the fair at Southwark had become so rowdy that it was ordered to be cried down by the bellman. In 1763 it was officially suppressed.

Sometimes the City Fathers or the Sovereign would arrange vivid pageants on the river. Typical was that which took place three days before Elizabeth's coronation, when the Queen made a ceremonial river journey from Westminster to the Tower accompanied by the Lord Mayor and City Corporation, 'their barges decked with banners of their crafts and mysteries, artillery shooting off lustily as they went, with great and pleasant melody of instruments, which played in a sweet and heavenly manner', as a contemporary noted. The colour of these progresses was brilliant: we hear of a pageant in the time of the first Tudor when the Mayor was robed in crimson velvet and sported a great velvet hat edged with fur, a girdle of gold round his middle and a 'bawdrike of gold about his neck trilling down behind him', while the attendant aldermen were dressed in scarlet with sanguine hoods.

⟨ SHAKESPEARE'S BANKSIDE

But the play was now the thing. There had been Mysteries and Mummeries and Miracle Plays in mediæval times, and these had been performed in any hall or church or in the streets on movable, wheeled platforms facing a demountable auditorium. Play-acting became associated with sin, and it is thus easy to forget that the churches were the first theatres.

Not until James Burbage, a joiner and a member of the Earl of Leicester's company of players, erected his timber playhouse, called the
Theatre, at Shoreditch in 1576 did the legitimate lay theatre really begin
in London. There Shakespeare, who came to town in 1586, first
achieved fame—not as a writer, but as an actor. The district, which
came to contain another theatre called the Curtain, was selected because
it lay outside the City's jurisdiction and the City was opposed to playhouses because 'plays do make assemblies of citizens and their families',
and assemblies were regarded with apprehension by those concerned
with keeping the peace. Moreover, theatres tended to spread the plague
—always a constant danger—so that all theatres were closed if the death-
rate from plague exceeded fifty in a week.

In 1596, a year before he died, Burbage built another theatre, this
time at Blackfriars; Playhouse Yard off Blackfriars Lane now marks the
spot. In 1598 Burbage's two sons, after a quarrel with the ground land-
lord, removed the Theatre—timber structure, furnishings, fittings and
all—'in the most forcible and riotous manner' to Bankside, where it was
called the Globe Theatre. It became so closely associated with Shakespeare's plays that its fame outlived that of all its contemporaries on
Bankside, such as the Rose and the Hope.

The memory of the Globe has been perpetuated by a bas-relief of
bronze inserted into the wall of Barclay's Brewery in Park Street,
Southwark. The tablet, unveiled in 1909, shows the head of Shakespeare reproduced from an authentic portrait and the inscription runs:
'Here stood the Globe Playhouse of Shakespeare, 1598–1613'.

In the 1640s most of the Bankside theatres were swept away by the
Puritans. The Globe was 'pulled downe to the ground by Sir Matthew
Brand, on Monday the 15th of April, 1644, to make tenements in the
room of it' (Howe's MS. continuation of Stow's *Survey*). The Hope,
used for both plays and bear-baiting, survived until 1656, when the
bears, by command of the High Sheriff of Surrey, were shot to death by
a company of soldiers.

⟦ SOUTHWARK AND ITS STEWS

We have mentioned the Stews shown in Wyngaerde's panorama. They
had existed on the south bank at least since the time of Henry II—probably since Roman times. In Henry VIII's reign Bankside became known
as the Stewes Bank, yet that incontinent king was the first to order the
closing down of these bordellos. As Stow tells: 'This row of stewes in

Southwark was put downe by the King's commandment, which was proclaymed by sounde of Trumpet, not more to be privileged, and used as a common Brothel, but the inhabitants of the same to keepe good order and honest rule as in other places of the realme.'

Not that Southwark was the only part of London at this time to contain houses of ill-fame; it was merely notorious for doing so. Stow mentions Stew Lane near Queenhithe (it still exists), so named 'of a stewe or hotte house there kept'.

A stewe was originally a sweating, or steam, bath which came to Britain from the Imperial City during the Roman occupation. This hygienic type of pleasure resort continued in Russia, Finland, Turkey and the Near East and was brought back to England again in the twelfth century by the Crusaders. Such bathing houses, through fleshly association, were usually bawdy houses—in Stow's phrase, 'for the repaire of incontinent men to the like women'.

Henry VIII's Act, like most other attempts to restrict this ancient profession, had little effect, and John Taylor, the Thames waterman and versifier of the seventeenth century, explained:

> '*The stews in England bore a beastly sway*
> *Till the eighth Henry banished them away.*
> *And since those common whores were quite put downe,*
> *A damnèd crew of private whores are grown.*'

Latimer also complained in a more solemn way: 'What availeth that you have but changed the places and not taken the whoredom away? There is now more whoredom in London than ever there was on the Banke.'

Back in Henry II's reign the stew houses had been accepted as an inevitable part of London's cultural pattern, but strict regulations were then issued for their management and Parliament ordered that 'certain stewe-houses privileged there (at Bankside) for ever should be kept within that lordship or franchise, according to the old customs that had been there used time out of mind'. Among the sensible regulations were the following:

'That no stew-holder or his wife should let or staye any single woman to goe and come freely at all times when they listed.'

'To take no more for the woman's chamber in the weeke than fourteene pence.'

'No single woman to be kept against her wille that would leave her sinne.'

'No single woman to take money to lie with any man, but shee lie with him all night till the morrow.'

'No man to be drawn or enticed into any stewhouse.'

'No stew-holder to keepe any woman that hath the perilous infirmitie of burning.'

The rents of these houses, as well as the fines imposed for breaking the regulations, increased the revenues of the Bishops of Winchester, and so the ladies of easy virtue on Bankside became known as Winchester Geese. The registered houses in early Tudor times were required to have signs painted on their walls facing the river, such as the Boar's Head, the Cross Keys, the Gun, the Swan, the Cardinal's Hat. (It is still often believed in the Orient that London's brothels are run by the Church.)

Early in the seventeenth century the Cardinal's Hat ceased to function as a brothel and, under Henslowe's ownership, became a meeting-place for actors. Attached to it was an ordinary, or *table d'hôte* eating-house. Probably the food there was good, as it certainly was at the famous inns along the Southwark high street, where travellers could find comfort and company near the great open fireplaces where glistening joints and plump capons turned above the flames. London had always possessed an international reputation for its cooking, and did so especially during the sixteenth century. The word Cockney may indeed come from *coquina*, meaning kitchen, a sad reminder of a tradition now lost.*

Good drink, as well as good food, could be had along Bankside, for 'the whole street is a continual ale-house', Dekker tells us in the early seventeenth century. Since Chaucer's day Southwark had owned a reputation for its 'nappy strong ale'. Late in the seventeenth century one

* Other derivations have been suggested. There is the curious tale—somewhat of the same sort as that which has suggested that the word Jazz comes from 'Jus' a tune'—given by John Minshen in *Ductor in Linguas*, 1617: 'A cockney or cockny—applied only to one born within the sound of Bow bells, that is within the City of London, a terme coming first out of this tale. That a cittizen's sonne riding with his father in the country, asked when he heard a horse neigh what the horse did; his father answered "neigh". Riding further he heard a cock crow, and said: "Does the cock neigh too?"' But the word seems to have applied originally to a small, misshapen egg, called a cock's egg, signifying something odd and misshapen. (See W. Kent, *An Encyclopædia of London*.)

of these Bankside pubs-cum-breweries (local house-brewing being usual until hops were introduced as a preservative from Germany) acquired a large trade under the ownership of one James Child. From that business grew the huge concern of Barclay Perkins, which today occupies so large an area to the south of Bankside.

No less than five prisons existed in unruly Southwark for the internment of 'such as should brabble, fray, or break the peace'. The most notable was the Clink, which stood near the river close to the stews and is now recalled by Clink Street, a gloomy canyon spanned by bridges between warehouses of dirty yellow brickwork. At one time the Clink was the small private prison of the Bishops of Winchester, a damp, unpleasant place lying below high-water level. The word, originally meaning a keyhole or a door-catch, is first mentioned in 1509 as 'clynke', and it came to signify not only the Liberty of the Bishops of Winchester, but also its gaol; in time it has come to serve as the vernacular, generic word for any gaol. The Clink ceased to be a prison in Cromwell's day, but the local inhabitants were still called Clinkers for a long time afterwards.

Bankside retained its notoriety even up to the nineteenth century as the libertarian home of debtors, felons and miscreants of every sort, who there could find the safe sanctuary of St Saviour's. The district was even used for a time by the City as a convenient dumping ground for undesirables. Then in 1550 the City bought a large part of Southwark from the King, and soon the whole of it came under the City's jurisdiction as the twenty-sixth ward, called Bridge Ward Without, to distinguish it from the Bridge Ward Within, which consisted of the Bridge itself and the area around the north bridgehead. Even when it had ceased to be a Liberty the general laxity of the place continued on its own momentum.

By Stow's time, at the end of the sixteenth century, Southwark had become fairly extensively built-up and stretched well over a mile along the river on either side of the bridgehead. 'The muster of men in this borough', Stow says, 'doth in number surpass all other cities, except London.' The building must have been rapid during the latter half of the sixteenth century, for Wyngaerde's panorama shows little building between Lambeth Palace and the cathedral-like structure of St. Mary Overy (or rather of St. Saviour's, as it became called after the Dissolution, when the prior and his monks were turned adrift). Stow says that almost the whole riverside between the Bridge and Lambeth had become built over by his day at the turn of the century.

⟦ THE NORTH BANK

Returning to our maps, we can survey the river, its great bridge and the whole north bank as it appeared in the sixteenth century. In Wyngaerde's panorama we see many large, sturdy, square-rigged ocean-going ships moored in mid-stream below bridge as far to the east as St. Katherine's Dock on the river, the precursor of Telford's enclosed dock of the early nineteenth century. Wherries and small sailing barges called hoys are scudding about among these trading vessels and a large timber raft is being poled down-stream by two men. Three large ships are squeezed into Billingsgate harbour. Above bridge many small craft are seen on the river: two more rafts, many little sailing-boats, a lighter or two and several state barges gay with fluttering flags and canopies and each moved by eight oarsmen. Just to the east of Lambeth Palace the horse ferry is approaching Stangate Stairs. Half a dozen small craft are moored in Queenhithe, for no large, tall ships have sailed above bridge since 1480, when it was decided that the drawbridge, in poor condition, should no longer be raised except to defend the City. East of the Bridge is that 'sure and most beautiful Roade for shipping', as William Camden, a contemporary of Stow and Shakespeare, calls it, where 'a man would say that seeth the shipping there, that it is, as it were, a very wood of trees disbranched to make glades and let in light; so shaded is it with masts and sailes'. Apart from these 'vessels of burthen', Stow says that 'there pertayneth to the cities of London and Westminster and the borough of Southwark above the number, as is supposed, of 2,000 wherries and other small boates whereby 3,000 poor men at the least be set on work and maintained'.

Old Paul's still has its steeple in Wyngaerde's drawing and to the west of the cathedral the Fleet Ditch runs down in a broad stream to the river, its two bridges being clearly shown. The Fleet was cleared out in 1502 and, under the name of Turnmill Brook, worked several flour and flatting mills. But then it returned to its usual unsavoury state. In 1560, some ten years after the time of Wyngaerde's drawing, Dr. Jones in his *Dyall of Agues* wrote of the Fleet Valley and its 'stinking lanes' that 'there died most in London, and were soonest inflicted and longest continued, as twice since I have known London, I have marked it to be true'. The Fleet was still capable of turning a snuff mill in the eighteenth century, but in 1734, despite Wren's efforts with the Fleet Canal after the Great Fire, it had become so vile a public nuisance that most

of it was then arched over to form a road. Pope's *Dunciad* described its
condition vividly:

> '*This labour past, by Bridewell all descend,*
> *(As morning pray'r and flagellation end)*
> *To where Fleet-ditch with disemboguing streams*
> *Rolls the large tribute of dead dogs to Thames.*
> *The King of Dykes! than whom, no sluice of mud,*
> *With deeper sable blots the silver flood.*'

Just to the east of the Fleet's mouth stands Baynards Castle in Wyngaerde's panorama, a range of towers lapped by the river, while to its
west the grand Palace of Bridewell is depicted as it was built by Henry
VIII for the entertainment of nobility and foreign potentates. The Emperor Charles lodged at Blackfriars on his visit to London in 1522, and
a wooden bridge was built across the Fleet here to link Blackfriars with
the palace. Stow says that the bridge existed in his time, but it is not
shown by Wyngaerde. Bridewell is a stately and beautiful house, says
Stow, and so it appears in the panorama, very large and four-square with
its two great internal courtyards. Henry himself often lodged there,
notably in 1529 when Cardinal Campeius, the Papal Legate, and Cardinal Wolsey were at Blackfriars judging whether or not the King's
marriage with Queen Katherine was lawful.

In 1552 Edward VI handed over the palace to the City for use as a
house of correction—'a workhouse for the poor and idle persons of the
city, wherein a great number of vagrant persons be now set a-work, and
relieved of the charges of the citizens' (Stow). Strype, in his 1720 edition of Stow, described it as a Hospital and 'now is for an House of
Correction, and to be a Place where all Strumpets, Night-walkers, Pick-
pockets, vagrant and idle Persons, that are taken up for their ill lives, as
also incorrigible and disobedient Servants, are committed by the Mayor
and Aldermen, who are Justices of the Peace within the said City; And
being so committed are forced to beat Hemp in publick View, with due
Correction of whipping, according to their Offence, for such a Time as
the President and Court shall see Cause.'

Bridewell was to suffer in the Great Fire, when the south quadrangle
was quite destroyed. But reconstruction was fairly rapid and was completed in 1676. A new stone bridge across the Fleet, Italianate and
arched high, was then built. After the reconstruction following the Great
Fire, a public whipping-room, draped in black and having a balustraded

F

public gallery, was built at Bridewell, and during the seventeenth and eighteenth centuries the public was admitted to watch the flagellation as one of the more sophisticated London delights. Bridewell continued as a reformatory until 1855 and the building was not demolished until 1863.

The palaces along the Strand are clearly delineated by Wyngaerde and even more clearly by Norden in his Westminster map—York, Durham (where Raleigh lived), Russell, Savoy, Arundel, Leicester and Essex. With their courtyards, formal gardens, great halls, chapels and irregular and picturesque variety, they are not unlike the colleges of Oxford. Between Arundel House and Savoy Palace, west of the Temple, a new house has appeared. This is Somerset Place, an important building in the history of English architecture, for it is almost certainly the first example of the Italianate Renaissance style in this country. Anne of Denmark added to it, so that it came to contain as many as three courts. Inigo Jones designed additions, including a chapel. A delightful engraving by Kip shows the great house and its formal riverside gardens as it appeared in its most complete form with Jones's work of 1638 and the new river-front of 1661 (see pp. 104-5). It became a Grace-and-Favour residence assigned to poor members of the aristocracy, and soon after its formation the Royal Academy was installed here in the royal apartments. Then in the 1770s the old, decayed palace was pulled down to make room for the great block of public offices designed by Sir William Chambers.

⁅ WHITEHALL

North of Westminster a huge complex has arisen by the riverside. Wolsey was residing here at the time of his disgrace, when it was the property of the See of York. Then called York Place, it was built originally by Hubert de Burgh, Henry III's minister, in the thirteenth century, but Wolsey rebuilt it in magnificent Tudor style with state rooms facing the river, a great hall, a chapel and a gallery, all richly furnished. There he lived in style attended by a household of eight hundred people until Henry VIII commandeered the place, annexed the neighbouring St. James's Leper Hospital and proceeded to make the domain even vaster than it had been. It then became the King's Manor of Westminster, but was generally known as Whitehall, and here the King moved with his Court from Westminster Palace, which had become rather dilapidated. As Shakespeare tells us in *Henry VIII*:

'Sir, you
Must no more call it York Place, that is past;
For since the Cardinal fell, that title's lost:
'Tis now the King's and called Whitehall.'

In the end the whole great palace precinct covered the area between Westminster and Charing Cross. As the Act of Parliament which Henry obtained reveals: 'The entire space between Charing Cross and the Sanctuary of Westminster, from the Thames on the east side to the park wall westward, shall from henceforth be deemed the king's whole Palace of Westminster.'

The Archbishops of York were compelled to move further east to a new London residence next to Durham House.

Below the palace on the east was a magnificent wine-cellar originated by Wolsey, but partly rebuilt by the King. When the miscellaneous jumble of eighteenth-century buildings which eventually developed on the site of the old palace were pulled down not long ago, some traces of the Tudor palace were discovered, including this wine cellar. It was found to be in a condition fair enough to make a restoration worth while —fair enough, indeed, to make worth while the wholesale moving of its four thousand tons a distance of twenty feet from its original position to make way for the foundations of the big new Air Ministry building. This dignified vault can now be seen on Saturday afternoons if special permission is first obtained.

In 1622 Inigo Jones added his classical Banqueting Hall to the palace, as a small part of a great new projected palace which was never to be executed; that hall was to survive to modern times in spite of the fire which consumed most of Whitehall Palace in 1698.

Two centuries of England's royal history are closely associated with Whitehall. There Henry VIII married Anne Boleyn and there he died on the 28th of January 1547. To this place the corpse of Queen Elizabeth was brought from Richmond on the 24th March 1603 to lie in state until burial. While six ladies watched round her coffin that night 'her body burst with such a crack, that it split the wood, lead and cerecloth; whereupon the next day she was fain to be new trimmed up' (Lady Southwell's MS). It was in the royal bedchamber here that Guy Fawkes was dragged before King James I from the cellar of the House of Lords. Asked what he intended to do with all those barrels of gunpowder, he is said to have replied: 'One thing I meant to do was to blow

Westminster towards the end of the sixteenth century (a detail from the map of Agas). Westminster Abbey and the great Hall are on the bottom left and running up north-east from them, with its two towered gateways, is 'Kinges Streete' now called Whitehall. Top centre is 'The Court', Henry VIII's Whitehall Palace, and above it Scotland Yard. St. James's Park lies on the top left and Lambeth Palace on the bottom right.

Scotchmen back to Scotland.' Charles I passed through a window of Jones's Banqueting Hall on to the scaffold for his execution 'in the open street before Whitehall'. Cromwell resided in the palace after the execution with his Lady Protectress and family and Milton his Secretary; and in spite of his asceticism he lived there in luxury, and there also he died.

[WESTMINSTER

South of Whitehall the old Westminster Palace, the Abbey and the surroundings underwent some changes after the Reformation. In spite of the destructions of the Dissolution, Westminster, alone of all the great abbeys of the Thames-side, survived, thanks to its links with the royal house. The King commandeered most of its revenues, but its fabric at least was spared and for nearly a decade the old abbey enjoyed a new status as a cathedral with a bishopric. In 1599 Queen Elizabeth turned the place into a collegiate church, and so it remains.

The old Palace lost its court gaiety after the King moved to Whitehall, but it achieved a new kind of life as the fixed parliamentary centre. The fine Chapel of St. Stephen, south of the Great Hall and close to the river bank, was fitted up for the Commons. The Star Chamber, to the east, became a court-house where the Lord Chancellor, the chief justices and members of the Privy Council dispensed any punishment except death and would hear plaints 'of riots, routs and other misdemeanours' (Stow). North of Old Palace Yard a huddle of smaller and meaner buildings sprang up, mostly lodgings for officials and also one or two taverns.

Wyngaerde shows the abbey church with a squat, square tower over the crossing without a steeple, while at the east end of the Abbey church the magnificently ornate late Gothic Lady Chapel of Henry VII is shown. Washington Irving, four centuries later, was to describe it well: 'The very walls are wrought into universal ornament, encrusted with tracery and scooped into niches, crowded with statues of saints and martyrs. Stone seems, by the cunning labour of the chisel, to have been robbed of its weight and density, suspended aloft, as if by magic, and the fretted roof achieved with the wonderful minuteness and airy security of a cobweb.'

In a broad courtyard, Old Palace Yard, just north of the Great Hall to which an arched gateway called the King's Stairs gives entrance from the river, stands a low, domed conduit head, and next to it a tall pointed tower. This is the Clock Tower, 'a tower of stone, containing a clock, which striketh every hour on a great bell, to be heard into the hall in sitting-time of the courts, or otherwise'. This is Stow again, who also tells us that 'the same clock, in a calm, will be heard into the city of London'. The domed building beside the tower he says is 'a fountain which at coronations and great triumphs is made to run with wine out of divers spouts'.

At Westminster great wealth rubbed shoulders with great poverty: it was not only a Sanctuary, but was inhabited by many hangers-on of the rich who were moderately well-off only when the Court was in residence. An Elizabethan statute refers to people living near the Abbey who are 'for the most part without trade or any other stay ... many of them wholly given to vice and idleness'. Norden tells us: 'The Citie of Westminster is known to have no generall trade whereby relief might be administered unto the common sort as by merchandise, clothing or such like ... had they not therefore some other meanes, the common sort could not be sustained. The first and principal meanes is her Majestie's residence at Whitehall or St. James', whence if her Grace be long absent the poore people forthwith complaine of pennary and want, and of a hard and miserable world.'

Before leaving Westminster in this sixteenth century we must not forget to look at the old parish church of St. Margaret's in the Abbey's shadow to the north. It provided then, as it does now, a valuable foil to the Abbey church, helping greatly to set off the Abbey's size. The church dates back at least to the twelfth century, and a tradition exists that it was founded by Edward the Confessor to please the monks, who disliked admitting to the south aisle of their church so many laymen consisting largely of refugees from justice taking Sanctuary. If this doubtful tradition is true, St. Margaret's has the oldest foundation of any London church excepting St. Paul's and Westminster Abbey. Apart from the chancel, it was rebuilt by the merchants of the Staple and the parishioners in the days of Edward I. It was again rebuilt in the reign of Edward IV. It was stripped of its external decorations in 1735, when its tower was cased and virtually rebuilt, and it was generally remodelled inside between 1876 and 1882, when the galleries were removed. From 1614 St. Margaret's has been used as the church of the House of Commons, and there fashionable weddings are now held.

⟮ THE TOWER AND THE BRIDGE

Let our eyes now swing with those of Wyngaerde from his hovering viewpoint high above Southwark right to the eastern corner of the City and the Tower. The White Tower is surrounded by a wide moat and a muddle of castellated buildings, and the space between the south part of this moat and the river is an open quay where a few people are to be seen strolling about; some primitive cranes stand by the water and, just as they do today, some cannons point towards the south.

To the west of the Tower lies the Customs House, presumably still the first one erected in 1382, when the King granted that 'the tronage of wools should be kept in the house and a counting place for customers'; it is a half-timbered structure with gables and a broad wharf in front of it. It was soon to be burnt down, rebuilt in the seventeenth century and burnt again in the Great Fire. In 1668 Wren built a large and noble new Customs House in a symmetrical classical style, all in stone decorated with pilasters and a central pediment. Then in 1718, for the third time, it was destroyed by fire and afterwards rebuilt.

West of the Customs House is Billingsgate harbour and then on the east of the bridgehead stands the mediæval church of St. Magnus Martyr, while on the west of the bridgehead is the Hall of the wealthy Fishmongers Company. The City stretching away behind to east and west is a forest of towers and spires, for, though the properties of the twenty-three religious establishments which had ornamented mediæval London are being turned into dwellings and their grounds being built over, the number of churches has not greatly diminished since the Dissolution, and many a conventual church has become the local parish church. We must imagine the winding alleys in that maze of buildings as being mostly unmetalled and muddy in wet weather. No public services, financed from rates, existed, and London had to wait until after the Great Fire for their beginnings. The streets of the City would have been crowded with inhabitants magnificent in dress and overbearing in manner, if we accept the view of a foreign visitor of 1592.

On the Bridge, the chapel and the old Drawbridge Tower are clearly visible in Wyngaerde's drawing. This tower, though rebuilt in 1428, is again in a bad state of repair and in 1577 it was demolished; in its place arose the fabulous Nonesuch House. This fantastic structure was built of timber framework joined together with wooden pegs only: it was, in effect, a piece of modern, dry, frame construction with parts prefabricated in Holland. In Elizabeth's reign the Bridge became very fashionable, and at Nonesuch House a number of noblemen resided. The building is shown clearly in Norden's print of the Bridge, and we can agree with Stow that it is 'a beautiful and chargeable peece of worke', or, as More imagined the houses in his *Utopia*, a work 'buylded after gorgious and gallante sorte'. Its four corners are turreted and crowned with cupolas and golden vanes; it is well fenestrated with leaded panes to illuminate the cheerful rooms within, which overlook the fascinating scenes of the river; its walls are encrusted with scrolls, carved panelling

Part of London Bridge drawn by Norden in the sixteenth century. To the left
centre is Nonesuch House, 'a beautiful and chargeable peece of worke'.

and pilasters painted green and white: altogether a magnificent example
of the type of lay building on which that good craftsmanship, formerly
dedicated chiefly to ecclesiastical buildings, is now being lavished.

Norden describes the whole Bridge at this time as 'adorned with
sumptuous buildings, and statlie and beautifull houses on either side,
inhabited by wealthy citizens and furnished with all manner of trades
comparable in itselfe to a little Citie, whose buildings are so artificially
contrived, and so finely combined, as it seemeth more than an ordinary
streete, for it is as one continuall vaute or roofe, except certain voyde
places reserved from buildings, for the retire of passengers from the
danger of carres, carts and droves of cattell, usually passing that way'.

The fronts of the various new turreted houses terminating the blocks
are embellished with 'armes and Scotishons' and 'a great lyon holdynge
a great fayne in his clowes, with the Kynge's armes crowned with a
crowne imperiall and garnyshed with flowers-de-lyces'. On the stalls
along the shop-fronts of the bridge street the merchants—milliners,
hosiers, haberdashers, silk men and 'stillers of strong waters'—display

colourful goods. The Bridge is now at its architectural peak and is marred only by some defacement of the chapel, for in 1538 Henry VIII issued a writ of summons against the long-deceased Thomas Beckett, sometime Archbishop of Canterbury, to answer a charge of treason against Henry II. Then the chapel was compelled to alter its dedication, and all the embroideries and 'dyvers pyctures of Thomas Beckett in our Lady Chapell', according to the Bridge House records, were maltreated. In 1553 it was degraded to the status of a grocery shop and warehouse, but it survived in its deformed state until the summer of 1760, by which year all the housing on the Bridge had been removed.

The greatest curiosity of London Bridge in these Tudor times was the waterwheel erected under an arch at the northern end in 1580. Turned by the tide, it served to pump up river-water. The drawing of water from the river by hand was laborious and the tributary streams were now either covered in or too sullied for household use, so that this new contraption proved to be a great blessing. It was the creation of a Dutchman, Pieter Morice, servant to Sir Christopher Hatton, and he had obtained permission to erect this machinery as a private enterprise.

In order to demonstrate its efficiency he had directed a jet of water over the tower of the Church of St. Magnus, and that so impressed the Mayor and his officers that Morice was given the lease of the northern arch of the Bridge for five hundred years on payment of ten shillings rent a year. In 1582 he acquired the second arch on the same terms. The water-bearers opposed the scheme from the start, of course, and the financial difficulties were overcome only by grants made by the City. But this primitive hydraulic apparatus worked well, and for a long while it supplied a large area of the City with water. After its destruction in the Great Fire, the apparatus and its water-house were rebuilt and continued in the ownership of the Morice family until 1701, when they were sold to one Richard Soames for £36,000. Later they became the property of a company and continued in operation until an Act of 1822 ordered their removal. Until the year 2082 compensation of £3,750 a year will continue to be paid by the Metropolitan Water Board to the heirs of this venture, in accordance with the original agreement.

⟦ VILLAGE OF PALACES

To complete this picture of the riverside in Tudor times, we must go off our maps westward and sketch in a small suburban community which grew up at Chelsea on the far side of the market gardens lying to the west of Westminster. It was considered then to be a particularly healthy spot, and so it was to be regarded for centuries afterwards. There the first of the famous people associated with Chelsea built a fine mansion round about the year 1520. This was Sir Thomas More, Master of Requests and high favourite (for a time) of Henry VIII, who set up his private Utopia here as a pleasant country retreat, having a large garden sloping to the river and a delightful view across the river to the woods and pastures of Surrey. It was a symmetrical Tudor design, 'not mean nor invidiously grand but comfortable', as Erasmus described it, and it stood half-way along the Beaufort Street of today. Originally called the Great More House, it became known as Beaufort House, and in 1597 it was acquired and partly rebuilt by Sir Robert Cecil, afterwards Lord Salisbury. It was pulled down in the eighteenth century by Sir Hans Sloane, the famous physician and Lord of the Manor of Chelsea, who owned much local property.

More was not the Lord of the Manor here, though he possessed the manorial privilege of a chapel—the one part of Old Chelsea Church which survived the Blitz. The lord of the manor was then Lord Sandys and from him about 1536 Henry VIII acquired the manorial property and built a manor house at Chelsea somewhat east of More's palace—east, that is, of the Oakley Street of our day. Fragments of the Tudor brick-work of this royal retreat have survived into the twentieth century and are still visible in the lower part of the walls between Nos. 19 and 26 Cheyne Walk. The King stayed there from time to time, but he used the place mainly as a royal nursery for his children, who spent much of their childhood there. Catherine Parr lived there later on and Anne of Cleeves both lived and died there. Lord Howard of Effingham, victor against the Spanish Armada, became tenant of the place in 1585 and there he was visited by Queen Elizabeth.

On account of these big houses and others which followed, Chelsea was often called the Village of Palaces. Defoe in his *Tour* of the 1720s called it a Town of Palaces at a time when Chelsea was beginning to join up with spreading London: 'A town of palaces and which by its new extended buildings seems to promise itself to be made one time or other a part of London, I mean London in its new extended capacity, which if it should happen, what a monster must London be.'

Beaufort House, Sir Thomas More's Tudor dwelling at Chelsea, 'not mean nor invidiously grand but comfortable'. (From a Victorian engraving)

THE SEVENTEENTH WAS a remarkable century in England: it saw the Civil War, the execution of Charles I, the Restoration, the last of the pandemic London plagues, the Great Fire, the bloodless revolution of 1688 and the foundation of the so-called Bank of England by that piratical Scot, William Paterson. This was a century of tremendous building activity in London, and one in which the City was to be pre-eminent for the last time in moulding the nation's history.

The movement out of the City by the nobility and rich traders caused by the Civil War was increased by the flight from the Plague and, a year later, from the Fire. Even at the beginning of the seventeenth century the wealthy began to move to the fashionable west and north-west because the overcrowding since the Dissolution had become serious. Moreover, the air was becoming fouled by the increased burning of sea-coal. The soot and fog were usually blown eastwards by the prevailing winds across the areas of Stepney, Wapping and Shadwell, where ship-owners, chandlers, shipwrights, sailors and many Protestant refugees were now living, mostly in poor dwellings. Thus the distinct, three-fold articulation of City, East End and West End—already evident in the sixteenth century—was definitely established in the seventeenth.

⟦ LONDON SPREADS

The chief topographical events of the century were the rebuilding of the City after the Fire and the considerable growth of London outside the ancient boundaries—a growth which the Fire, of course, stimulated be-cause it compelled people to live outside the walls during the time of re-construction when the housing problem was acute. As Thomas Free-man wrote in his odd ode, *London's Progresses*:

> 'London has got a long way from the streame,
> I think she means to go to Islington,
> To eat a dish of Strawberries and creame.'

And in 1648 John Evelyn wrote: 'To such a mad intemperance is the age come of building about a city by far too disproportionate already to the nation, I having in my time seen it almost as large again as it was within my memory.'

There was a distinct break in architectural development in London between the first decades of the century and the last, for the two halves were parted first by the years of the Civil War and their dull aftermath and then, following soon, the Great Fire. Though Inigo Jones inaugurated the architecture of the High Renaissance in London, its full flood did not arrive until the age of Wren which followed the Fire.

Speculative building and estate development began in a big way in this century and the professional architect supported by the enlightened patron emerged. Westminster and the City finally became joined firmly together, as the Strand became built up, to form a continuous town. North of the Strand in the 1630s the first landowner's estate development for the upper classes was completed at Covent Garden by Inigo Jones for the Earl of Bedford: a dignified piece of deliberate town planning of which other examples were to follow, most of them a century later, especially in the form of squares. But most of the expansion was as haphazard, piecemeal and uncontrolled as it had always been. Kings and Councils continued their attempts to control the expansion, but with little success.

In the end attempted restrictions merely helped to increase the overcrowding and, until the Fire brought a great clearance, London in the middle of the seventeenth century was at its most unhealthy. Between 1580 and the beginning of the Stuart period the population of the City, Westminster, the Liberties and the out-parishes had doubled to about a quarter of a million. By 1660 it had risen to over four hundred thousand. The Plague of 1665, which killed one hundred thousand and caused a large evacuation into the country, reduced the population greatly, but by the end of the century it was touching seven hundred thousand.

 ⟦ LIVING CONDITIONS

Overcrowding was largely responsible not only for the Great Plague of 1665 but also for the general plague which prevailed during the first six decades of the century in London. Whole families lived in single rooms, often in basements; Count Cominges, French Ambassador to England in the early years of Charles II's reign, mentions the difficulty of estimating the population owing to the great number of poor people who were living in cellars. Added to this overcrowding was the poor state of sanitation, the narrow, airless streets, the old and dilapidated houses and the increasing foulness of the air. Both Pepys and Evelyn complained of the City's dirt, smoke and narrow, crowded and unpaved streets. Evelyn also complained of the 'troublesome and malicious disposal of the spouts and gutters overhead' which rendered the labyrinth of principal passages 'a continual wet day after the storm is over'.

And how splendidly Evelyn—that 'most excellent person' as Pepys called him—fought against the 'hellish and dismall Cloud of Sea-Cole', notably in his polemical work of 1661 called *Fumifugium: or the aer and smoake of London dissipated. Together with some Remedies humbly proposed.* London's impure mists and filthy vapours, he pointed out, caused among the inhabitants in this one city more than in the whole Earth besides the raging 'of vile Catharrs, Phthisicks, Coughs and Consumptions '. Unfortunately the authorities did not discourage the burning of coal, as Edward 1 had done, because considerable taxes were raised from its import into London.

The fresh and open river was a mitigation, for there the citizens continued to travel in the watermen's wherries from bank to bank and from wharf to wharf, whether bent on business or pleasure. And as further lungs for the City after the Restoration, several of those riverside gardens which were to provide so important a feature of riverside life during the next century came into existence. But the streets, created originally for the pedestrian and the pack-horse, were rendered the more incommodious during the seventeenth century by the increase of wheeled traffic.

Some three thousand watermen were working the river between Westminster and the Bridge and as many as forty thousand between Windsor and Gravesend. They continued to feel anxious lest their livelihoods would be taken from them by these so-called Hackney Hell Carts and the sedan chairs which arrived in London in 1634. That lively, articulate pamphleteer and versifier, John Taylor (1580–1653), the Water Poet who became royal waterman to a succession of sovereigns and was the self-appointed publicity agent for all his kind, called attention to the plight of his fellows in 'a rattling, rowling and rumbling age' and broke into song thus:

> 'Carroaches, coaches, jades and Flanders mares
> Do rob us of our shares, our wares, our fares;
> Against the ground we stand and knock our heeles,
> Whilst all our profit runns away on wheels.'

One reason for the increase of passenger travel by road in London to the detriment of water travel is a curious one and shows the extent to which even fashion in dress can affect the environment. It is revealed by Z. C. von Uffenbach in a travel book of 1710, where he comments that though travel on the river in London was far more comfortable and swifter than by carriage through the streets, there was always a wind on the water, and this made a mess of men's wigs. But the chief cause of the increase of road vehicles was that London had grown to such proportions that horse-drawn vehicles had become essential to her economic life.

In spite of that the river remained London's high street, for the wherry was still the most pleasant, safe and rapid means of conveyance, even for long journeys to London from Gravesend or as the first stage out of London to the west as far as Putney. As late as 1822, nine thousand watermen were earning their livings on the river.

⟨ RIVER VIEWS

A number of contemporary maps and panoramas of seventeenth-century London and its river are in existence. The most beautiful one is an engraving of London Bridge, and the City beyond, made by John Visscher in 1616. But the most important are those by the Bohemian artist, Wenceslaus Hollar (1607–77), whom that patron of the arts, Thomas, Earl of Arundel, brought to England with him from Prague. Though Hollar lived a richly creative life he was often hard up, and his last request to the bailiffs was that they should not remove the bed on which he lay dying. More than fifty of his drawings and maps have been reproduced in a work of 1922 by A. M. Hind, and they depict London both before and after the Fire.

The first real plan survey of London and the most accurate and important map of the century is that of Ogilby and Morgan published in 1677, and eight feet long. Hollar engraved most of it. It was produced to assist in the plotting out of the City affected by the Fire and so it does not include Westminster or anything east of the Tower, or Southwark, or even the whole of the Strand. It is mainly from Hollar's masterly etchings that we can obtain a picture of the London of the Stuarts and the Commonwealth, particularly from his magnificent Long View of London from Bankside.

Visscher's etching of 1616 shows the Bridge clearly with its large houses, smoking chimneys and southern bridgehead. St. Saviour's is close to us in the foreground, with a central square tower; the river is filled with craft of all kinds, while the background shows the City in great detail with its forest of proud towers and tapering spires; along the

riverside is a tight jumble of gables and here and there stands a large
castellated structure. It is all still mediæval in its chaotic charm—
beautiful at a distance, dark and unhealthy down in the alleys.

Hollar's view of 1647 shows little change except on the Bridge. Nonesuch House has appeared and is clearly shown. The shrivelling heads on
their poles have gone; so also have many houses at the northern part of
the Bridge, for in February 1633 a maidservant employed by a needle-
maker living at the north end had carelessly left a pail of hot ashes under
some stairs and within a few hours all the old Tudor houses lying on the
City side of the Chapel House had been reduced to ashes. Some time
after Hollar had made his engraving—it must have been near the time of
King Charles's execution—these houses were rebuilt as a three-storey
block without gables but with dormered roofs. 'Over the houses,' writes
a contemporary, 'were stately platforms, leaded with rails and ballasters
about them, very commodious and pleasant for walking and enjoying so
fine a prospect up and down the river, and some had pretty little gardens
with arbours.' This was a period of fine wood carving, a craft which
was no doubt displayed in the details of this attractive group. Unfortunately it did not last long. The Great Fire destroyed it, together with
Morice's churning water-wheels below, but by good fortune the intervening space between the old houses and the new had not been filled and
the gap acted as a fire-break. Luckily only the new block caught fire
and the rest of the houses on the Bridge were preserved. But some
of the timbers of the burning houses fell into the roadway and there
caused a barrier to those trying to flee from the holocaust across the
Bridge.

London still owned only one bridge, and this formed a serious bottle-
neck on the way out of London to the south, especially when the wheeled
traffic had increased and London had expanded east and west. In spite
of the obvious need and the increasing agitation, London was compelled
to wait another century for its second bridge. In 1664, as we can read in
a letter from Ambassador van Goch to the Estates General in Holland,
a project for a bridge between Westminster and Lambeth had been
brought before the City Council, but the opposition from the City
authorities, whose Bridge channelled the traffic into the City and concentrated trade there, had been too strong. On that occasion the citizens
had sent delegates to Charles II to implore him to oppose the scheme,
offering him a loan of £100,000 as an inducement. The King, always
hard up, agreed, as is recorded in the archives of the Common Council.

Part of Visscher's panorama of 1616, showing the Bridge. The church in the foreground is St. Saviour's, now Southwark Cathedral.

❨ PLAGUE AND FIRE

Let us turn now from the visions of Hollar and Visscher to the written records of the calamitous mid-century. The dreary, humourless years of the Commonwealth, when even the festivities of Christmas and May

G

Another part of Visscher's panorama of 1616 showing Old St. Paul's and, in the foreground, Bankside with two of its round theatres for bear-baiting and play-acting.

Day were banned, ended with Cromwell's funeral in London—'the joyfullest funeral I ever saw', in Evelyn's experience. The gaiety of the Restoration was hardly forgotten when the first calamity began early in the hot summer of 1665 out in the suburb of St. Giles's-in-the-Fields. As the plague's death-roll mounted through the months more and more people fled from the City until, as a contemporary recorded, 'there is a dismal solitude in London streets. Now shops are shut in, people rare, and very few that walk about, insomuch that the grass begins to spring up in some places and a deep silence in every place, especially within the walls. . . . The nights are too short to bury the dead; the long summer days are spent from morning unto twilight in conveying the vast number of dead bodies into the bed in their graves.'

The river was the safest place, though this too was largely deserted, and many watermen and their families had rowed up-river to camp in the riverside fields until the terror had departed. In mid-stream for some way down the river ships were moored two or three abreast and these provided relatively safe refuges for many hundreds of frightened people.

The months passed and all movement on the water ceased. There seemed to be no end to the horror. Pepys entered in his diary as late as September 20th: 'But, Lord! what a sad time it is to see no boats upon the river; and grass grows all up and down White Hall court, and nobody but poor wretches in the streets! And, which is worst of all, the Duke (of Albemarle) showed us the number of the plague this week, brought in the last night from the Lord Mayor, that it is encreased about 600 more than the last, which is quite contrary to our hopes and expectations, from the coldness of the late season.'

When the plague at last began to die down as the autumn advanced and the death-carts no longer rumbled towards the pits, over one hundred thousand Londoners out of a total population of less than half a million had perished from the contagion. Less than a year later came the second calamity. As Evelyn records on the 2nd of September 1666: 'This fatal night, about ten, began the deplorable fire, near Fish Street, in London!' The story has been told again and again, and so it will be until London has ceased to exist. No descriptions are so evocative as those of eye-witnesses of the event. Pepys, still in his nightshirt, watched from an ale-house on Bankside: 'As it grew darker, appeared more and more, and in corners and upon steeples, and between churches and houses, as far as we could see up the hill of the City, in a most horrid malicious and bloody flame . . . one entire arch of fire from this to the other side of the bridge, and in a bow up the hill for an arch of above a mile long: it made me weep to see it.'

Evelyn too watched from Bankside the following day:

'The heat, with a long set of fair and warm weather, had even ignited the air, and prepared the materials to conceive the fire, which devoured, after an incredible manner, houses, furniture, and every thing. Here, we saw the Thames covered with goods floating, all the barges, and boats laden with what some had time and courage to save, as, on the other side, the carts &c., carrying out to the fields, which for many miles were strewed with moveables of all sorts, and tents erected to shelter both people and what goods they could get away. Oh, the miserable and calamitous spectacle! . . . All the sky was of a fiery aspect, like the top of a burning oven, and the light seen above forty miles round-about for many nights. God grant that mine eyes may never behold the like, who now saw above 10,000 houses all in one flame! The noise and cracking and thunder of the impetuous flames, the shrieking of women and children, the hurry of people, the fall of towers, houses, and churches, was like a hideous storm; and the air all about so hot and inflamed, that at the last one was not able to approach it, so that they were forced to stand still, and let the flames burn on, which they did, for near two miles in length and one in breadth. The clouds also of smoke were dismal, and reached, upon computation, near fifty miles in length. Thus, I left it this afternoon burning, a resemblance of Sodom, or the last day . . . London was, but it is no more!'

A few half-hearted efforts were made to pull down or blow up the houses on the rim of the Fire, but there was no hope in this tightly built-up area of dry old timber structures. 'The conflagration was so universal,' continues Evelyn, 'and the people so astonished, that, from the beginning, I know not by what despondency, or fate, they hardly stirred to quench it.' The fire lasted four days and destroyed four-fifths of the City within the walls—thirteen thousand houses, most of the Halls of the City Companies, the Royal Exchange, the Guildhall and eighty-six parish churches, thirty-five of which were never to be rebuilt. The riverside with its warehouses of wood and its inflammable stocks suffered particularly severely, and the old cathedral, surrounded by timber scaffolding for its repair, was a calcined ruin. 'London was, but it is no more.'

⟦ LONDON REBUILT

Both Plague and Fire were generally believed to be just punishments imposed by an all-merciful God, which, according to Evelyn, 'we highly deserved for our prodigious ingratitude, burning lusts, dissolute court, profane and abominable lives'. But ours is a practical, improvising

'One entire arch of fire . . . above a mile long.' (A painting of the Great Fire by Thomas Wyck)

nation and a few days after the Fire had died down the problem of re-building was being tackled with a will. This was primarily a domestic problem of rehousing the tens of thousands of homeless people, at first largely solved by 'doubling up' in the suburban homes.

Evelyn, for one, presented to the King a survey of the ruins and his 'plot for a new City with a discourse on it'. Dr. Christopher Wren, who had been appointed Assistant Surveyor-General in 1662, also prepared his famous street plan with its monumental lay-out, and there were several others, among them one by Robert Hooke. Nothing came of any of them, for, though they would have transformed the City's whole street lay-out and therefore its character, they were only hypothetical projects, paper sketches, which were quite unrelated to the psycho-logical and economic realities of the situation. A town is, in a sense, a living thing, in that it is always changing and always adapting itself half-consciously through the collective will to new conditions in an *ad hoc*, compromising way; except under ruthless despotism, when it is a dead, dull thing, it can hardly ever be created as a complete entity all at once as the work of art of one single mind. As Sir Nathaniel Hobart, Master in Chancery, sensibly observed: 'The rebuilding of the Citty will not

bee soe difficult as the satisfying all interests, there being so many proprietors.'

Speed in rebuilding was essential but, though a tidy lay-out and
grand, baroque vistas were out of the question, some improvements,
especially in road widening, were imperative. Considering all the difficulties, the accomplishments in the end were remarkable enough; at
least London would never again be reduced to cinders, nor would she
suffer any severe plagues until cholera came with the industrial slums of
the nineteenth century.

The Council and City were finally responsible for the work of rebuilding, under which a group of Commissioners was appointed to
undertake a survey and then guide the reconstruction. The King appointed Dr. Wren, Hugh May (who had been the King's Paymaster of
the Works and in that capacity had supervised such structures as the
royal palaces), and Roger Pratt (who had already designed four fine
mansions and had been surveyor of St. Paul's). To these the City
added Robert Hooke (later to become famous as a scientist), Edward
Jarman (about whom little is known, though he seems to have had practical experience in City building), and Peter Mills (for some years the
City Surveyor, with whom Jarman may have been associated). It was a
rapidly improvised but admirable band. As T. F. Reddaway writes in
his *The Rebuilding of London After the Great Fire* (1940): 'They [the
documents] show no hero, no presiding genius. The focal point is the
struggle of the community to survive destruction. Their mass, often
unindexed, seldom calendared, sometimes unsorted, gradually yields a
picture of difficulties faced and surmounted. In spite of mistakes and
misconceptions, the splendour of the community's achievement is their
only final conclusion. . . . To a disinterested observer there is an element of unconscious greatness about it all.'

As Reddaway points out, it is an interesting sign of the size of the
calamity of the Fire and of the energy, speed and common sense with
which it was faced by the citizens, that after the destruction of Tokyo in
1923, over two and a half centuries later, the Japanese sent inquiries to
London seeking to know how London had once faced its time of trial.

Two bold projects, connected directly with the river, were included
in the Rebuilding Acts, as they had also been included in the ideal plans
of both Wren and Evelyn. These were the Fleet Canal and the Thames
Quay. Both were achieved in part, but both may be considered to have
been failures.

The Fleet River and its valley had been a nuisance for a long time, as we have seen, and the river, once navigable for half a mile up to Holborn Bridge, had degenerated into an open, shallow sewer which could take no useful navigation. The plan was to dig the river out as far as Holborn Bridge and turn it into a navigable cut fifty feet wide, crossed by high bridges, and lined on either side with wharves thirty-two feet wide with storage vaults beneath and uniform lines of houses and warehouses lying back on either side in an orderly Dutch manner. The scheme, which evolved under Wren's direction, was carried out after many setbacks by that excellent contractor Thomas Fitch. Though it did achieve reality, the Fleet Canal was never a success, and in Strype's words, 'that project did not take'. Too few took up storage space or houses to make the scheme financially successful and the wharves became used illicitly for parking carts and coaches, for stacking timber, for rubbish dumping and other purposes; they were also used too much as traffic routes, so that the pavements became broken and the roofing of the vaults was threatened.

Clearly, a road was needed here much more than a canal. In 1733 the canal was arched over from Holborn Bridge to Fleet Bridge, the wharves became roads and the central strip accommodated a covered market. In 1766 the lower reach of the Fleet was also covered over, and three years later the building of Blackfriars Bridge ended the visible life of the Fleet Canal. The canal scheme was a success in the end, but, as so often happens in the planning of towns, not in the way its planners had at first intended.

The projected commodious and continuous Thames Quay was a more obvious failure and was never fully realised, even though the King himself had proclaimed: 'We do resolve and declare that there shall be a fair key or wharf on all the river side.'

Before the Fire the riverside had been a mess of sheds, yards and half-derelict gear with here and there a rough landing-place and a stinking lay-stall—all reached by lanes, very steep and narrow and both inconvenient and dangerous for the dray-carts. The waterfront had been an offence to a great city. Now the broad new quay was to run all the way from the Tower to the Temple, forty feet wide and overlooked by handsome buildings. It would not only provide a dignified waterfront of which Londoners could feel proud but it would serve usefully for landing goods and passengers anywhere along the City's riverside. The project had almost universal support from the King down, though in the

first of the Rebuilding Acts it was implied only in the brief enactment that 'noe House, Outhouse or other building whatsoever (Cranes and Sheds for the present use onely excepted) shall be built or erected within the distance of Forty foote of such part of any Wall, Key or Wharf as bounds the River of Thames from Tower Wharfe to London Bridge and

Old Somerset House, one of the Strand palaces with their riverside gardens. In the left foreground is the pleasure-boat, *The Folly*. (From a seventeenth-century engraving by J. Kip)

from London Bridge to the Temple Staires . . . before the fower and twentieth day of March (1669)'.

Not until the second Rebuilding Act of 1670 was statutory provision made for the Thames Quay, but by that time a provisional, unplanned quay, developed by private enterprise, was actually in being below the Bridge and was serving well enough, even though it had a number of indentations and no architectural pretensions. The new Act therefore concentrated on the riverside above the Bridge. Here, however, requirements were quite different from those below Bridge because traffic here consisted only of lighters, barges and small craft (the days of Queenhithe's precedence had long since passed) and the goods they deposited needed less a broad quay than ample storage accommodation. Eight months after the statutory time for clearing the riverside above Bridge had expired, Wren reported to the King: 'Every where inclosed and incumbred with Pales or Brickwalls irregular houses and buildings Piles of Timber Billetts Faggots and heapes of Coles many boarded sheds and several great Laystalls . . . the old Towers of Baynard's Castle . . . yet standing.'

Very little was done for some time, but meanwhile the City had devised a new scheme by which the north bank of the river should be pushed forward into the river to run more or less parallel with the lines of existing warehouses. This idea caught on, but somehow in the end that grand scheme of a properly planned waterfront was nowhere fully realised. Neither did that project 'take'. The main trouble, of course, was lack of money with which to pay owners' compensations. Nevertheless, piecemeal developments along the river were accomplished. If Ogilby's map of 1677 is a reliable guide, some good vaulting and wharfing appeared at Dowgate and Puddle Dock and to the east of the mouth of the Fleet. And a monumental new Fishmongers' Hall arose just west of the Bridge in 1671 as a pleasant, Wrennish building of red brick and stone with a central pediment. The architect was Edward Jarman, who died young but carried out a good deal of work in the new city, notably on the handsome Royal Exchange, which was to be destroyed by fire in 1838. Jarman's Fishmongers' Hall was replaced by the present classical structure in 1833, erected when the new London Bridge was built.

Ogilby's map shows that most of the new warehouses on the north bank were set back some distance from the river to provide landing-quays, but there was no continuous 'fair key or wharf'. In spite of such lack of decisiveness, London and the riverside were transformed after the Fire and considerable improvements came to the City as a whole with the new legislation. The major step was the 1667 Rebuilding Act.

It covered some tidying-up of the old meandering, chaotic labyrinth of alleys, courtyards and bottle-necks; the standardisation of materials, designs and heights of new houses, with a special stress on fire-resistance; and the power to raise money for the new public buildings by means of a tax on coal. Some streets were widened and a continual way was formed from the Guildhall down to the Thames. Thames Street was widened to thirty feet to take the heavy carts to and from the wharves, and the steepness of the alleys running down to the river was reduced by levelling.

The standardisation of house-building in the new Act was of great importance and the City's first major step in building control. There were to be four classes of building for the sake of better regulation, uniformity and gracefulness, and none were to be higher than four storeys. The houses were to be of brick or stone, and the thickness of walls, the sizes of floor-joists and the heights of rooms were fixed. The larger houses were to have a balcony at first-floor level and there was to be protection for pedestrians against rainwater falling from the eaves. But the decoration of exteriors was left to individual taste. The result produced an unprecedented orderliness in the streets, to some extent monotonous in comparison with the old picturesque confusion, but relieved with varied and charming details, especially in the fine wood carving of this period of Grinling Gibbons.

Rebuilding seems to have been fairly rapid, considering the ruined state of the merchants and companies and the lack of modern insurance and long-term lending. By the time Ogilby's map was published, ten years after the Act was passed, a good part of the City had been rebuilt. The Monument inscription declares that the time of rebuilding was 'three short years', but that is an exaggeration. By the end of 1670, however, most of the private building had been completed, new and special markets were forming away from the main streets, and life in the City was returning to normal. Building was still very compressed and most of the mediæval streets had reappeared under their old names. To quote Reddaway again: 'No single one of the improvements sketched can be described as spectacular. . . . The changes were far-reaching but utilitarian. The rebuilt area had its splendour, but it was the sober splendour of the Dutch towns—exemplars of burgherdom—of row upon row of seemly, well-built brick houses. . . . The parish churches, its first adornment, owed their beauty almost to an accident. No effort was made to site them to greater advantage. . . . Monuments to pious

The City rebuilt after the Great Fire from the riverside gardens of Old Somerset House; a detail from a sketch by Canaletto in Windsor Castle Library.
(Reproduced by gracious permission of Her Majesty The Queen)

conservatism, they might well have been dull or mediocre. Only the
chance genius of one man raised them to a splendour undreamt of by
their parishioners.'

London rose again in a new and more urbane form, but it had lost
something of the old, informal rural county-town atmosphere. The appearance from the river was quite changed by the beginning of the
eighteenth century, when the rebuilding was at last complete—as different from the mediæval look as from the look we know today. One grand
feature remains to us even though it is now insulted by the heavy and
insensitive great blocks of modern commerce which surround it—the
dome of St. Paul's. That too looked different from the dome we know,
for then the Portland stone was not veiled and patched with soot as it is
now (by no means a displeasing effect and an important and mitigating
part of the City's modern, neurotic personality); it then gleamed as white
and fresh as a wedding cake against the greys and blues of the sky.

From the river the scene must have had a homogeneous, friendly
charm and a unity of scale that have long since vanished, with its low
tiled and slated roofs, pierced here and there by the variegated steeples,
surmounted by their glinting vanes, of the fifty-one churches, mostly of
Portland stone, which were all the product of Wren's fertile fantasy. The

whole scene, held together by the great dome, swelling and matriarchal, must have appeared from the river as one of the most beautiful in Europe, a complete new town beautiful enough to inspire some of Canaletto's most memorable pictures. All the colouring was new—the fresh reds of the tiles and the russets and yellows of the brickwork, to which the informal patches of living, leafy green, the occasional low, grey geometrical patches of the leaded church roofs and the ivory steeples thrusting joyfully through them provided vigorous foils.

The gay, urbane freshness of it all must have been its most striking characteristic—an elegant freshness, for the age of cultivated taste had arrived, and pride in fine craftsmanship was strong. With its brickiness and its rhythmical, ubiquitous and uniting pattern of wide windows with their mullions and transoms, the picture had a look of domestic Dutch vernacular, yet it was peculiarly English in its *ad hoc* informality.

Wren not only altered the silhouette of London with his church spires and his central dome, but he also altered the look of the riverside itself by providing a number of important structures on its banks: the great military hospital to the east and the great naval hospital to the west, the short-lived Customs House and a number of delightful churches along Thames Street at the centre.

Wren's Custom House, erected in 1668, as depicted in a contemporary engraving. In the distance is the Tower of London and to its left the Great Storehouse in the Tower, presumed to have been designed by Wren. (From a print in the Guildhall Library)

⟦ THE MONUMENT

The Monument, completed in 1677 close to the bakery in Pudding Lane where the Fire started, was one of the many vertical features in the new City. Though situated on the axis of the old Bridge, its position near the bottom of a hill was not dramatic then, and is even less so today, when it no longer lies on the Bridge axis and is closed in by tall buildings. We shall find it near Billingsgate on the last of our walks—a fluted Doric column of Portland stone surmounted by a railed platform and a rather mean little vase of gilded flames. Defoe described it quaintly as being 'built in the form of a candle'. This typical piece of English visual understatement was, until recently, believed to have been Wren's work, but the diaries of Robert Hooke which were published not long ago suggest that Hooke was the creator. That frail but brilliant man is best known for his scientific work, but he had a considerable hand in the rebuilding of the City; he was one of the City Surveyors and worked closely with Wren on many schemes, including St. Paul's.

Wren did prepare a design, and it was more exciting than the one that was built. It consisted of a column in flames having great bronze-gilt tongues of fire sprouting from the loopholes which lit the internal stairs, and on the summit was poised a golden phœnix. Another proposal was to surmount the column with a statue of Charles II, fifteen feet high, but the cost was thought to be prohibitive.

The base of the existing column bears bas-reliefs and inscriptions, the bas-relief on the western side being by Cibber, the Dane who was much favoured by Wren and received the appointment of carver to the King's closet. We can examine these more closely on our walk. An inscription we shall not read is the following, which was placed there in 1681 by order of the Court of Aldermen at a time when Titus Oates was giving trouble: 'This pillar was set up in perpetual remembrance of that most dreadful burning of this Protestant city, begun and carried on by ye treachery & malice of ye Popish faction in ye year of our Lord 1665, in order for carrying on their horrid plott for extirpating the Protestant and old English liberty, and introducing Popery and slavery.'

In 1685 under James II this was obliterated, but in 1689 under William III it was reinstated, and upon it Pope was to comment:

> *'Where London's column, pointing at the skies,*
> *Like a tall bully, lifts its head and lies.'*

The inscription was finally removed in 1830.

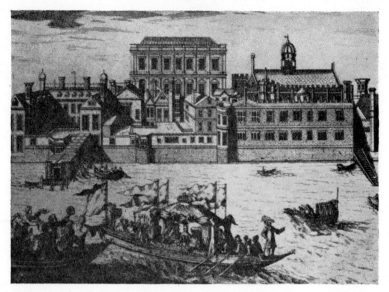

Part of Whitehall with the Banqueting House by Inigo Jones seen from the river in the time of William and Mary. The Royal Barge is in the foreground. (From a contemporary print in the Guildhall Library)

❲ THE BANQUETING HALL

At Greenwich, at Somerset House on the Strand and at Whitehall, Inigo Jones had changed the scene before Wren. The Queen's House at Greenwich and the Banqueting Hall at Whitehall survive to this day in perfect preservation.

The Banqueting Hall, though invisible now from the river, did show its rear elevation to river voyagers during the seventeenth and eighteenth centuries and so it belongs to the river's story. It was built in 1622 and it was to form part of a new royal palace designed by John Webb, Jones's nephew, heir and pupil: an enormous classical palace which would cover twenty-four acres and be as large as Versailles. It survived the fire which consumed most of the Tudor palace in 1698, and though the asthmatic King William preferred the cleaner air of Hampton Court, the rebuilding of the Palace was then reconsidered. Wren prepared a scheme somewhat on the lines of Webb's project in which Jones's Hall was to form the central feature. Later Wren proposed a less ambitious scheme, but in the end the whole idea was abandoned and efforts were concentrated on Hampton Court.

The Banqueting Hall is a most important building in two historic ways—as a symbol and as an architectural innovation. It was almost a sacred structure designed as a glorious setting for the divine figure of the King—a banqueting hall maybe, but in those days a banqueting hall was more than a place for dinner-parties. The seventeenth-century royal banquet appealed to all the senses, for eating and drinking were combined with music, masques and rose-scented air. The Calvinists had not yet laid their blight on the land. Charles I commissioned Rubens to decorate the ceiling with paintings representing the apotheosis of James I who, as we can still see today, is being assisted towards his Crown and Orb by the spirited exertions of plump cherubim. In Charles's time it was still serving its intended purpose, for we read in *The Present State of London* (1681) that:

'There were daily in his court eighty-six tables, well furnished each meal; whereof the king's table had twenty-eight dishes; the queen's twenty-four . . . There was spent yearly in the King's house, of gross meat, fifteen hundred oxen; seven thousand sheep; twelve hundred calves; three hundred porkers; four hundred young beefs; six thousand eight hundred lambs; three hundred flitches of bacon; and twenty six boars. Also one hundred and forty dozen geese; two hundred and fifty dozen of capons; four hundred and seventy dozen of hens; seven hundred and fifty dozen of pullets; fourteen hundred and seventy dozen of chickens; for bread, three hundred and sixty-four thousand bushels of wheat; and for drink, six hundred tuns of wine and seventeen hundred tuns of beer; together with fish and fowl, fruit, and spice, proportionately.'

Architecturally, in Horace Walpole's words, the building stood 'as a model of the most pure and beautiful taste'. This building was the first decisive step away from the crude provincialism of the half-Gothic Jacobethan towards the sophisticated and learned taste of the pure classical Renaissance. 'The freshness, the stark novelty, of Jones's work in Jacobean London cannot be overstressed', writes John Summerson in his classic work, *Georgian London*. 'Here was a city built by generations of closely organised carpenters and masons, a city of gables, mullioned windows, carved barge-boards, corner posts and brackets. . . . To put up a pure Italian building in such a setting was sensational—almost like realising a stage set in permanent materials.'

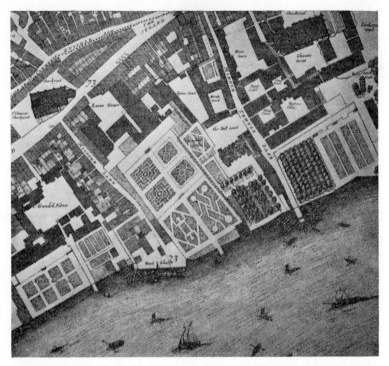

A detail of Ogilby's map of 1677 showing the Temple Gardens and part of the area between the river and the Strand.

⟦ THE STRAND

Ogilby shows the Fleet River still uncovered as far as Holborn and marked 'New Canal'. Bridewell, now largely rebuilt, is still there on its west bank with its two great courtyards. West of it lies the Inner and Middle Temple complex with its riverside gardens. On its western boundary Middle Temple Lane runs down from the Strand to a landing-stage on the river where wherries are thickly clustered like a shoal of nosing fish. West again of that, three of the Strand palaces are shown —Essex, Arundel and Somerset—with their formal parterres and gardens along the river-front. And there, unfortunately, the map ends.

But we can reconstruct this old link between the City and Westminster from other evidence. We can see on Ogilby's map that the three palaces he does show are becoming embedded in a medley of small

H

buildings and streets. The Strand is losing its old exclusive tone of a Millionaires' Row, because the aristocratic owners, many of them reduced in circumstances by exile and by the general difficulties of the times, are selling off their properties here for high prices. By the end of the seventeenth century almost the whole district between the Strand and the river had been built up in streets of comparatively small but high-class houses with attendant shops.

The fate of the Tudor manor of Essex House is typical. As Exeter House it had been originally the London inn of the Bishops of Exeter; Henry VIII passed it to Sir William (later Lord) Paget, when it was called Paget House. In 1563 Robert Dudley, Earl of Leicester, Elizabeth's favourite, obtained possession of it and more or less rebuilt it. At his death in 1588 it passed to Robert Devereux, second Earl of Essex, when its name was again changed, this time to Essex House. In 1674 one Dr. Nicholas Barbon bought the property and demolished most of the house for purposes of speculative building in the area now marked by Essex Street.

London's West End development in the seventeenth and eighteenth centuries was due in large part to speculative builders, among whom the most notorious was this Dr. Barbon. He was the son of the fanatical mob-raiser, Commonwealth parliamentarian and leather-seller, Praise-God Barebone, and though he obtained the diploma of Doctor of Medicine after studying medicine at Leyden for about four months, he gave up this calling for the more profitable activities of real-estate development and fire insurance. (The Phœnix Office claims him as its founder.) Energetic adventurer, confidence trickster, economist, financial wizard, part crook, part altruist, he was an early arch-type of the puritan business man who was to come into his own in the nineteenth century and is with us still. Roger North described his activities thus: 'He was the inventor of this new method of building by casting of ground into streets and small houses, and to augment their number with as little front as possible, and selling the ground to workmen by so much per foot front, and what he could not sell build himself. This has made ground rents high for the sake of mortgaging, and others following his steps have refined and improved upon it, and made a super-fœtation of houses about London.'

Barbon also initiated the principle of standardisation in building, for all his houses were much alike, with mean plans and rather coarse, mass-produced detailing. Many of his houses were jerry-built and in one case 'all the vaults fell in, and the Houses came down scandalously'.

He was the first of the worst kind of speculative builder that our own century has known too well. His activities and influence extended all over London, but nowhere did they have so great an effect as in the area lying between the Strand and the river. Within a year the dignified abode of earls and prelates had been replaced by streets of houses, taverns and cookshops and the garden on the riverside had become a range of wharves for brewers and wood merchants.

Once the development of some of these old Thames-side palace sites had begun, the rest soon followed. Arundel House, for instance, was demolished in 1678. This had originally been the inn of the Bishops of Bath, and Stow tells us that it had been 'lately new built or a great part thereof by the Lord Thomas Seymour, admiral'. It came in 1603 to the Earl of Arundel and Surrey, a great patron of the arts. Both Van Dyck and Hollar stayed and worked there, and Hollar made etchings of the house and of the view of London from its roof. According to one of Hollar's etchings, the house contained a fine chapel. In 1666 the Royal Society began to meet there. Then the Earl died in 1677 and was succeeded by his brother, who, in the following year, pulled the place down. The site was then covered by streets, and is now represented by Howard, Norfolk, Arundel and Surrey Streets, just north of the Temple Underground station.

Old Durham House, where the plot to make Lady Jane Grey the Queen of England was hatched and where Raleigh lived for a time, is now recalled by Durham House Street. The house was replaced as early as 1609 by an emporium called Britain's Bourse or the New Exchange; this included an arcade of shops with living-quarters above. Pepys records that he shopped there and Strype describes it as 'furnished with shops on both sides the walls, both below and above stairs, for milliners, sempstresses and other trades, that furnish dresses; and it is a place of great resort and trade for the nobility and gentry and such as have occasion for such commodities'. There were about one hundred and fifty shops there in 1708, half of them milliners and mercers, but this New Exchange ceased to be profitable and was pulled down in 1737. In 1740 David Garrick, then calling himself a wine merchant, was living in one of the houses built on the courtyard of the old palace, and later the Adam brothers were to erect their Adelphi housing estate on the site.

On the site of Salisbury House streets and houses were built and also one of the local markets in the form of the Middle Exchange. According to Strype it consisted of a very large, long room 'with shops on both sides which from the Strand ran as far as the water side, where there was a handsome pair of stairs to go down to the water side, to take boat at, but it had the ill-luck to have the nickname given it of the "Whore's Nest"; whereby, with the ill-fate that attended it, few or no people took shops there, and those that did were soon weary and left them. In so much that it lay useless except three or four shops towards the Strand.'

Though Somerset House was re-erected in the eighteenth century as a public building and still stands, the last of the Strand mansions to be demolished was Northumberland House, which had been built in 1605 on the site of the Hospital of St. Mary Rounceval, close to Old Scotland Yard, for the Earl of Northampton. It became known as Suffolk House when it came to the first Earl of Suffolk in 1614 and then it assumed an appearance somewhat like the White Tower in miniature as a quadrangular structure having four corner turrets. It passed into the hands of the Northumberlands and the name was changed again. Here the Restoration was planned. In 1774 Robert Adam decorated its famous ballroom, a section of whose elaborate wall decoration of coloured glasses and filigree is now preserved at the Victoria and Albert Museum. Not until 1873 was the house sold, and then it was pulled down to make way for the building of Northumberland Avenue.

Between the Strand and the Embankment, just west of the approach to Waterloo Bridge, a relic of another palace remains today—the Savoy Chapel. This was built in 1508 as part of the Hospital of St. John, soon after Henry VII had bequeathed a large sum for the restoration of the ruined Savoy Palace and for its endowment as a hospital for a hundred 'pouer, nedie people'. The hospital was dissolved in 1702, but the chapel still survives, having been altered several times, the last time being by Sydney Smirke in the 1860s. In 1940 George VI gave the chapel the title 'The King's Chapel of the Savoy' and appointed it for the use of the Royal Victorian Order; at that time the interior was completely refitted.

(SOUTHWARK

What has been happening across the river during this century? Though Southwark escaped the Great Fire, it suffered severely in a conflagration in 1676. Chaucer's Tabard Inn and a number of others in the High Street were badly burnt, including the George, which still survives and looks like a Tudor building, although it was, in fact, rebuilt after this Southwark fire.

As a pleasure resort of inns, public gardens and theatres the district retained its old reputation throughout the century, but, like the north bank, it became more and more built up as the century progressed, expanding south and along the riverside. Defoe describes it in his *Tour* as it was in 1728 and very much as it must have been at the end of the seventeenth century: 'A long street of about nine miles in length . . . reaching Vauxhall to London Bridge and from the Bridge to Deptford, all up to Deptford bridge, which parts it from Greenwich, all the way winding and turning as the river winds and turns.'

⟦ THE TWO HOSPITALS

At Greenwich a great deal has been happening. James I walled in the park and settled the whole estate on his wife, Anne of Denmark, who in 1617 commissioned Inigo Jones to build a simple and charming small palace standing some way back from the river. Called the Queen's House, it was not completed until 1635, when Henrietta Maria, the wife of Charles I, acquired it and called it her House of Delight. Inigo Jones called it a 'curious device', and so it may have seemed at the time, though to us it looks like a most staid small rectangular mansion of stone with familiar classical features and a balcony inset into the first floor. It now houses the National Maritime Museum, a splendid visual record of English seafaring history, and on either side of it stretch long rhythmical colonnades erected in the eighteenth century which link the house with the end pavilions.

Cromwell took the place over, and in his time the old Tudor palace on the riverside was badly treated, part of it being used for a biscuit factory and part as a prison for Dutch sailors. When it came back to the monarch, Charles II demolished the old and dilapidated Tudor building and in 1664 began as part of a new palace the north-west wing of what became in the end the Royal Naval College. He was short of funds and the work was not completed in his time. Set at right angles to the river, this wing had nominally been designed by Sir John Denham, but the architect was in fact John Webb, who worked on designs by his uncle, Inigo Jones. Denham was an ineffectual Surveyor-General and altogether an unhappy person. As a widower in 1665 he married a young wife, was cuckolded by the Duke of York, was generally believed to have ended the liaison by poisoning his wife, and died two years after her under the impression that he was the Holy Ghost.

William III at the instigation of his Consort decided to complete this wing, add a balancing one and turn the whole place into an asylum for England's many superannuated and disabled naval seamen. A commission was set up, of which Evelyn was appointed treasurer, but the response to appeals for funds was poor. Then a lottery was organised, fines for smuggling were imposed, sixpence a year was docked from every sailor's pay, prize money was forfeited and £6,000 was commandeered from the gains of Captain Kidd, the pirate who ended his life on the gibbet at Execution Dock. Finally Queen Anne gave another £6,000, and so the establishment was financed, created and maintained for its first purpose until the nineteenth century.

Wren was asked to design the new buildings and he generously waived his fees. He had no easy task, for he was not permitted by the Queen to demolish the 'House of Delight' and had to incorporate it in the general scheme. The little palace was charming but it was out of scale with the new, grand conception. Wren did his best by making the Queen's House the central climax at the end of the main axis so that the house had a clear view to the river, but it is the one weakness of the whole, for it is much too small. Wren added new wings and colonnades in Portland stone around a great open courtyard, and he incorporated two balancing domes, one above the chapel and the other above the Painted Hall. In spite of the climactic weakness, the final result was one of the grandest pieces of baroque architecture to be seen anywhere in England.

The foundation stone of the Hospital was laid jointly by Wren and Evelyn at precisely five o'clock on the 30th June 1696, the time being fixed by Flamsteed's instruments in Wren's Royal Observatory on the hill behind. The work proceeded slowly on account of the financial difficulties, but nine years after the foundation stone had been laid the first inmates took up their residence there. Wren did not live to see his work completed, for the last wing was not ready until the reign of George II, and by then other architects had left their marks. In 1702 control of operations passed into the hands of Sir John Vanbrugh, whose special contribution was the designing of the King William block to the west, a structure of stone and brick, typical of the architect's work in its theatricality and boldness of scale. Vanbrugh wanted to cut off the view of the Queen's House by building a great oval courtyard having a central chapel with a tall tower above it, but Wren's lay-out prevailed in the

Greenwich Hospital, depicted by C. A. Pugin in 1806, showing Nelson's funeral procession setting off for Westminster. (From a print in the Guildhall Library)

end. Finally no less than seven architects contributed to the design of the whole of Greenwich Hospital, though the general conception must be attributed to Wren.

In 1779 a fire destroyed the chapel in the south-east wing which had been designed by Ripley, and it was rebuilt by James (Athenian) Stuart in the elegant way we can see today. Stuart (1713–88) began his career as a painter of fans, but in 1751 he explored Athens with Nicholas Revett. Four years later these two published their *Antiquities of Athens*, which was to have its influence on architecture in due time. His most notable work is this sculptured interior at Greenwich, which is not in the least influenced by Adam, the innovator, but is remarkable for its individuality.

Another pleasure of the place is the mural decoration in the Painted Hall by Sir James Thornhill. Thornhill, who—without being asked— became Hogarth's father-in-law, was the first Englishman successfully to enter this field of applied art, and his heroic work of Baroque theatricality at Greenwich, which took him nineteen years to complete (at the fee of £2 per square yard for walls and £3 for the ceiling), has great character, strength and competence. It has not survived the years too well, but is now being restored. Another detail of the place is the statue of George II by Ruysbrack which stands in the great quadrangle.

Greenwich Hospital is a grand and monumental complex, but it is hardly functional. It is indeed more suitable for its present purposes as a naval college and museum than for the one for which it was designed—the domestic comfort and happiness of retired old seamen. Nathaniel Hawthorne wrote an enlightened criticism of the Hospital in this respect in the 1850s. It was, he reflected,

'a series of edifices externally more beautiful than any English palace that I have seen, consisting of several quadrangles of stately architecture, united by colonnades and graceful walks, and enclosing grassy squares with statues in the centre, the whole extending along the Thames. It is built of marble or of light coloured stone in the classical style of pillars and porticoes which (to my taste, and I fancy to that of the old sailors) produces such a cold and shivery effect in the English climate. Had I been the architect I would have studied the characteristics, habits, predilections of nautical people at Wapping, Rotherhithe, and the neigh-

Chelsea Hospital from the river with its two decorative canals, long since filled in. The riverside gazebos have also gone. (An eighteenth-century engraving)

bourhood of the Tower . . . and would have built the hospital in a kind of ethereal similitude to the narrow, dark, ugly, inconvenient, but snug and cosy homeliness of the sailor-bearing houses there. There can be no question that all the above attributes, or enough of them to satisfy the old sailors here might be reconciled with architectural beauty, and the wholesome contrivance of modern buildings, and thus a novel and genuine style of building be given to the world.'

On the far side of the City and on the opposite bank to Greenwich stands its military equivalent, the Royal Hospital of Chelsea, one of Wren's finest works, and still in use for its original purpose. Charles II founded it, and in that he was more likely to have been following the example of the Hotel des Invalides than the advice of Mistress Gwynn. The establishment was necessary because England now had a standing

Chelsea Pensioners. (From a children's book of William IV's period)

army and the welfare of its veterans and invalids was becoming a problem.

Chelsea Hospital was begun in 1682 and completed in 1689, when four hundred and seventy-six N.C.O.s and men settled in, according to Evelyn, 'as in a college or monastery'. Today over five hundred pensioners live there, and in their special uniforms dating from Marlborough's time, whether the bright scarlet of summer or the dark blue of winter, are a familiar and picturesque sight in the streets and pubs of Chelsea.

As we shall see on our walk, this is a large symmetrical building with projecting wings forming a wide courtyard open on the riverside and set behind a large open space of grass surrounded with trees. The central entrance is marked by a bold Tuscan portico, above which, from the roof, rises a baroque lantern containing a clock. It is all of homely red brick with stone dressings, somewhat Dutch in character. Three fine features are its long, low, covered way on each side of the main portico to the south, the Dining Hall to the west and the balancing Chapel to the east, which has an apse decorated with a painting of the Resurrection by Sebastiano Ricci. In the centre of the courtyard stands a statue of Charles II by Grinling Gibbons.

Though grand in size, the atmosphere of the place is domestic enough and, in the way so characteristic of Wren, it has dignity without pomposity. The whole is more unified, much less ambitious and, in its internal arrangements and planning, far more suitable for its purpose than Greenwich.

❲ THE PORT

Notwithstanding the Plague and the Fire with their depressing deprivations, overseas trade increased during the century, and by its end the tonnage of shipping entering the port was more than a third of the whole tonnage of the country. Though Defoe made his Tour early in the following century, the picture he gives cannot have altered greatly during the comparatively quiet intervening decades. On London's river he found 'about two thousand sail of all sorts, not reckoning barges, lighters or pleasure boats or yatchts (sic)'. From the Pool down to Blackwall he discovered three wet docks for laying up, twenty-two dry docks for repairs and thirty-three yards for building merchant ships.

During most of the seventeenth century, and right through the eighteenth, the docking accommodation was inadequate and most ships were compelled to anchor in mid-stream and to unload into lighters. In 1665 three more legal quays where customs could be collected (in addition to the seventeen which had been created in 1558 between the Bridge and the Town) were established, but these were not enough, and new sufferance wharves were added where certain goods with low customs duties on them could be handled. The East India Company built an early dock at Blackwall in 1614 where its ships could be fitted out, and Howland's wet dock was built at Rotherhithe in 1696, remaining London's largest dock for more than a century. It merely provided shelter and anchorage; it was planted around with rows of trees and no warehouses were built there. As we have already mentioned, it came to be used mainly by whaling-ships and changed its name to Greenland Dock; finally it was absorbed into the Surrey Commercial Docks. In 1699 Billingsgate became exclusively a free wharf for fish and here sea food straight from the boats was sold from stalls around the harbour.

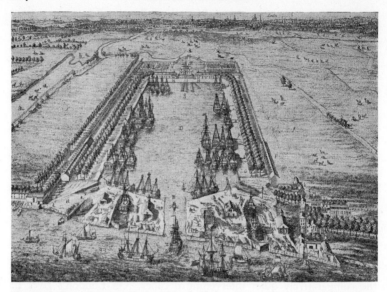

Howland Great Dock at Rotherhithe built in 1696 and London's largest dock for a century. In the distance is the mansion of the Howland family. (From an engraving by Kip)

Much of the fish landed and sold at Billingsgate was caught in the Thames itself, for the river even at London was 'fishful' right up to the 1820s, when serious pollution of the water began. Howell in his *Londinopolis* (1657) tells us that 'the Boryall stremys plesaunt and pre-clare' was only sullied after heavy floods which 'do oftentimes thicken the fineness of the River, in so much that after a Land flood, tis usual to take up Haddocks with ones hand beneath the Bridge, as they float aloft on the water, their eyes being so blinded with the thickness of the water, that they cannot see whither they swimme.'

Floods, before the embanking, were frequent and caused great damage, especially on the south bank. Ben Jonson recalls the flooding of the Thames in his lines:

> *'It was the day, what time the powerful moon*
> *Makes the poor Banksider creature wet its shoon*
> *In its own Hall.'*

As early as 1236 a flood was recorded when the Woolwich marshes were like a sea, many people were drowned and in the Great Hall of

Westminster men rowed about in wherries. In 1242 the river overflowed at Lambeth to a distance of six miles and in the Great Hall men rode through the water on horseback. Pepys recalls that on 7th December 1663 all Whitehall was under water. Only quite recently, after the serious flood of 1928, when ten people were drowned in their basement homes at Westminster, has the river at London come under full control.

The lack of adequate wharfage and warehousing was to remain a serious brake on trade until the early nineteenth century, not least on account of the appalling amount of easy pillaging which went on. Smuggling too was rife. So serious was the lack of port facilities at one time, with its consequent delays in unloading, that scarcity prevailed on shore while plenty lay undistributed upon the water. Only one port authority existed—the City of London—and its docking monopoly brought the City great profit in its customs charges. The warehousing system as we know it today did not come into being until 1714, when for the first time traders were allowed to warehouse tobacco in bond on payment of only a small part of the import duty. But the general situation did not begin to improve until the start of the nineteenth century, when the first enclosed docks were built.

❡ RIVER PAGEANTRY

In spite of the congestion in the Pool and below it, the river during the seventeenth century was colourful—perhaps more so than it had ever been before or has ever been since. The pleasure-loving Charles II brought in the new sport of yachting when the Dutch East India Company presented him with a delightful little pleasure craft like a miniature and highly bedizened battleship, all carved and gilded. In this the Merry Monarch delighted to race. Evelyn sailed with him in his 'yatcht' in the autumn of 1661; there was a wager, he records, 'between his other new pleasure-boat built frigate-like, and one of the Duke of York's; the wager 100 L., the race from Greenwich to Gravesend and back'. He goes on:

'The King lost it going, the wind being contrary, but saved stakes in returning. There were divers noble persons and lords on board, his Majesty sometimes steering himself. His barge and kitchen boat attended, I brake fast this morning with the King at return in his smaller vessel, he being pleased to take me and only four more, who were noblemen, with him; but dined in his yatcht, where we all sat together with his Majesty . . . he was pleased to discourse to me about my book inveighing against the nuisance of the smoke of London, and proposing expedients how, by removing those particulars I mentioned, it might be reformed; commanding me to prepare a Bill against the next session of Parliament, being, as he said, resolved to have something done in it.'

In the early days of the century the annual Lord Mayor's Show upon the river was at its most spectacular and, in competition with the grandeur and theatricality of the Court with its current love of Masques, the City fathers and Companies devised sumptuous and impressive tableaux. On one occasion the Grocers spent nearly £900 on their display and on another the Fishmongers presented eight magnificent features. Here is John Tatham describing in *The Royal Cake* an eye-witness account of the Show of 1660:

'The livery, assistants, master, and wardens, and their gentlemen ushers, do pass to their barges laid at the stairs at the east end of Three Crain Wharff. The lord mayor, aldermen, and their attendants passe into their barge, laid at the accustomed place. The barges, and all other companies, adorned with streamers and banners, and fitted with hoeboyes, cornets, drums, and trumpets, being in the water, move towards Westminster, and by the way his lordship is saluted with twenty pieces of ordnance, as peals of entertainment and joy; against White-hall appears a large stack or fabrick, at the one end whereof is a ship, floating, rigg'd and man'd; at the other end a rock with various figures; one representing Oceanus, who is said to be God of Seas, and the Father of Rivers; he was son of Coelum and Vesta: Archelous was his son, begat of Thetis; and the syrens are said to be the daughters of Archelous and Calliope. To shew his majesty, he walks or treads upon his watery regiment, severall fishes are discovered to play at his feet, and Trytons sporting themselves; four virgins cloathed in white loose garments, and their brows circled with sage, representing the nymphs that frequent rivers.'

London enjoyed one of its Frost Fairs during the latter part of the century. At Christmas time in 1683 the Thames began to freeze, and at the beginning of the new year formal streets of booths and tents had been set up on the river, where not only were commodities sold but various trades were carried on, including printing. Coaches plied on the

A Frost Fair on the Thames in the time of Charles II. (Reproduced from a contemporary engraving)

ice from Westminster to the Temple and there was bull-baiting on the ice, horse and coach racing, puppet plays, cooking, tippling.

Perhaps the greatest ceremony of the century was the procession which crossed the Bridge on the 29th May 1660. Again Evelyn has preserved the scene for us:

'This day his Majestie Charles II came to London after a sad and long exile and calamitous suffering both of the King and Church, being 17 yeares. This was also his birth-day, and with a triumph of above 20,000 horse and foote brandishing their swords and shouting with inexpressible joy; the wayes strew'd with flowers, the bells ringing, the streets hung with tapistry, fountaines running with wine; the Maior, Aldermen, and all the Companies in their liveries, chaines of gold, and banners; Lords and Nobles clad in cloth of silver, gold and velvet; the windowes and balconies well set with ladies; trumpets, music, and myriads of people flocking, even so far from Rochester, so as they were

seven houres in passing the Citty, even from 2 in the afternoone till 9
at night. I stood in the Strand and beheld it and bless'd God.'

Such public shows were occasional only, but a permanent place of
pleasure floated on the river. This was Folly Barge, a whimsical house-
boat with turreted corners which was normally moored opposite Somerset House in the summer months and sometimes off Bankside. It appeared soon after the Restoration, and Pepys visited it in 1668. It was
intended, says Thomas Brown in his *Amusements Serious and Comical*
(1708): 'as a musical summer-house for the entertainment of quality
where they might meet and ogle one another . . . but the ladies of the
town finding it as convenient a rendezvous for their purpose . . . dash'd
the female quality out of countenance and made them seek a more
retired conveniency'. Brown goes on to describe a visit he made at the
end of the century. Some ladies were dancing and tripping about on the
deck, and down below in the boxes sworded bullies sat smoking and
drinking burnt brandy. Perhaps there were other goings-on too because Brown, not often squeamish, found here 'a confused scene of folly,
madness and debauchery'. The Folly became in time a gambling den
and survived well into the eighteenth century. Then it was suppressed,
fell into decay and was broken up for firewood. (See pp. 104–5.)

From the Folly those on pleasure bent might row to Cuper's Gardens
close by on the south bank where Waterloo Bridge now runs ashore.
These gardens were opened in 1691 by Boydell Cuper, an old servant of
the Howard family, and, naturally enough, they became called Cupid's
Gardens. Here, according to Wroth in his *London Pleasure Gardens*,
you could find 'young attorneys' clerks and Fleet Street sempstresses
with a few city dames, escorted by their husbands' 'prentices, who sat in
the arbours singing, laughing and regaling themselves with bottle-ale'.

Some way to the west beyond Lambeth Palace was another public
garden by the river which was to become the most lasting and famous
of its kind. This was the Spring Gardens of Fawkes Hall or Foxhall,
later called Vauxhall. Evelyn visited 'this prettily contrived plantation'
soon after it opened in 1661. So later did Pepys with his wife, two maids
and a boy. Brown refers to the windings and turnings in the little wilderness which were so intricate that the most experienced mothers often
lost themselves there when looking for their daughters.

And with this talk of pleasure gardens we are in the eighteenth century
and their Golden Age.

5 | Rocque's Georgian River

IN SPITE OF its disordered and shambling—though picturesque—line of warehouses, wharves, piers, stairs and water-gates, the river achieved its most civilised look during the eighteenth century, especially so in its latter half, when the Adelphi, the new Somerset House and the Westminster and Blackfriars Bridges had been built, and when the Pool was filled with square riggers which were approaching their full development and beauty.

The importance of the City as a financial centre increased until, with the collapse of the Bank of Amsterdam during the Napoleonic wars, it became the powerful financial headquarters of the whole world. Industries continued, especially in the suburbs and in particular those engaged on the skilled making of luxury goods, but banking, shipping and exchange were the City's main activities.

In this century the control of production by the Livery Companies declined and eventually died out; the Companies lived on (and still do), but mainly as ritualistic survivals.

(NEW TRENDS

The eighteenth was a lively century for the country, and yet, though commerce in the mercantile metropolis and upon its river continued to grow, the look of the riverside changed little. This was the sunny, urbane river depicted so clearly by Canaletto and Samuel Scott, and surveyed and mapped so accurately by Rocque: the river that flowed through those decades when wars were waged elsewhere for commerce and colonies, when lands were lost in America but gained in Canada and India, when the British Empire was founded and foreign markets were always expanding.

It was a century of contrast and paradox: of coarseness and refinement, tolerance and tyranny, gaiety and melancholia, beggar and buck, press gang and tea-garden, cock-pit and coffee-house, slave-ship and Grand Tour, Wesley and the Hell Fire Club, Chelsea porcelain and the Gordon Riots, Handel's Water Music and the sobs of the condemned at Tyburn Tree.

It was, in fact, a century in which the ground was being prepared unseen for the Industrial Revolution and the tremendous social and

I

economic upheavals of the nineteenth and twentieth centuries—not least through the improvement in communications. In this we see the greatest of all the eighteenth-century paradoxes—and one which was to extend well into the next century—the birth and brief life of that splendid child of early industrialism produced by the happy honeymoon of architecture and early engineering to be seen in the functional bridges, mills, warehouses, docks and canal works of the period. In 1820 London and its river was linked, by means of the Regent's Canal and the Grand Junction, with the nation-wide network of inland navigations which had begun with the opening of the Duke of Bridgewater's Canal in 1761. These new canals were an essential element in the creation of the Industrial Revolution, for they linked coal with iron. Unlike the other lanes of transport—the new turnpike roads and the railways to come—the inland waterways did not converge on London, but on Birmingham and the Midlands, and in that they represent the one concession in transport convergence to the change from an agrarian to an industrial economy with its geographical shift to the north. It was during this Canal Era that England, including London, enjoyed its swan song of visual design. This was the Regency period (called so somewhat inaccurately, since the Regency started in 1811 and the swan song had begun some time before that as a continuation from the Golden Age, and went on after the Regent had been crowned).

In the first half of the century there were only a few minor changes in the fabric of London and its riverside. Parapets tended to replace eaves on the houses, and after 1709 the Georgian sash, imported from Holland, began rapidly to replace the Stuart casement with its transoms and mullions; brown-yellow tended to replace red in the colour of brickwork; roofs were mostly covered with red tiles until the last decades of the century, when London's hair began to turn grey as cheap slates arrived from the Welsh quarries.

❲ THE PORT

The City Wall disappeared between 1760 and 1766 and the gates were soon pulled down too. New waterworks were formed at Chelsea in 1722. In 1737 the Fleet Ditch was covered in as far down as Holborn and above it a long arcaded market with skylights, designed by the Clerk of the City Works, George Dance the Elder, was erected, and remained active until it was demolished in 1829 to make way for the new Farringdon Street. But apart from that very little happened until past mid-century. The population changed in numbers hardly at all in the first half: in 1700 it was about 674,500 and by 1750 it had increased by only two or three thousand. After that the rise was rapid: to nearly nine hundred thousand in 1801, the year of the first official census, and 1,654,994 by 1831, when London had become Cobbett's Wen.

In the country's trading, London's port was pre-eminent, so that the river became ever more congested with East Indiamen and West Indiamen, merchant ships from the Continent, from Spain and Africa, whalers from Greenland and fat colliers from Newcastle and Durham—as well as the lighters, barges, brigs, hoys, dinghys, bum-boats, ferry-boats, packets and wherries which scuttled around the Pool, right up to the old Bridge and beyond. In the last decade of the century well over twelve thousand ships, large and small, sailed to the port each year. The scene they created was a fascinating one, for all these ships carried masts, rigging and sails—the products of a highly-evolved craftsmanship.

All this traffic was controlled, as we have seen, by a port monopoly—the City of London itself—and in order to reduce the ever-growing smuggling and pilfering and to ensure that as many as possible of the customs dues were paid, the authorities continued the old system of Legal Quays where merchant vessels were compelled to unload. The City in this way made large profits, in spite of the congestion, the delay, the pilfering and the smuggling. So serious did the smuggling become that in 1750 an Act was passed which forbade the bum-boats to use the river after dark—boats which would float around seeking a ship whose officer, for a bribe, would be prepared to unload sugar, coffee or rum into their black bags or bladders, often with the connivance of the revenue officers who had been blinded by hush-money. Under the new Act penalties were harsh—fourteen years' transportation, for example, for buying or receiving goods direct from the vessels lying on the river.

By the end of the century the congestion and delay were so serious, and the agitation for reform so compelling, that something had to be done, in spite of the opposition of the City, which had, of course, a strong vested interest in maintaining its monopoly and the *status quo*. A Parliamentary Committee was set up in 1796 and an official report soon followed. The main trouble was lack of docking space, and this was remedied when new, enclosed docks were built east of the Tower in the first decades of the nineteenth century.

⟦ NEW CHURCHES

The only important buildings of a serious, monumental sort to be built along the river during the first half of the eighteenth century were a few impressive churches of Portland stone, most of which still stand. In the General Election of 1710 the Whigs suffered a sudden defeat when a Tory government was returned for the first time in twenty-two years. It was a major victory for the Right and, as a gesture of Tory High-Church policy, the event was sanctified in the ninth year of the pious Queen Anne by an Act for the 'building of fifty new churches in or near the Cities of London and Westminster or the Suburbs thereof of Stone and other proper Materials with Towers and Steeples to each of them'. The finance, as usual, was to be raised by taxing coal.

The ultimate results of the new Act were the erection of only eight new churches, a few new steeples, some works on Westminster Abbey, the completion of Greenwich Hospital and the payment of the arrears on Wren's salary as Surveyor of St. Paul's, which the Whigs had been withholding. Of these eight new churches the riverside was graced with one by Thomas Archer, Groom Porter to Queen Anne,* and two of the six remarkable examples designed by Wren's favourite pupil and assistant, Nicholas Hawksmoor. Archer's church is odd but interesting, while Hawksmoor's examples by the river are splendidly strong and original, especially in their tall, square towers. One of them is St. Anne's, Limehouse (1712–24) and the other St. George-in-the-East (1715–23). They can still be seen on either side of, and not far from, the Regent's Canal Dock in Stepney, just south of the Commercial Road —a road which, when the churches were built, was a narrow thorough-fare running between fields and rope walks under the name Rose Lane. Unfortunately, St. George-in-the-East, with its unusual apse, is now a bombed-out shell, but its outer form can still be enjoyed. The tower of St. Anne's is particularly fine, though neither church perhaps quite reaches the dignity and power of Hawksmoor's Christ Church, Spital-fields (1723–29), which lies some way inland from the river.

Archer's church is that of St. John's, in Smith Square, Westminster (1714–28). This also is a casualty of the Second World War. (We can inspect its shell on our walk along Millbank.) Walpole scoffed at the design as a '*chef-d'œuvre* of absurdity', Lord Chesterfield said it looked like an elephant with its legs in the air, while in *Our Mutual Friend*

---

* This was a post of distinction and Archer was an educated man.

St. John's Church, Smith Square, Westminster, from an eighteenth-century engraving; 'the most definitely baroque church in England'. (From a print in the Guildhall Library)

Dickens calls it 'a very hideous church . . . generally resembling some petrified monster, frightful and gigantic, on its back with its legs in the air'. It is a strange, square temple with cylindrical towers at each corner ornamented around with Corinthian pillars and at the tops with huge pineapples. It has been too greatly maligned, for it has virtues in its rich carving and its reasonable adaptation to the shape of the square place in which it stands; it has the distinction, too, of being the most definitely baroque church in England—a country not rich in that exuberant style. Sir Walter Besant has told the story that 'Queen Anne, being troubled in mind by much wearisome detail, kicked over her wooden footstool and said, "Go, build me a church like that".' Besant adds: 'This sounds apocryphal.' But the nickname, Queen Anne's Footstool, has stuck. The future of the shell of St. John's is uncertain, but a hopeful rumour (1957) suggests that it may soon be converted into a small concert hall.

In 1713 Wren made a report on Westminster Abbey, recommending that the stunted western towers should be completed 'in the Gothick Manner' and should be high enough to take bells. Some years later he designed, as one of his last works, a strange superstructure for the low central tower over the crossing. These projects were not executed and, after Wren's death in 1723, when he followed Wren as Surveyor of the Abbey Hawksmoor designed the two western towers we see today. They are a curious mongrel of a design, but they are effective enough, and unmistakably stamped with their creator's strong touch. They were not finished until a few years after Hawksmoor had died in 1736.

(EARLY WATERWORKS

In about 1747, Canaletto made a delightful pen-and-wash drawing of the river looking west from a point on the river near the north bank below the Strand. In the centre distance rises Westminster Abbey with its new western towers clearly shown, as well as the squat stump above the crossing. To the left in the distance is Westminster Bridge, half built. The river is filled with small boats of all kinds, including a state barge, while moored by the bank quite close to us is a boat with its mainsail brailed up, floating below a strange but elegant tower, tall and tapering, apparently of timber boarding. This tower marks the York Buildings Waterworks established in 1675, and it must be that 'Water House, very considerable, serving abundance of water at this end of the town' at the bottom of Villiers Street, which Strype mentions in his 1720 edition of Stow. The site is now occupied by part of Charing Cross Railway Station. Behind the tower are two tall chimneys, for these were the first waterworks to apply steam power for raising water, and Savery in 1712 and Newcomen in 1726 each installed steam-driven pumps here. Near the tower and closer towards us can be seen the York Water Gate, which is still preserved in the Embankment Gardens east of Charing Cross Station.

Samuel Scott painted this very same scene a few years after Canaletto made his sketch, and a water-colour by Philip James de Loutherbourg of 1780 also shows the waterworks with the two chimneys boldly puffing smoke. When Newcomen's engine was first installed here, a pamphlet on the works was published, being probably inspired by the rival interests of the New River Company. It is entitled:

The York Water Gate erected in 1626 and, on the left, the York Buildings Waterworks, as depicted in one of Malton's famous aquatints published at the end of the eighteenth century.

'*The York Buildings Dragons; or a full and true account of a most horrid and barbarous murder intended to be committed next Monday, on the bodies, goods, and name of the greatest part of his Majesty's liege subjects dwelling and inhabiting between Temple Bar in the East, and St. James's in the West, and between Hungerford Market in the South, and St. Mary-le-bone in the North, by a set of evil-minded persons, who do assemble twice a week, to carry on their wicked purposes, in a private room over a stable by the Thames side, in a remote corner of the town.*'

The pamphlet reveals that when fed with live coals by 'a Lancashire wizzard, with long black hair and grim visage . . . and a Welshman bred on top of Penmaenmaur, the monster will clap his wings several times successively with prodigious force, and so terrible will be the noise thereof, that it will be heard as far as Calais, if the wind set right'. Then from the Thames will be sucked 'such a prodigious quantity of water that barges will never be able to go through the bridges' and 'being of a *huffing, snuffing* temper, he will dart out of his nostrils perpendicularly up to the skies two such vast, dense, and opake columns of smoke, that those who live in the Borough will hardly see the sun at noonday'. Finally he will poison the population with the vile effluvium which he will draw from the river 'through a long proboscis, something like an elephant's trunk'.

(ROCQUE'S SCENE

Let us now look at the river panorama as it appeared towards the mid-century, guided by the splendid great map which John Rocque completed in 1745. Very little is known about Rocque, but he seems to have been French. His map, however, is famous and can be seen at the British Museum as measuring no less than thirteen feet long—a model of accuracy and careful detailing. Thereon built-up London extends some four miles from east to west and not much more than two from south to north. To the west Chelsea is growing into a fashionable suburban village and Chelsea Hospital is shown with a long formal avenue, flanked by two decorative canals (long since filled in) and running down to formal riverside stairs. To the east of these the Westbourne falls into the Thames after running along the boundary of Ranelagh Gardens with its great Rotunda. To the east of the Westbourne the ponds of the Chelsea Water Works, established in 1723, are shown. Then come Neat House Gardens and Tothill Fields—mostly open ground partly cultivated as market-gardens and dotted with a few cottages and houses, some of them, no doubt, holiday lodgings and others tea-houses set in small rustic gardens, in Canning's rhyme:

> *'Where each spruce nymph, from city compters free,*
> *Sips the frothed syllabub, or fragrant tea;*
> *While with sliced ham, scraped beef, and burnt champagne,*
> *Her 'prentice lover soothes his amorous pain.'*

This district of Tothill Fields and the Five Fields, now occupied by the houses of Belgravia and Pimlico, was right into the nineteenth century a lonely, marshy locality, where footpads prowled on dark nights.

Across the river here on the south bank the ground is open still. Two windmills are marked beside the river at Battersea. Nine Elms is mostly composed of orchards and market-gardens which run eastward and surround Vauxhall. Fairly close building along the river begins at Lambeth and stretches as far as Rotherhithe, but even so the south bank was far less congested then than it is today, and even as late as 1772 a foreign visitor named Grosley observed that 'opposite Westminster

there is only the country in which are scattered up and down pleasure
houses and agreeable gardens, the number of which increases every
day'. He goes on: 'Opposite London it has only Southwark, a quarter
of the town ill-built, having but two streets in its breadth, and almost
entirely occupied by tanners and weavers.'

On Rocque's map we see that on the north bank close building begins north of Horseferry Road and reaches as far as Shadwell, but there
are market-gardens still in the depths of Wapping. There is no sign
of the ancient City Wall on the map, but many of the old names of
wharves and river stairs remain—Trig Stairs, Broken Wharf, Queen
Hythe, Three Cranes Stairs, Steel Yard Stairs, Billingsgate Dock,
among many. Two new bridges—Westminster and Blackfriars—are
delineated but, as we shall see, they are not yet in use.

Unless you lived on London Bridge, or stood in Temple Gardens, or
on a roof-top or on the deck of a vessel moored in the river, or on some
river stair, you never could enjoy a full river scene. As Grosley wrote:

'The spacious canal formed by the Thames might present us with as
noble and striking an object as the great canal of Venice, lined with
palaces of the most sumptuous magnificence and the most pleasing
variety; but the banks of the Thames are occupied by tanners, dyers, and
other manufacturers, who there have an opportunity of easily supplying
themselves with water. The streets where these manufactures are carried on are the dirtiest in the city; in fine, the bridges have no prospect of
the river, except through a balustrade of stone. In a word, in the first
excursion which I made in order to take a survey of London, I could not
have a full view of the Thames, either on the side of the city, or in that
of Southwark, unless I entered the houses and manufactories which
stand close to the river. . . . All possible measures have been taken to
conceal the prospect of this fine river, and the passages that lead to it.'

Grosley gave an odd reason for this lack of river prospect—that it
tended to keep people from drowning themselves in the river, there
being a 'natural bent of the English, and in particular the people of
London, to suicide'.

〖 TWO NEW BRIDGES

Before mid-century was reached the opposition from the City (as
well as of the vested interest of the Watermen's Company, which was
under the control of the City) to the building across the river of any

bridge in addition to its ancient edifice was at last broken down and London acquired two fine new river monuments—the bridges of Westminster and Blackfriars. (I do not include among new London bridges the rough wooden toll bridge, designed by the surgeon Cheselden and executed by John Phillips, the King's carpenter, which had been erected at Putney in 1729.)

Westminster Bridge was the first to be built in the metropolis since old London Bridge had been erected in the thirteenth century. It was England's first major work of engineering, almost in its modern sense, and, since no engineers then existed in this country, the work was entrusted to a competent foreigner, Charles Labelye, an authority on land drainage and on river and harbour works, the type of skilled Swiss technician. The scheme was sponsored by the ninth Earl of Pembroke, an amateur architect with a reputation as a bridge designer who in partnership with Roger Morris designed the Palladian bridge at Wilton Park. The first stone was laid by Lord Pembroke in January 1739 and the work was finished twelve years later at the considerable cost, for those days, of £393,000.

Labelye carried out his work in a cloud of professional jealousy, but he accomplished the job in the end as a graceful and ingenious piece of Palladianism. It served well until replaced by the present bridge of 1861, and it might be with us still if the substructure had been less experimental. We can see exactly how the bridge looked in the paintings of Samuel Scott. (See p. 21). Of Portland stone with spandrels of darker Purbeck, it crossed the river with fifteen semi-circular arches which increased regularly in size from either end up to the central arch of seventy-six feet span. It was grand in scale and had a high parapet broken with alcoves above the piers where one could sit and watch the traffic pass. A feature of the construction was the new method of caissons used in building the foundations of the piers.*

The second of the two major London bridges erected across the Thames during the eighteenth century was Blackfriars. The designer was Robert Mylne, whose plan was selected and its execution begun early in 1760. It was opened ten years later under the name Pitt Bridge in honour of the statesman who had, according to the foundation tablet now in the Guildhall Museum, 'recovered, augmented and secured the British Empire in Asia, Africa, and America, and restored the ancient reputation and influence of his country among the nations of Europe'.

* See my *Bridges of Britain* (Batsford, 1954).

Blackfriars Bridge under construction, as visualised by Piranesi in 1764 from drawings and descriptions; only half of the engraving is shown here.

It was a fine bridge in Portland stone, unusual in having semi-elliptical arches only nine in number, over which the road ran in a graceful curve, the central arch being a hundred feet in span. In 1863 it was taken down owing to its narrowness and decay; so London lost another fine bridge. The present bridge was opened in 1869 by Queen Victoria on the same day that she opened Holborn Viaduct.

A third but less important bridge than either Westminster or Blackfriars was erected in 1771 at Battersea, by the same concern that had built Putney Bridge. For over a century this rough timber structure stood, a unique and picturesque landmark, as Chelsea's only river crossing. Its construction was supervised by Henry Holland, then a budding young architect working for his father's building firm at Fulham. He married the daughter of 'Capability' Brown and reached renown as the architect to the Prince of Wales and the Grand Whiggery. Battersea Bridge, immortalised in Whistler's *Nocturne* (in the Tate Gallery, see p. 204), stood until 1890, when it was superseded by the present undistinguished structure by Sir Joseph Bazalgette of Embankment fame.

❨ THE OLD BRIDGE

Changes came to old London Bridge in this century. By 1710 all the houses on the Bridge had been rebuilt in Restoration style with hipped roofs and deep eaves, and they now projected further over the river so that the road might be increased in width to twenty feet. The houses were in regular terraces and the old picturesque jumble had gone. By mid-century the houses were already in a bad condition and the whole Bridge had lost caste, in spite of the building soon after 1745 of a new regular block of colonnaded Georgian houses at the north end designed by George Dance the Elder, the City Clerk of Works; called The Piazzas, this block stood for only some sixteen years. There was talk at this time of completely rebuilding the Bridge. The cost was thought to be prohibitive, but a committee announced that they were 'humbly of the opinion that the houses upon London Bridge are a public nuisance, long felt and universally censured and complained of'. In 1757 down they came. The Bridge was then widened and partly reconstructed by the sculptor-architect, Sir Robert Taylor, working in collaboration with Dance.

They built a wide new centre arch and refaced the piers, decorating them with Gothic panels. At road level were built hooded alcoves at regular intervals like those on Westminster Bridge.* In that state the Bridge was to last another sixty years, but during those years there was continual trouble with the foundations of the Great Arch caused by the strong scouring of the current. The pools around the piers were always being fed with rubble, until the authorities at last came to their senses and built a new bridge. If the City had taken Wren's advice, a century earlier, to remove every other pier of Old London Bridge, the scouring would have been distributed and a lot of money and trouble would have been saved.

* One of these alcoves is now in a courtyard of Guy's Hospital and two others are in Victoria Park.

Old London Bridge after the houses had been removed in the 1750s and the bridge had been partly reconstructed. In the distance are the Monument and the spire of St. Magnus (From an aquatint of 1790 by Joseph Farington, R.A.)

❡ THE ADELPHI SCHEME

About the time the Building Act of 1774 was passed, London's two major constructions of the century were erected along the river front: the Adelphi housing by the Adam brothers, and the new Somerset House by Chambers. The whole of Somerset House exists today, but only a few relics of the Adelphi scheme remain.

Robert Adam and Sir William Chambers were the dominating architectural personalities of their time and represented the new type of professional gentleman-architect as opposed to the civil-servant surveyor or aristocrat's artist-protegé of the past. Both men exercised great influence, especially Adam, whose Adelphi terraces were as revolutionary in their way as Jones's Banqueting Hall had been in its time.

In 1764, Adam was thirty-six. His youthful work was in complete contrast to that of Chambers, being playful, fantastic and ornamented in an entirely new way. The staid Palladians had designed everything, including country houses, as though they were Roman temples, but Adam argued reasonably that the Romans themselves did not decorate

The Adelphi: a contemporary print by Ben Green

their houses in the same way as their temples, but in the light and delicate manner which his foreign researches had revealed. So he produced his charming cosmetics of honeysuckle and swags, pilasters and plaques which, in their novelty and inventiveness, had an immediate appeal and a powerful effect on all later domestic façades and interiors. Adam continued to accept the Palladian massing and symmetry, and his innovations were almost entirely decorative, as the Adelphi buildings showed.

The Adelphi was a big speculative enterprise launched by Robert Adam and his brother James (hence its name which is Greek for brothers). The land where Durham House had stood was leased in 1768 from the Duke of St. Albans; by 1772, the riverside wharf, the substructure of brick catacombs and some of the houses were going up, but the whole scheme running back to the Strand was not to be completed for some years, because the brothers were beset by difficulties, mainly financial. A major blow fell when the Ordnance Department refused to honour its promise to rent the vaults for storage, on the grounds that by a miscalculation the wharf had been built too low and was therefore liable to flooding at high tides. And the houses were slow in selling, even though the actor Garrick, a great friend of the brothers, had given a helpful lead by taking a house in the centre of the Royal Terrace facing the river. Undaunted, the Adams not only raised mortgages on the property in order to avoid bankruptcy, but resorted to a lottery, selling over four thousand tickets at £50 each with the offer of one hundred and eight prizes. Eventually the situation was saved and the houses were built, but the brothers had suffered great worry as well as the loss of their art collections and most of their modest fortunes.

Opinions of the scheme when it was finished were loud and varied. Men like Chambers not only found the work meretricious, but objected to the commercial adventuring of the promoters, who had even been vulgar enough to advertise themselves in the very name of the place. Horace Walpole declared that the Adelphi looked like a warehouse; perhaps it did in a way, but what a magnificent one! From what we can see of the Adelphi now in the old prints and in the few remaining relics, it was a successful piece of architecture. Quite symmetrical in lay-out, it consisted of a row of arches along the wharf supporting a generous promenade above as the first piece of public riverside embanking the riverside had enjoyed. Behind this promenade, and facing the river, lay the Royal Adelphi Terrace, with gaily decorated pilasters in the centre and at the ends. Two streets ran back to the Strand at either hand, and the southern ends of the returns of the outer rows of houses were also pilastered and pedimented. Most of the structure was yellow brickwork with a ground floor of stucco; well-wrought ironwork balconies and railings helped to decorate the geometric simplicity of the whole.

In 1872 the Royal Terrace was remodelled and debased with a heavy central pediment, so that when the houses were pulled down in 1936, the loss was less than it might have been if the whole of the Adelphi had been preserved in its original state. The present overpowering and inhuman office block which covers a large part of the site was opened in 1938, but Adam Street still exists on its east side and there a few of the original houses remain, the most perfect fragment being the offices of *The Lancet* at No. 7. Another good fragment is the headquarters of the Royal Society of Arts in John Adam Street, where the Society has been housed since the place was built.

Many people of renown lived at the Adelphi at various times. Garrick, as we have seen, was the first, and there in 1772 Fanny Burney visited him. 'A sweet situation,' she wrote. 'The house is large and elegantly fitted up.' In 1781, two years after Garrick had died, Dr.

Johnson dined there with Mrs. Garrick, Boswell, Dr. Burney, Sir Joshua Reynolds and Hannah More. At No. 8, The Royal Terrace, Thomas Hardy studied architecture as an apprentice to Arthur Blomfield and from there he saw Charing Cross Railway Bridge being built. On the top floors of No. 10 lived Bernard Shaw and his wife after their marriage in 1896 until 1927. At the vanished Adelphi Hotel on the corner of Adam and John Streets (the latter is now called John Adam Street), Thomas Rowlandson, the caricaturist, died in 1827; the house figures as Osborne's Hotel in *Pickwick Papers* and was originally the Adelphi New Tavern and Coffee House.

(SOMERSET HOUSE

Old Somerset House had served many notable inhabitants and purposes during its long life, and in the later years it housed the schools of design of the Royal Academy; there the first official dinner of the Academy had been held in 1771. Now it was decayed, and in 1775, after much discussion, an Act was passed to enable a new building to be erected on the site of the old mansion—a grand new public edifice to form a suitable centre for a number of administrative and academic bodies which were at the time lodged ignominiously in scattered and inadequate premises. This kind of building was a novel conception and one of its aims was to act as a prestige symbol for a country which had gained an Empire.

Being Surveyor-General, Treasurer of the Royal Academy and a friend of the King, Sir William Chambers was the natural choice as its architect. In 1776 the monumental work was begun. The only thing it had in common with the Adelphi, lying less than a quarter of a mile to its west, was in possessing a riverside terrace with an arcade below, like an embankment promenade. In every other way it was different, being a heavy, studied, conservative and classic design in Portland stone. With its rustications, its rhythmical windows, its 'correct' detailing, its competent carving and its fine central water gate, it is a dignified and accomplished building but rather a dull one, and its small domes are weak. It can be seen at its best from Waterloo Bridge, and from there it is easy to realise how much the building lost when the Victoria Embankment divorced its arcaded basement from the river.

The main central buildings, completed in 1789, were designed to contain the Offices for the Navy, the Ordnance and Taxes, and here the Royal Academy resided from 1780 to 1838. The Royal Society and the Society of Antiquaries also met there until they both moved to Burling-

View from a pier at Wapping across the river to Rotherhithe; on the left is the eighteenth-century tower and steeple of St. Mary's Church.

ton House in 1856. Today the rooms are inhabited by officials of the Registrar General and the Probate Registry. The whole edifice was not completed during Chambers's life, but as it stands it is in accordance with his original designs. The east wing was finished in 1835 under Sir Robert Smirke as King's College, while the west wing was not finished until 1856 under Sir James Pennethorne, being inhabited today by the Board of Inland Revenue.

A good deal of symbolic sculpture decorates the building and is worth looking at. Most of it was executed by Chambers's fellow academicians, Bacon, Carlini and Wilton.

⟦ TWO OTHER BUILDINGS

Two lesser buildings appeared in the eighteenth century along the riverside. One is St. Mary's Church on the south bank near the Surrey

K

Commercial Docks in Rotherhithe (called Redriff at one time). It adds a charming and civilised touch to the confusion of warehouses when seen across the river from Wapping. It was completed in the summer of 1715, but the steeple was not added until 1738. The building is of red brick with stone dressings and a stone steeple decorated with Corinthian columns and standing on a square tower.

The second building was of some symbolic importance, though it stood for only three years. In March 1783 a company was formed with the object of building some large corn mills on Bankside upon the site now covered by the end of the railway bridge running across the river from Blackfriars. Called Albion Mills, these were to be no ordinary sort of mills driven by wind or water, for they were to be powered with the new steam engines of Boulton and Watt. For the next three years the big block was building under the supervision of the brothers James and Samuel Wyatt.

The Albion Mills. (From a Victorian engraving)

The engines which James Watt installed in the mills were the most powerful he had yet devised, and for the first time steam power was here applied to drive millstones and machines for fanning, sifting and dressing corn as well as to hoist and lower the corn and to load and unload the sacks into barges. John Rennie, then only twenty-five, was given the job of fitting up the machinery and this established his reputation as an engineer. When completed the two great engines drove twenty pairs of millstones, each pair grinding ten bushels of wheat per hour, day and night if demanded.

The mills were the great mechanical wonder of the day and caused a good deal of consternation and hostility within the trade. They were opened in 1788 and were working well and realising handsome profits when, on the night of the 3rd of March, 1791, they were completely destroyed by fire. They were never rebuilt. Luddite incendiarism was suspected but was never proved.

The devastating fire at the Albion Mills had important repercussions because it stimulated the rapid development of fireproof construction of industrial buildings. Mill-owners were suffering heavy losses by fire and rates of insurance were exorbitant. Thus the new system of iron columns and beams with brick-tile floors developed by William Strutt and Charles Bage soon set an important precedent in that structural revolution from which have evolved the steel-frame buildings of today, including the skyscrapers of New York.

(VAUXHALL GARDENS

I have left the most enchanting additions to the riverside in the eighteenth century to the last. They are those places of Polite Amusement, the two famous pleasure-gardens of Vauxhall and Ranelagh, with their plantations, illuminations and playful structures—baroque, rococo, Chinese and Gothick—which were, as Dr. Johnson pointed out in describing Vauxhall, 'so peculiarly adapted to the taste of the English nation, there being a mixture of curious show, gay exhibition, music vocal and instrumental not too refined for the general ear, for all which only a shilling is paid'.

We have already seen that Vauxhall was a public pleasure resort in the seventeenth century under the name Spring Gardens, but it was not until 1728, when Jonathan Tyers took a thirty years' lease of the property and set about improving it, that Vauxhall entered its long and successful career. He opened it on the 7th of June 1732 with a select *ridotto alfresco*, which the Prince of Wales attended. This was the start of a highly successful enterprise which was to survive for one hundred and twenty-seven years. Nearly every Londoner of the eighteenth century must have visited the place at one time or another in their lives and, to quote a contemporary song, have

> '*Sail'd triumphant in the liquid way,*
> *To hear the fiddlers of Spring Garden play.*'

Hogarth helped to beautify the place, for he painted pictures in several of the rooms; Roubillac produced a statue of Handel for the gardens. In 1758 an elaborate new orchestra structure was built in Strawberry Hill Gothick, topped with a dome surmounted with feathers. Another building Tyers erected was the Prince's Pavilion in honour of his royal patron, and there Prince Fritz would often sup and listen to the music.

Goldsmith was enchanted by Vauxhall. He wrote in a letter about 1760: 'The lights everywhere glimmering through scarcely moving trees; the full-bodied concert bursting on the stillness of the night; the natural concert of the birds in the more retired part of the grove, vieing with that which was formed by art; the company gaily dressed, looking satisfied; and the tables spread with various delicacies,—all conspired to fill my imagination with the visionary happiness of the Arabian law-giver, and lifted me into an ecstacy of admiration. "Head of Confucius," cried I to my friend, "this is fine! This unites rural beauty with courtly magnificence."'

A print of 1751 drawn by Wale shows us how Vauxhall looked in its earlier years. In the foreground to the left is a row of Georgian terrace houses with the so-called Water Gate Entrance, not in fact a true water-gate, for the gardens lie a little way back from the river. Attached to the houses is the Prince's Pavilion, facing on to a square surrounded by trees, at the centre of which stands the orchestra structure, complete with organ—an ornate bandstand, in fact. To the left of the quadrangle across the Grand Walk we see the roof of a round building; this is the Rotunda, nicknamed the Umbrella, which is entered through a colonnade. The Rotunda's interior is seventy feet in diameter and has been delineated by Wale as an elegant room gaily decorated with rococo swirls and a scalloped ceiling embellished with bows and garlands. Here the orchestra performs on wet evenings. Connected with the Rotunda is a long room called the Saloon or Picture Room. In 1786 a Supper Room, not shown in Wale's general view, was built to the left

A general prospect of Vauxhall Gardens depicted by Wale in 1751.

of the Rotunda. Around the quadrangle are arranged, in long colonnades or in semi-circular sweeps, rows of supper-boxes decorated with
paintings of such light-hearted scenes as a cricket match or a dance
around a maypole; there cold collations of ham and chicken may be
enjoyed. (It is plain to see in Wale's clear drawing, with its ogee domes
and exotic detailing, the inspiration for the designing of the structures
of the 1951 Festival Gardens in Battersea Park.)

A number of avenues run between plantations to the distance where
the open country begins. The avenue to the right, called the South
Walk, is decorated at intervals with ornamental archways, and it ends
with a great painting representing the Ruins of Palmyra. On the extreme
right lies the intimate Lovers' Walk, below a canopy of tall trees where
the wild birds build their nests and sing. This is one of the Dark Walks
of the garden which in 1763 Tyers was compelled to rail off following
complaints about the number of lascivious characters therein. Happily
the railings were soon torn up by a gang of young bucks when the next
season opened.

Various entertaining spectacles were dotted about the twelve-acre
grounds, including the Cascade to the north, whither the visitors would
be summoned at nine o'clock by a bell; a curtain would be drawn aside

to reveal a brightly-lit landscape in miniature in which a waterfall turned a mill-wheel. At the Musical Bushes a subterranean band would play fairy music until it was discovered that 'the natural damp of the earth' was 'prejudicial to the instruments'. *England's Gazetteer* of 1751 thus describes Vauxhall:

'This is the place where are those called Spring Gardens, laid out in so grand a taste that they are frequented in the three summer months by most of the nobility and gentry then in and near London; and are often honoured with some of the royal family, who are here entertained, with the sweet song of numbers of nightingales, in concert with the best band of musick in England. Here are fine pavilions, shady groves, and most delightful walks, illuminated by above one thousand lamps, so disposed that they all take fire together, almost as quick as lightning, and dart such a sudden blaze as is perfectly surprising. Here are among others, two curious statues of Appollo the god, and Mr. Handel, the master of musick; and in the centre of the area, where the walks terminate, is erected the temple for the musicians, which is encompassed all round with handsome seats, decorated with pleasant paintings, on subjects most happily adapted to the season, place and company.'

It was all very pleasant in its simple way and more democratic than this description indicates, for the company came from all classes. Tyers died in 1767, having made a fortune by his enterprise. His two sons succeeded him, and in their time there was a good deal of high-spirited rowdyism in the gardens, particularly on the last night of each season. We read in *Evelina*, published about 1778, that on such occasions 'there's always a riot—and there the folks run about—and then there's such squealing and squalling! and there all the lamps are broke, and the women run skimper scamper'.

Fireworks began at Vauxhall in 1798 and entertainments grew more sophisticated, such as those performances of Madame Saqui from Paris, who, spangled and plumed, would slowly descend an inclined rope 'in the face of a tempest of fireworks'.

In 1821 the gardens passed out of the Tyers family and in the following year became, through the patronage of George IV, the Royal Gardens, Vauxhall. Some changes came to the look of the place, which was now brightly lit by twenty thousand additional lamps. Equestrian performances were given in the Rotunda, there was a submarine cavern in the grounds and a Hermit's Cottage; in the Saloon a device called the

C. H. Simpson, 'that kind, smiling idiot', for thirty-six years Master of
Ceremonies at Vauxhall Gardens, in a contemporary lithograph by J. W. Gear.

Heptaplasiesoptron was installed—an exotic spectacle of moving lights
and reflections giving visions of pillared halls, palm-trees, writhing ser-
pents, gushing fountains *inter al*, a forerunner of Daguerre's Diorama.

A survey plan of 1826 marks a theatre in one of the plantations, a Smugglers' Cave, a Firework Tower and a new Chinese Entrance on the south.

But the most memorable sight of Vauxhall in the early nineteenth century was the Master of Ceremonies, 'the gentle Simpson, that kind, smiling idiot', as Thackeray described him. His short, eccentric figure, frilled and dapper, has been immortalised by Cruikshank.

The Ranelagh Rotunda drawn by W. Newton and engraved by A. Walker in 1761—'an immense amphitheatre, with balconies full of little ale-houses'.

In early Victorian days Vauxhall was still lively enough, but it had lost some of its earlier freshness and charm. On Monday the 25th of July 1859 the set-piece of fireworks displayed the device 'Farewell for Ever'. And that was the end. In that year Battersea Park was opened to the public and Cremorne Gardens were flourishing. On the site of the gardens many new streets and buildings arose; but the place is still recorded in the name Tyers Street, which marks the eastern edge of the old gardens.

⟨ THE ROUND OF PLEASURE

On the other side of the river from Vauxhall, a little to the north-west, was the more fashionable and more sedate resort of Ranelagh. At Runnelow, as it would have been pronounced (London was then Lunnon), a large round building was erected in 1741 just to the east of Chelsea Hospital, in the grounds of a property previously owned by Lord Ranelagh, Paymaster-General to the Forces, who about 1690 had built himself a house there and laid out some fine gardens. This great Rotunda, a kind of Roman Pantheon, was built by a company to the design of William Jones, a furniture designer and architect to the East India Company. The chief shareholder of the company was Sir Thomas Robinson, Bart., M.P., an amateur of the arts who was to become Ranelagh's Director of Entertainments.

The place was opened on the 5th of April 1742, and ten days later Horace Walpole, an early chronicler of Ranelagh, wrote in a letter to Sir Horace Mann: 'I have been breakfasting this morning at Ranelagh Garden: they have built an immense amphitheatre, with balconies full of little ale-houses: it is in rivalry to Vauxhall and costs above twelve thousand pounds.' In another letter written in the following month he describes again the 'vast amphitheatre, finely gilt, painted and illuminated; into which everybody that loves eating, drinking, staring or crowding, is admitted for twelvepence'. Two years later we read in a letter to the Hon. Henry Conway that Walpole goes 'every night constantly ' to Ranelagh, 'which has totally beat Vauxhall . . . nobody goes anywhere else; everybody goes there'. The floor of the Rotunda, he writes, 'is all of beaten princes . . . you can't set your foot without treading on a Prince of Wales or Duke of Cumberland. The company is universal; there is from his Grace of Grafton down to children out of the Foundling Hospital—from my Lady Townshend to the kitten—from my Lord Sandys to your humble cousin and his friend Hor. Walpole.' Four years later 'Ranelagh is so crowded, that going there t'other night in a string of coaches, we had a stop of six and thirty minutes'.

The Rotunda was indeed something worth going to see, quite apart from the people—'much nobility and much mob' in Walpole's phrase—who strolled therein. Its internal diameter was one hundred and fifty

feet, about the size of the British Museum Reading Room. It was entered
by four Doric porticoes; an arcade supporting a gallery encircled the
building outside, while inside a circle of supper boxes ran round the
edge of the floor and supported a similar circle of boxes above, each of
which was entered from the outside gallery. Above the gallery ran a
row of sixty round-headed windows. At the centre stood an elaborate
construction which was nothing more than a huge open fireplace and
chimney, though it had been designed originally to hold the orchestra;
for acoustical reasons the orchestra was later moved to the side. From
the olive-coloured ceiling hung many scintillating chandeliers holding
thousands of candles. The whole structure was almost entirely of wood
and it is surprising that in its life of sixty years it never caught fire.

In *Humphrey Clinker*, Lydia Melford describes the place with youthful enthusiasm: 'Ranelagh looks like the enchanted palace of a genio,
adorned with the most exquisite performances of painting, carving, and
gilding, enlightened with a thousand golden lamps, that emulate the
noonday sun; crowded with the great, the rich, the gay, the happy and
the fair; glittering with cloth of gold and silver, lace, embroidery, and
precious stones. While these exulting sons and daughters of felicity
tread this round of pleasure, or regale in different parties, and separate
lodges, with fine imperial tea and other delicious refreshments, their
ears are entertained with the most ravishing delights of music, both instrumental and vocal.'

Defoe thought the Rotunda 'a fine Structure' which had been 'erected
in the Gardens, to propagate Sound for Sense, and to feast the eyes of
Belles and Beaux, who crowd thither to become Spectacles to one another, for the Benefit of the Proprietors of the Undertaking'. Dr. Johnson thought the interior of the Rotunda was 'the finest thing he had ever
seen', which gave to his mind 'an expansion of gay sensation' he had
never experienced elsewhere, even if, sir, such things 'are only *struggles*
for happiness'. A French visitor of about 1749 merely shrugged: 'On
s'ennuie avec de la mauvaise musique, du thé et du beurre.'

The music was by no means always bad; some of the world's finest
singers and instrumentalists performed there. On the 29th of June
1764, for a 'Public useful charity', a child of eight played 'several fine
select Pieces of his own Composition on the Harpsichord and on the
Organ which has already given the highest Pleasure, Delight and Sur-
prize to the greatest Judges of Music in England or Italy'. The child
was Mozart.

The normal charge for admission became half-a-crown and the price included refreshments of tea or coffee with bread and butter. The main season began at Easter, but the Rotunda was open earlier in the year for dances. In its earlier days, breakfast could be had there too, and morning concerts were frequent. The gardens were much less elaborate than those at Vauxhall, but they possessed their special attractions—their broad, tree-lined avenues, their Temple of Pan, illuminations, great fountain and, not least, their decorative canal on which stood a little island temple, half-Chinese, half-Venetian. After 1767 firework displays were often given and sometimes special masquerades were organised. But the chief diversion of the place was the promenade around the Rotunda—that 'ring of Folly', of which Robert Bloomfield was to write in a satirical poem inspired by a visit there in 1802:

'*A thousand feet rustled on mats,*
A carpet that once had been green;
Men bow'd with their outlandish hats,
With corners so fearfully keen!
Fair maids, who at home in their haste
Had left all clothing else but a train,
Swept the floor clean, as slowly they pac'd
And then—walk'd round and swept it again.'

Among the bright occasions at Ranelagh was the Grand Jubilee Masquerade, in the Venetian taste, held on the 26th of April 1749 to celebrate the peace of Aix-la-Chapelle. There was nothing Venetian in it, wrote Horace Walpole in an enthusiastic letter,

'but was by far the best understood and prettiest spectacle I ever saw; nothing in a fairy tale ever surpassed it . . . when you entered you found the whole garden filled with masks and spread with tents, which remained all night very commodely. In one quarter was a Maypole dressed with garlands, and people dancing round it to a tabor and pipe, and rustic music, all masked, as were all the various bands of music that were disposed in different parts of the garden; some like huntsmen with French-horns, some like peasants, and a troop of harlequins and scaramouches in the little open temple on the mount. On the canal was a sort of gondola, adorned with flags and streamers, and filled with music rowed about. All round the outside of the amphitheatre were shops, filled with Dresden china, Japan, &c., and all the shopkeepers in mask. The amphitheatre was illuminated, and in the middle was a circular bower, composed of all kinds of firs in tubs, from twenty to thirty feet high; under them, orange trees, with small lamps in each orange, and below them all sorts of the finest auriculas in pots; and festoons of natural flowers hanging from tree to tree. Between the arches, too, were firs, and smaller ones in the balconies above. There were booths for tea and wine, gaming-tables, and dancing, and about two thousand persons. In short, it pleased me more than the finest thing I ever saw.'

Perhaps the most brilliant occasion ever held at Ranelagh was the great Regatta and Ball of the 23rd of June 1775, six days after the Battle of Bunkers Hill. Though the Coat and Badge race—the Watermen's Derby—had been instituted in 1716 by the Irish comedian Doggett and was an annual event (as it still is), a Thames regatta was a novelty. All day the church bells rang and a race was rowed by pairs of hearty watermen from Westminster to London Bridge and back, the first prizes being ten guineas with Coats and Badges. Thereafter a grand procession moved up-river to the Chelsea Hospital Stairs, flags fluttered, military bands played on cymbals, fifes and drums, pleasure-boats and barges filled the river and on the banks the buildings and the temporary stands were filled with people.

At eleven o'clock that night the doors of the Rotunda were thrown open and inside, at long tables radiated from the centre, one thousand three hundred people who had been lucky enough to obtain tickets (in the form of a splendid allegorical engraving by Cipriani and Bartolozzi depicting Father Thames and attendants) sat down to a supper provided by the celebrated Mrs. Cornelys. An orchestra of two hundred and forty under Giardini's baton gave a concert and later there was more music in the garden, while in an 'antique amphitheatre' representing the Temple of Neptune, the guests danced minuets, cotillions and country steps to a band of musicians all 'in sylvan dresses'.

On the 8th of July 1803 the Rotunda opened its doors for the last time and on the 30th September of the same year the proprietors ordered its demolition. The eighteenth century and the peak of England's civilisation were nearly over. By 1807 the grounds were already desolate and overgrown with weeds, but in 1826 they were bought by the Chelsea Hospital and to this day a large part of them remains a public garden—part of them only because in 1853 the Chelsea Bridge

Road was built along the eastern side, and the Chelsea Embankment a few years later cut off its southern tip.

Today visitors to the annual Chelsea Flower Show can, like Dr. Johnson, struggle for happiness there and achieve in mind what he did on this very spot—an expansion of gay sensation.

A Vauxhall ticket of admission struck in
silver after a design by William Hogarth.
(From an engraving of 1825)

6 | Mogg's River and the Explosion

THE NINETEENTH CENTURY falls into two fairly distinct parts—Georgian and Victorian. The whole century was one of fantastic building developments and improvements in communications throughout the country and particularly in London, which, in the furious crescendo of industrial expansion, firmly consolidated its position as the Imperial City. That position was to be maintained well into the twentieth century until the two world wars did for the United States what the Napoleonic wars had done for Britain, and the centre of financial power shifted to New York.

Along the river many new bridges were built, warehouses sprang up everywhere and great new enclosed docks were dug east of the Tower. During the Regency, taste was at its highest peak, but unfortunately building was then hindered to some extent by the wars and the consequent shortage of Baltic timber. After the Great Reform Act of 1832, which killed the old landowning oligarchy, taste declined as rapidly as London expanded.

In this century the Palace of Westminster went up in flames and was reborn as a mediæval dream; the Brunels ferreted under the river, Bazalgette relieved the traffic and the sewage with his ponderous embankments and, under the remorseless pressure of the ever-growing population, major civic reforms came in local administration and social services. The arrival of steam changed life both on land and water; more bridges were built to carry the snorting iron horses over the Thames, and at Cannon Street, Charing Cross, and London Bridge terminal stations, the great cathedrals of the Victorian age, arched into life. In 1889, a big administrative advance came with the creation of the London County Council, which absorbed the older Metropolitan Board of Works, born in 1855. Gas light came to the streets and in the 'seventies electric lights began to take their place. As congestion increased there was burrowing underground for the tube railways, and these, extending ever outwards, spread the cultural deserts over the outlying fields. Along the riverside two oases brought spacious green relief, first at Cremorne, to the west of Chelsea, and later on, south of the river at Battersea.

By the end of the century hardly a sail was to be seen on the river or in the docks, and in 1909 came another major reform on the river with

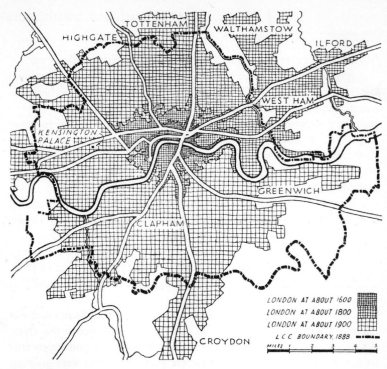

Map showing the growth of London between 1600 and 1900. (Reproduced by courtesy of the Trustees of the London Museum)

the creation of the Port of London Authority. During all this confused and rapid development of the nineteenth century, the City lost its control of the river to the Crown but managed, by virtue of its ancient pride, prestige and power, to retain many of its corporate rights and privileges. It remains to this day outside the jurisdiction of the LCC, and in this there is no logic but only an understandable sentiment; as a Commission of Inquiry into London government declared, the only justification it could find for the separation of the small City area from a wide municipal one was that it had long existed.

The central London we know today is still largely the London of the nineteenth century—along the riverside as elsewhere. The soot is now more deeply encrusted, the bombs have left their wounds, the tinkling trams have gone, a noble new bridge has appeared, there are more office blocks, new power-stations and in Battersea Park the trees have grown to middle-aged maturity. But on the whole the changes of the past seven decades have been comparatively few compared with those of the seven that went before—at least within London itself.

As I write I have beside me a map published on the 1st January 1827, which proves the point. This map gives us an admirable guide to the riverside during the first decades of the century. Its florid title reads: *'London in Miniature with the Surrounding Villages—An Entire New Plan in which the Improvements both present and intended are actually produced (by permission) from the surveys of the Several Proprietors—The whole laid down from the best Authorities and Carefully corrected to the present time by Howard Mogg.'* It is an admirably clear map, hand-tinted in green to show parks and gardens and in vermilion to show intended improvements. I have reproduced its main river features on pages 184–5.

❰ MANY NEW BRIDGES

Seven bridges are shown. Far to the east is the old wooden bridge of Battersea; next, at the western end of Chelsea Reach, stands Vauxhall Bridge (opened in 1816), approached from the north-east by the New Road (now Vauxhall Bridge Road) and running into Kennington Lane by Vauxhall Gardens. Then comes Labelye's Westminster Bridge, decked since 1813 with gas lamps, Waterloo Bridge (opened in 1817), Mylne's Blackfriars Bridge, Southwark Bridge (opened in 1819) and finally old London Bridge. On the west of the old Bridge a stripe across the river indicates New London Bridge, then nearing completion.

Waterloo Bridge was Rennie's finest work. Begun in 1811 as Strand Bridge, its name was later altered for patriotic reason when it was opened by the Prince Regent in 1817 on the second anniversary of the Battle of Waterloo. The Act for the change of name states that 'the said bridge when completed will be a work of great stability and magnificence and such works are adopted to transmit to posterity the remembrance of great and glorious achievements'. Indeed, with its nine semi-elliptical arches of granite, each spanning one hundred and twenty feet and built with superb precision and craftsmanship, it was justly described at the time by the Italian sculptor Canova as 'the noblest bridge in the world worth a visit from the remotest corners of the earth'.

Southwark Bridge, opened in 1819, was Rennie's next job, and in order to provide as wide a central span as possible to aid shipping, he

L

decided to use iron; the piers were of stone, but the three flat segmental arches were of cast iron and made with diagonal strutting in the spandrels. The central arch was no less than 240 feet wide, and the whole was the largest cast iron structure that had so far been built. It was demolished in 1914.

The last great work of Rennie's life was the conceiving of New London Bridge, and it was still only on paper when its designer died. His sons, George and John, carried on the work to full realisation. It is the only one of Rennie's London bridges which still stands, though it is not exactly as he planned it, for it was widened in 1902-4.

After the opening of the new bridge in 1831, the old one was gradually demolished and by the second year of Victoria's reign the last sign of it had vanished forever.* The current was increased by the removal, and this had its scouring effects on the bridges above. Today they have all been rebuilt either because they failed, like Labelye's Westminster or Rennie's Waterloo, or because they were inadequate for the growing traffic both above and below.

An interesting bridge which appeared in 1845 and vanished soon again when Charing Cross Railway Bridge took its place in 1863 was Isambard Kingdom Brunel's Hungerford Footbridge, a chain suspension between two square Italianate towers. When the bridge was demolished the chains were acquired for a low sum and were used to complete Brunel's Clifton Suspension Bridge after Brunel had died.

Another interesting bridge of Victorian times is Ordish's Albert Bridge, built at Chelsea in 1873 and now threatened with demolition. It is not exactly a beauty, but it has great individuality and is now regarded by many with a growing affection. It is a hybrid invention of the designer, combining cantilever and suspension principles; tie-bars radiate from the tops of the towers to points all along the deck sides, while an eye-bar chain takes some of the deck load by means of suspenders.

A bridge which came much later during the century than the year of 1827 was Tower Bridge. Designed by the City Architect, Horace Jones, and J. W. Barry, it was begun in 1885 and opened by the Prince of Wales (later Edward VII) in 1894. It is the first bridge to be built below London Bridge and still the last of the Thames bridges before the sea. With its double-leaf bascule, it is a curious, intricate struc-

---

* A lover of London tells me that a sign of the old Bridge can be seen at low water when an eddy marks the place of the submerged stump of one of the piers.

Old London Bridge with its starlings immediately before its demolition. In the background is Wren's St. Magnus Martyr Church and the top of the monument. (From an engraving by E. W. Cooke made in 1831)

ture and the only movable bridge on the whole river. It has two ornate towers of some sort of mongrel of Mediæval and Flemish Renaissance bred to harmonise with the Tower of London close by. The two towers are linked high up by a pair of fixed steel footways reached by lifts and stairs within the towers, and these were used by foot-passengers for some time whenever the bascules were up to allow ships to pass, but they have been closed to the public for many years. Each of the giant bascules weighs over one thousand tons and is moved by hydraulic machinery.

Aesthetically the bridge is a fraud, for the abutments and the main towers contain steel framework faced with granite, and Portland stone with brick backing, all resting on concrete foundations within iron caissons. Yet this bridge has 'got something'. Perhaps we have grown fond of it for purely subjective reasons, but it does form an imposing river gateway to London and provides a few of those features which the London skyline of today so badly needs—pinnacles.

⟦ THE TUNNEL

To return to Mogg's map and to that last of the new communications across the river—the Thames Tunnel. This was a pioneering work by Sir Marc Isambard Brunel, a Norman by birth who married an English lady *née* Kingdom. A progeny of the marriage was Isambard Kingdom Brunel, who became even more famous as an engineer than his father, particularly on account of his work for the Great Western Railway. Both father and son had a number of connections with the Thames, and they lived for a time at Lindsey House by the river at Chelsea. During the French Revolution the elder Brunel, then a young man, was threatened as a Royalist, fled to New York, and eventually became an American citizen. He came to England in 1799 and continued his work of mechanical invention, notably in block machinery for the Navy. In his early seventies he tackled his last and biggest job—one which was to become a world wonder and yet, in the end, a white elephant—the uniting of the two river banks by a subterranean passage at a point below the Pool where a bridge could not, at that time, be built. As far back as 1798 the digging of a tunnel between Gravesend and Tilbury had been contemplated by the indefatigable Dodd (a proposal which now, after more than a hundred and fifty years, is to become a reality). Several other schemes were also projected, and one to join Limehouse and Rotherhithe was actually begun in the early years of the nineteenth century under Richard Trevithick, but was ultimately abandoned.

Then early in 1824 a company was formed to carry out Brunel's proposal for a tunnel of twin arches to join Wapping and Rotherhithe. A few months later a Parliamentary Bill was passed for its construction and the following year the digging of a shaft was begun at Rotherhithe. The first stone was formally laid by the chairman of the company on the 2nd of March and afterwards 'upwards of two hundred persons partook of a sumptuous collation; the bells from the steeple of Rotherhithe rang out their joyful acclamations, and success to the undertaking was echoed from a thousand voices', as Beamish (who was connected with the work) records in his *Life of Brunel* (1862).

This formidable undertaking—one of the most heroic works of the heroic age of the early engineers and, apart from some Cornish mine-workings, the first sub-aqueous tunnel ever to be constructed—was finally successful, but only after many heartrending troubles, many delays and many deaths. In October 1825 the shaft was ready and the tunnelling began with the use of Brunel's patent shield. This shield consisted of twelve cast-iron frames supporting a wall of timber boards and it was moved forward in stages by propelling screws. Each frame was divided into three floors or compartments and in each compart-ment a miner could work at one end and a bricklayer at the other. The timber boards were removed separately and the earth behind was then dug to a depth of four and a half inches and later nine inches, the board then being replaced in the new position. The frames moved forward in alternate stages, while the construction of the brick arches kept pace behind. When all was going well, the work proceeded at the rate of about eight feet a week, but there were many stoppages caused by flood-ing, silt and uneven soil strata, while at one point the bed of the river was accidentally pierced.

The elder Brunel was under too great a strain for his age, and his son, then only twenty years old, took over a great deal of the supervision and responsibility. In May 1827 the first trouble began: the Thames water burst into the tunnel. The workmen fled back to the shaft and luckily no one was drowned. The cause of the flooding was found to be a dredged pit in the bed of the river. This was filled from above with bags of clay on which was sunk a large raft loaded with clay, but that did not work. The raft was removed with the help of a diving bell and then gravel and more clay bags were dropped into the pit. This move succeeded, and towards the end of June the tunnel was pumped out. By November the work was going on so well that young Brunel decided to celebrate by inviting a group of fifty friends to dinner in the tunnel.

But two months later a much worse flooding occurred, and so sudden was the influx of water that six men were drowned. Young Brunel,

A longitudinal section of the Thames Tunnel during construction showing the moving shield. (From an illustrated souvenir of 1840 sold in the Tunnel when it was nearing completion)

though injured, was by good fortune carried by the force of the water to the surface in the shaft.

By now the company's funds were exhausted and the work was suspended. But the tunnel was regarded as a great national undertaking and its completion was generally desired as a matter of national pride. More funds were subscribed, but not enough, and finally an appeal was made to the Government. But a slump was on and work hung fire for some time; indeed for a while the shield was bricked over and a great mirror was fixed in front of it so that some revenue might be obtained from sightseers. A Tunnel Club was formed, William IV showed personal interest in the Great Bore, as it had come to be called, and in 1834 an adequate Treasury loan was at last granted.

By now the younger Brunel was deeply engaged at Bristol, and Beamish took over the post of resident engineer (soon to be followed by his assistant, Thomas Page). The old shield was removed and a new and stronger one was inserted, while large drains were formed above the inverted arches of the tunnel to carry away the water more rapidly. By the end of August 1836 the centre of the river had been passed. A year later the river broke into the works for the third time, then a fourth time and in March the next year for a fifth time. There was some scoffing now, and Thomas Hood wrote an ode to Brunel in one verse of which he suggested that the tunnel should be used as a wine cellar. Another verse reads:

'Alas! half-way thou hadst proceeded, when
Old Thames, through roof, not water-proof,
Came, like 'a tide in the affairs of men';
And with a mighty stormy kind of roar,
  Reproachful of thy wrong,
  Burst out in that old song
Of Incledon's, beginning 'Cease, rude Bore—'.
Other great speculations have been nursed,
  Till want of proceeds laid them on a shelf;
But thy concern was at the worst
  When it began to liquidate itself!'

At one period sewer gas from the polluted river came in with the black, half-fluid mud and flashes of fire would sometimes pass twenty-five feet across the shield. Thus to work in the tunnel was not only highly dangerous but also unhealthy, and men would sometimes fall senseless in their frames or be suddenly struck blind by Tunnel Sickness. The relentless, tragic struggle went on, the northern shaft was

Sir Marc Isambard Brunel as he appeared during his progress through the Thames Tunnel on the opening day. (From *The Illustrated London News*, 25 March 1843)

sunk, old Brunel was knighted and on the 15th of December 1841 the
tunnel at last reached the northern shaft. On the 25th of March 1843
the tunnel was ceremoniously opened to the public, and the little old
engineer, 'his face all head', took part in the procession through the
the Great Bore behind a band of fifes and drums. Nineteen years had
been required 'to put a pipe into old Thames' mouth'; the first esti-
mated cost had been £160,000 and the final cost was over half a million
and a number of lives. That Brunel had survived all the anxieties is a
remarkable tribute to his resilience of spirit. This charming, unworldly

St. Katherine's Docks engineered by Thomas Telford, as proposed. (A print from *The Gentleman's Magazine*, January 1826.)   The planning of three basins enabled one of the inner ones to be emptied and cleaned out while the other remained in use.

yet able old man was to live for another six years, but faded away quietly at last in 1849 at the age of eighty-one.

Though it excited much curiosity when first opened, the tunnel was little used. Nathaniel Hawthorne visited it in 1855 and described it as 'an arched corridor, of apparently interminable length, gloomily lighted with jets of gas at regular intervals—plastered at the sides, and stone beneath the feet'. He goes on: 'It would have made an admirable prison. . . . There are people who spend their lives there, seldom or never, I presume, seeing any daylight; except perhaps a little in the morning. All along the extent of this corridor, in little alcoves, there are stalls or shops, kept principally by women, who, as you approach, are seen through the dusk, offering for sale views of the Tunnel, put up, with a little magnifying glass, in cases of Derbyshire spar; also cheap jewelry and multifarious trumpery; also cakes, candy, ginger-beer, and such small refreshment. . . . So far as any present use is concerned, the Tunnel is an entire failure.'

The tunnel never became a passage for vehicles because the intended spiral ramps at either end were never built. In 1865 it was acquired by the East London Railway Company, and today the tunnel serves usefully to carry the Underground railway beneath the river and at night steam trains too. The two great staircase shafts remain, but are filled with lifts and pumping machinery.

The second tunnel to be built under the Thames was the Tower Subway running from Tower Hill to Tooley Street and intended for foot passengers only. It was begun in 1869 and constructed rapidly of iron tubes in less than two years; since Tower Bridge was built it has contained water mains. Today there exist some dozen tunnels serving various purposes. A new one is now under construction between Dartford and Purfleet which will take a London by-pass road; a second is being built at Blackwall and a third between Gravesend and Tilbury to replace the present ferry. Such new tunnels do not excite us much these days; but when Brunel was boring beneath the river the first Thames Tunnel must have appealed to the whole world as a wonderful, romantic and courageous work—as indeed it was, for its period.

(THE NEW DOCKS

Both to the east and to the north-west of the red stripe of the tunnel on Mogg's map a number of new, large, enclosed docks are shown. Big steps had by now been taken to remedy the appalling shipping conditions. By the beginning of the century trade had increased tremendously, and the East India Company alone was sailing to London a greater number of vessels than had come to the port each year a hundred years before. The ships were still moored in mid-stream and unloaded into open lighters which then transported the goods to the legal quays. Supervision was lax and inadequate and the goods would lie about untended for days, and even weeks, for there were not enough warehouses and these were mostly mere sheds. The quays, originally intended to serve only as temporary areas of transit, had perforce become storage places where sugar hogsheads would stand in piles eight high and all kinds of wares would lie around in picturesque and colourful confusion. The amount of pilfering that went on was enormous. In 1797 the West India Company, for instance, wrote off the year's loss from pilfering at £150,000 and total losses on the quays were put at half a million. Port life became an organised racket on a huge scale with its River Pirates, Night Plunderers or Light Horsemen, its Day Plunderers or Heavy Horsemen, and its grubbing Mudlarks.*

The formation of Colquhoun's and Harriott's river police force in 1798 (the first fully organised police force in the country which came thirty-one years before the Peelers) had some effects, but not enough. And so congested and inefficient was the whole system that a ship might take as long as two months to turn round. If the Port was to retain its trade and position something had to be done. Something was indeed done, and within three decades a whole new system of protected and enclosed wet docks came into being, built by private companies, and with them arose a whole new dockland district to add to the East End squalor.

The London docks stem from the early quays or hithes of Saxon times—small cuts formed in the river bank, their sides protected by stakes. The first wet dock was at Blackwall, and was mentioned by Pepys in 1661, and towards the end of that century Howland Dock, as we have seen, was dug at Rotherhithe. It was a ten-acre lake surrounded, not by warehouses, but by trim rows of poplars to reinforce the banks while at the end of the vista stood the brick mansion of the Howland family (see p. 124). This became the Greenland Dock, associated with whalers, and was to be absorbed into the Surrey Commercial Docks.

The first wet enclosed and protected dock with adequate warehousing

---

* Pilfering still goes on today in the docks but at a comparatively low level. A Special Correspondent in *The Times* in an article, 'Busy Thieves in the Ports' (18 June 1957), wrote that 'in the years before 1920, when the rum was stored in the open in London docks, there were more dockers charged with drunkenness in a week than are now charged in a year. During a single year before 1920 the PLA police presented to one hospital 150 rubber hot-water bottles confiscated from workmen who had been caught taking rum from the docks.' He went on: 'In the early 1920s thefts in the London docks reached such a pitch that shipping companies banded together in recruiting their own men specially to guard cargoes. The system worked and within a year or two these men were absorbed by the PLA police force.'

in the modern sense was that completed in 1802 for the West India Company just to the north of the Isle of Dogs between Limehouse and Blackwall, having lock exits and entrances to the river both on the east and the west, and a long row of warehouse blocks on the north side of the import dock. Here ships could lie at the quayside free from the rise and fall of the tides and well secured against robbers by the high brick walls. The engineer in charge of this work was Ralph Walker, though John Rennie, at that time working on his Kelso bridge, was consultant; from the Minutes of the West India Dock Company, however, we gather that to George Gwilt and his son must go the honour for designing the sturdy five-storey warehouses which finally stretched along the dockside for nearly two-thirds of a mile. With its impressive lines of warehouses, the West India Dock was a splendid job, and even today, in spite of the newer buildings there, something of its original nobility can still be seen. If we consider the dock conditions of the time it was built, the reason for its fortress-like external appearance—including guard houses—is easy to understand.

The West India Dock proved its worth, and other docks rapidly followed. The London Docks (later extended) were begun at Wapping in 1802, the engineer being Daniel Alexander, who constructed the gaols at Dartmoor and Maidstone. He was something of a poet in structure and was strongly inspired, like many of his contemporaries, by the engravings of Piranesi, especially those of imaginary Roman prisons. His warehouses at Wapping were magnificent and it is unfortunate that only part of his work now survives there.

In 1804 the Surrey Docks on the south of the river were started. These were the work of Ralph Dodd, who was both speculator and engineer. His complex of irregular sheets of water and attendant buildings was extended and altered greatly in Victorian times. An interesting part of his scheme was the digging of the Grand Surrey Canal, which runs westward from the docks. The original idea was to extend the canal to Epsom, and even beyond to link up with the Wey navigation, but in the event it reached no further than Camberwell. Though the short-lived Croydon Canal was linked with it for a time, it became in the end less of a canal than a long dock.

The fourth dock was begun in 1805 at Blackwall for the East India Company, the engineer being John Rennie. To link these docks with the Company's city warehouse a broad road was constructed, and this is now called Commercial Road and East India Dock Road.

A dramatic brick wall of the St. Katherine's Docks in Wapping which survives
from the early nineteenth century.

The final one of these early nineteenth-century docks was St.
Katherine's, which was squeezed into the area between London Docks
and the Tower. It is marked in vermilion by Mogg because it was not
opened until 1828. The engineer was Thomas Telford, and we can still
see his bold and distinguished work in yellow brick with its rhythmical
arched recesses and strong Doric columns almost in its original form—

almost, because much damage was caused there by bombing in the Second World War.

With the completion of these docks the river was at last cleared of congestion, but the wharfingers and the lightermen were not pleased, because their livelihoods were threatened. To compensate them the wharfingers received cash payments and the lightermen were given a free run of all the new dock waters, a right they still retain. For a time all went well and the dock shareholders 'basked in the sunshine of ten per cent'. But then this Free Water Clause of the lightermen, combined with Free Trade and the arrival of the railways, which, like the lightermen, bore away the cargoes as soon as landed, brought bad times to the dock companies. Profits, which had been obtainable from the long storage necessitated by the seasonal rushes of the great sailing-ships, dwindled, and Free Trade meant that imported goods need no longer be placed under the King's Lock and could be deposited with wharfingers anywhere along the river. And though the dock companies could take fees from the large vessels using their berths, the goods they brought were too often whisked away to cheaper warehouses by the lightermen, those aristocrats of riverside workers, who could enter any docks unmolested and without charge. Moreover, the East India Company lost its monopoly in the early 'thirties, and rival companies, including American ones, had entered the shipping race with ever leaner and faster vessels; the Port of Liverpool was a growing competitor too.

South of the West India Dock the City Canal had been dug in 1805 to enable sailing-ships to dispense with the difficult tack round the Isle of Dogs, but this canal was not very successful, and in 1829 it was sold to the West India Dock Company and turned into a dock; later it was enlarged and is now called the South Dock. In 1855 the St. Katherine Company completed the great Royal Victoria Dock east of Bow Creek: the first London enterprise to cross the River Lea into rural Essex. This was extended in 1880 by the London Dock Company and St. Katherine's, who had now amalgamated, in the form of the even larger Royal Albert having three miles of quay. Finally in 1921 came the King George V Dock, south of the Albert, to complete the inter-communicating Royal Dock group as the largest area of impounded dock water in the world—two hundred and forty-six acres.

In 1868 the Millwall Dock was opened on the Isle of Dogs. In the difficult, competitive circumstances the dock companies were amalgamating, and in mid-century the East and West India Companies joined forces and countered their rivals by opening in 1886 a sea outpost at Tilbury equipped with huge docking facilities, convenient railway links and a hotel. These were to be greatly extended in 1929. The warfare became ruinous and strikes of dockers were frequent. Towards the end of the century John ('Liquid History') Burns, the dockers' leader, who was a great student of the river's life-story and was the first Labour M.P. to reach the Cabinet, began to agitate for the amalgamation of all the dock companies into one municipal enterprise; it was he who led the historic strike of 1889—the dockers' Tanner Strike for sixpence an hour. Once more drastic action became imperative. A Royal Commission reported in 1902 that the Port of London was neglected, ill-equipped and inefficient, that it possessed too many rulers and that its long supremacy was threatened; it advised the formation of a new Port Authority representing all the interests concerned. Not until 1909 did the Port of London Authority take charge of London's river and its docks, when it began its constructive and beneficent work by improving the river and its port and by administering all the tidal parts of the river as one unit.

The tidal river from Teddington down to the Nore, a distance of some seventy miles, was taken over by the PLA from the Thames Conservators and the powers of the old Watermen's Company were relinquished. The River Police continued their independent watch and the Elder Brethren of Trinity House were confirmed in their long-held supervision of pilotage, lights and sea-marks.*

One of the first and most useful actions of the new PLA was to dredge a channel in the river which could be navigated by vessels drawing up to thirty-seven feet—that is to say, the largest in the world. Today the shipping which arrives and departs from the Port of London amounts to some fifty million tons, and all the docks of the Port, with the one exception of the Regent's Canal Dock, are under the jurisdiction of the PLA, who can now store a million tons of goods under cover. London has been made the longest and largest deep-water port in the world.

* This noble fraternity, founded early in the fifteenth century as a religious guild, received a charter from Henry VIII in 1514 with the title of 'The Brotherhood of the Most Glorious and Undivided Trinity of Deptford-Stronde,' and was thereby given charge of all sea marks and appointed advisors to the new Navy. It built its first lighthouse in 1680 and in 1836 the Corporation of Trinity House, as it came to be called, was given complete control of all English lighthouses. It works closely with the Navy and its Younger Brethren, numbering two hundred, have all reached the naval rank of Captain. During all their centuries of existence they, more than any other body, have advanced the river's good order and prosperity.

Something of the original grandeur of the early nineteenth-century docks can still be grasped from what remains of them. The two original basins of the West India Dock, for instance, still retain their pristine shapes; and to the north-west a few remains of their first warehouses, which the bombs did not destroy, can still be seen, as they also can at St. Katherine's and at London Docks. And many of the original purposes of each dock continue to this day—softwood at the Surrey Docks, grain at Millwall, sugar, rum and hardwood at the West India.

❲ RIVER CRAFT

Today London's Port is more lively than it has ever been before in its long history; yet it has lost much of that old romance which existed when the speedy Blackwall frigates and the elegant clippers berthed here. Throughout the nineteenth century steamships were gradually ousting sailing-ships, which passed away at the height of their glory as the windjammers with their splendid, carved figureheads; they plied the tea and wool trades and finally took to carrying passengers during the Australian gold rush. The first steam-boat was seen on the tidal river in 1801, and after 1815 steam-packets, with their thin, tall funnels and their frothing paddle-wheels, were a daily sight on the river. Yet even as late as 1869 one of the most famous of all sailing-vessels, the *Cutty Sark* (now permanently berthed at Greenwich for all to see), was launched at Dumbarton. All that is left of sail on London's river today is the Thames barge, and soon that too will be seen no more except as a museum specimen; it is a tribute to the superb design of this type of vessel (handled by one man and a boy) that it has survived so long.

The ocean-going steamer arrived during the second half of the century, the Suez Canal was opened and the commercial sailing-vessel was doomed. The end of the river as a popular means of passenger transport and a local means of communication also came in this century. From 1840 local passenger steamboats were plying up and down the river at London, but soon the Penny Steamers seemed slow compared with the new means of transport on land and they too faded away. The days of the jolly watermen were over.

The satirical young journalist Dickens, writing in his *Sketches by Boz* of his London of the time of William IV, gives a lively picture of a scene on one of these river-steamers as it moves off from the wharf below London Bridge one Sunday morning in the early 1830s:

Penny Steamers at Westminster on Boat Race Day. (A drawing by Gustave Doré from *London*, by Doré and Jerrold, 1872)

'Telescopes, sandwiches, and glasses of brandy-and-water cold without, begin to be in great requisition; and bashful men who have been looking down the hatchway at the engine find to their great relief, a subject on which they can converse with one another—and a copious

M

one too—Steam. "Wonderful thing steam, sir." "Ah! (a deep-drawn sigh) it is indeed, sir." "Great power, sir." "Immense—immense!" "Great deal done by steam, sir." "Ah! (another sigh at the immensity of the subject, and a knowing shake of the head) you may say that, sir." Novel remarks of this kind, are generally the commencement of a conversation which is prolonged until the conclusion of the trip, and, perhaps, lays the foundation of a speaking acquaintance between half-a-dozen gentlemen, who, having their families at Gravesend, take season-tickets for the boat, and dine on board regularly every afternoon.'

The Thames-side shipbuilding industry also passed away, partly because London was badly situated for the supply of the new material, iron, and partly because the river was not wide enough for launching the larger ships that were being built. Though shipbuilding went to the Clyde and to Belfast, we must not forget that the younger Brunel's huge and famous *Great Eastern* was launched from the yard of John Scott Russell and Company at Millwall in 1858. Because of the narrowness of the river here she was launched sideways on rails. She was a leviathan nearly seven hundred feet long, powered with both paddle-wheels and a screw, and designed to travel to Australia and back carrying her own coal all the way. Launching her was a considerable technical feat for the time and it is not surprising that the first attempt failed with loss of a life (but through no fault of Brunel's). From the start she was an ill-fated ship, and on her maiden voyage she suffered a severe explosion, the news of which finally killed Brunel, already an ailing man. The relationship between Brunel and the unscrupulous and jealous Scott Russell had not been cordial during most of the difficult times of the ship's construction, when there were many delays and false under-estimates of costs. In the end the *Great Eastern* served the most productive part of her life in laying the first cable across the Atlantic during the early 1860s. She laid many other cables after that and then, for a time, reverted to passenger service, in which she was never a great success. This great pioneering steamship ended her days sadly, like an ageing trollop, moored on the Mersey as a gaudy showboat, and in 1888 she was sold for breaking up. We need not take too seriously the well-known tale of the discovery, in one of the cells of the iron hull during demolition, of the corpses of a riveter and his boy. It is one of those small myths that stick as hard as the big myths which alter human history.

Other strange craft could have been seen on London's river during the first half of the century: the grim hulks of worn-out and rotting ships of the line which were used as prisons. Many of the prisoners there were employed on dock-building while awaiting transportation, and their lives and deaths aboard were worse than in the prisons on shore, where conditions throughout the century were appalling enough. Round about mid-century a more cheerful sight was the Chinese junk which was visited by Charles Dickens. Like its fore-runner, *The Folly*, it was a floating pleasure-haunt, and when the London season began each year it would be towed up from its winter station at Blackwall to a mooring near Waterloo Bridge.

Though squalor spread around the docks as the century progressed, the scene upon the river must have been a splendid and an inspiring one, for there the clustered masts soared upwards like winter groves and everything connected with them had that robust and honest beauty of form which seafaring produces. And they possessed more than good form, for 'masts are always dreamy to look at', writes Richard Jefferies: 'They speak a romance of the sea; of unknown lands; of distant forests aglow with tropical colours and abounding with strange forms of life. In the hearts of most of us there is always a desire for something beyond experience. Hardly any of us but have thought, Some day I will go on a long voyage; but the years go by, and still we have not sailed.'

Listen to another piece by Jefferies, which evokes the scene more vividly than I can, for he saw it with his own eyes round about the late 1870s when sail and steam were mixing on the river:

'It is a great plain: a plain of enclosed waters, built in and restrained by the labour of man, and holding upon its surface fleet upon fleet, argosy upon argosy. Masts to the right, masts to the left, masts in front, masts yonder above the warehouses; masts in among the streets as steeples appear amid roofs; masts across the river hung with drooping half-furled sails; masts afar down thin and attenuated, mere dark straight lines in the distance. They await in stillness the rising of the tide.

'It comes, and at the exact moment—foreknown to a second—the gates are opened, and the world of ships moves outwards to the stream. Downwards they drift to the east, some slowly that have as yet but barely felt the pull of the hawser, others swiftly, and the swifter because their masts cross and pass the masts of the inward-bound ships ascending. Two lines of masts, one raking one way, the other the other, cross and puzzle the eye to separate their weaving motion and to assign the rigging to the right vessel. White funnels aslant, dark funnels, red funnels rush between them; white steam curls upwards; there is a hum, a haste, almost a whirl, for the commerce of the world is crowded into the hour of the full tide. These great hulls, these crossing masts a-rake, the inter-tangled rigging, the background of black barges drifting downwards, the lines and ripple of the water as the sun comes out, if you look too steadily, daze the eyes and cause a sense of giddiness. It is so difficult to realize so much mass—so much bulk—moving so swiftly, and in so intertangled a manner; a mighty dance of thousands of tons—gliding, slipping, drifting onwards, yet without apparent effort. Thousands upon thousands of tons go by like shadows, silently as if the ponderous hulls had no stability or weight; like a dream they float past, solid and yet without reality. It is a giddiness to watch them.

'This happens, not on one day, not one tide, but at every tide and every day the year through, year after year. The bright summer sun glows upon it; the red sun of the frosty hours of winter looks at it from under the deepening canopy of vapour; the blasts of the autumnal equinox howl over the vast city and whistle shrilly in the rigging; still at every tide the world of ships moves out into the river.'

The fine, tall vessels have gone, but some romance still hangs around those docks where the great squat liners berth today. You can gain a good whiff of it if you go for a jaunt in one of those PLA passenger boats which run down-river and through the Royal Docks in the summer months.

[EAST END AND SOUTH BANK

In 1827, as Mogg's map shows, the area around the docks was still fairly open, except around St. Katherine's and the London Docks. Stepney was still almost an isolated village; so was Bow, and Bromley. Poplar was a ribbon of buildings running between the West India Docks and the East India Dock Road. Essex east of the River Lea was all un-spoiled country, while the Isle of Dogs was an open marsh marked with a few tracks. And so it was still in 1857, when a reporter, on the *Illus-trated London News*, writing at a time when the *Great Eastern* was building there, described 'those marshy fields, sparsely studded with stunted limes and poplars, muddy ditches, with here and there a medi-tative cow cropping the coarse herbage'. In 1880 Charles Dickens Junior wrote in his *Dictionary of the Thames* that 'the isle itself is pretty well covered with ship-building and engineering yards, and was a few years since one of the busiest spots on the river bank'.

Today the Isle of Dogs is densely built up and contains within it the

Millwall Dock and most of Poplar, Cubitt Town and Millwall. Back in the time of Rocque's map in the mid-eighteenth century, Poplar was a hamlet to the north, along Limehouse Reach were windmills for pumping and to the south stood a gibbet with its rotting fruit suspended as a warning against piracy. The origin of the strange place-name is obscure; one theory suggests that here on the Isle of Dogs (rather an isthmus than a true island) were at one time the royal kennels of Greenwich Palace lying across the river. Timbs in his *Curiosities of London* (1867) says that 'traditionally, it was named from the hounds of Edward III, being kept there, for contiguity to Waltham and other royal forests in Essex. Again Isle of Dogs is held to be corrupted from Isle of Ducks, from the wildfowl upon it'. The latter seems the most plausible explanation. Incidentally, before the large ironworks and shipyards sprang up during mid-nineteenth century there stood the works of Captain (later Sir Samuel) Brown, R.N., who around 1813 was producing iron chains for the Navy and for his suspension bridges—an important development in bridge construction. With James Walker he later proposed the erection of a high-level suspension bridge across the Thames near the Tower, but the project came to nothing.

The Regent's Canal is clearly marked by Mogg and runs like a boundary around the north of London, eventually skirting Regent's Park and joining up with the Paddington Canal. In this way, by means of the Regent's Canal Dock, lying midway between the London Docks and the West India Docks, London was linked with the national network of inland navigations. London was, and still is, a terminus of the Grand Junction Canal (1805), which has its main outlet into the river a long way up-stream at Brentford. By now the network of canals was so widespread in England that hardly any place in the whole country was more than fifteen miles from water transport. Just to the south-east of the Regent's Canal Dock is a smaller dock joined to the river—the end of the Poplar Cut (now Limehouse Cut), which runs north-east for about a mile and a half to the navigable River Lea. The confused industrial landscape around these waters is often squalid, but sometimes in a fortuitous way it is superb. To stroll along the banks of these waters affords a rare experience in visual drama.

On the south of the river from Deptford around the Surrey Docks as far as Southwark, which is now very congested, there is building all along the bank in Mogg's map, but behind that verge down to the Grand Surrey Canal and beyond, the landscape is flat and open again.

The Lion Brewery and Shot Tower on the south bank in an engraving of about 1865. Compare this with the same view today, p. 235.

A square shot tower had appeared on the south bank in 1789 and not far to its west another, a round one, was built in 1826. It still stands and was incorporated in the South Bank Exhibition of 1951 as a radar tower, sending messages to the moon. Close to it, where the LCC Festival Hall is now, the Lion Brewery was built in 1836 with its red lion perched on top, a familiar sight for over a century from the north bank until it was demolished in 1950. The building of yellow brick was designed by a pupil of that neurotic genius, Sir John Soane, one Francis Edwards, who had already built the works and offices of the Imperial Gas Company on the Regent's Canal at Hoxton. This was the beginning of the commercial patronage of architecture, and at the start the results were not so bad as they later became. The red lion of the brewery survives not far away from its original perch and now stands guard at the northern entrance to Waterloo Station.

Within fifty years, all the open whiteness shown by Mogg around the docks was built over, mostly in yellow brickwork, by numberless speculators who ran up their cheap, insanitary and rat-infested warrens at a tremendous pace. It was the age of uncontrolled opportunism and *laissez-faire* in which the bleak, sordid and congested London jungle of Mayhew, Dickens and Doré was formed. With it came the vice, drunkenness, brutality and general misery which produced literary protests, as well as lurid paper-backs, about opium dens, Bluegate Fields and the notorious Ratcliff Highway. Social conditions are different today: gas-and-water Socialism may not be romantic, but without its common-sense altruism the poverty and exploitation of Victorian England would surely have produced a violent revolution. Ask any policeman on his beat in Wapping today what his life is like, and he will tell you that it is quiet enough and that the Wapping folk are a decent lot (many of them descendants of the Irish labourers who first came here to dig the docks); he will tell you that it is in the West End around Piccadilly where the London policeman now finds most trouble.

Before we turn westward we must mention the changes that came to the building which for so long had been associated with the shipping of the river—the Customs House, lying between the Tower and London Bridge. A rebuilding of the Queen Anne structure by Wren began in 1814 after the peace, and the new work was then entrusted to the Customs Surveyor, David Laing, another pupil of Soane. His design,

A dockyard brawl in the 'London jungle of Mayhew, Dickens and Doré'. (A drawing by Gustave Doré in *London*, 1872)

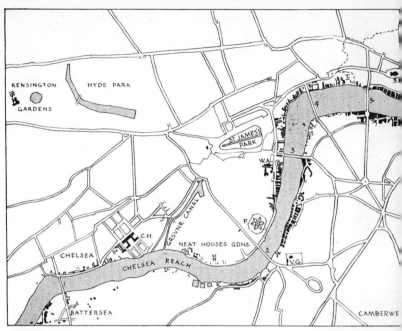

completed in 1817, featured an unusual hall with three domes, and it was much praised at the time. But Laing was not very experienced, and in 1825 part of the central hall subsided owing to the decay in the piling. The work of restoration was given to Robert Smirke, designer of the British Museum, who demolished the whole of the centre and rebuilt it as it can be seen today: a dignified but rather dull affair in stone, somewhat harmed by bombing.

⟦ THE NORTH BANK

Let us take our bearings again from Mogg and work our way along the north bank from Chelsea to the east. From the old timber bridge of Battersea, Cheyne Walk runs along the riverside, for the Embankments have yet to be built. It turns inland towards the north-east to become Paradise Row (now Royal Hospital Road), which runs into the north part of Chelsea Hospital grounds. No definite riverside way beyond Cheyne Walk is marked until we reach Vauxhall Bridge. The area south of the spot where Victoria Station now stands is all open, marshy, market-garden land still.

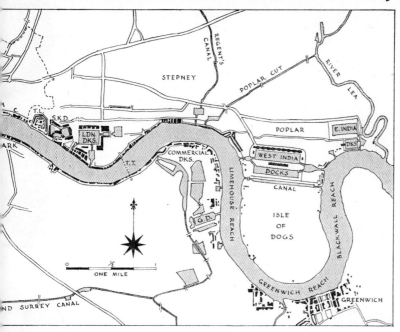

The river from Chelsea to Greenwich according to Mogg's map of 1827. Only the main roads, main buildings and riverside buildings are reproduced here. BRIDGES: 1. Battersea; 2. Vauxhall; 3. Westminster; 4. Waterloo; 5. Blackfriars; 6. Southwark; 7. London. BUILDINGS etc.: C.H., Chelsea Hospital; P., Penitentiary; V.G., Vauxhall Gardens; W.A., Westminster Abbey; T., Temple; S.P., St. Paul's Cathedral; M., Monument; C., Customs House; T.L., Tower of London; S.K.D., St. Katherine's Docks; T.T., Thames Tunnel; G.D., Greenland Dock.

This area was to be developed in the first half of the nineteenth century as Pimlico by the great speculative builder Thomas Cubitt. Already on Mogg's map his formal stucco squares and terraces in Pimlico (and in Belgravia to its north) are taking shape as the architectural links between Georgian and Victorian London.

Neat House Gardens on the Mogg map is bounded on the west by the Grosvenor Canal, a short waterway running up from the river by the Chelsea Water Works to the Victoria Station area, and culminating at Pimlico Wharf, a large basin. The northern end of this canal was filled in at the end of the century when Victoria Station was built, but part of the canal still exists and can be seen just to the east of the point where

The Millbank Penitentiary and Steamboat Pier. (A Victorian print of 1860)

Chelsea Bridge Road joins the Embankment. It came to be used by the Army and Navy Co-operative Society, but in recent years it has been employed by the City of Westminster for the collection and treatment of rubbish; from the buildings on its banks the rubbish is dropped into barges and carried downstream to be dumped on the Essex marshes.

[THE TENCH

Beyond Neat House Gardens and the New Road (now Vauxhall Bridge Road) an enormous star-shaped building is shown. This is the Penitentiary Prison (later called Millbank Prison)—the dreaded 'Tench'.

   Wandsworth Prison and many others of the nineteenth century were built like the Penitentiary, on a principle of radiating wings from a centre so that the ranges of cells could be seen by the warders from certain vantage points in a central tower. The principle was evolved from an idea proposed by the radical philosopher, Jeremy Bentham, for a Panoptikon, or Inspection House, and it is a typical paradox of life that such grim results should have stemmed from so congenial a character who believed that all punishment is evil and should be admitted only 'so far as it promises to exclude some greater evil'. Conditions had been horrible enough in the old Fleet Prison, at Newgate or in the gaols of Southwark, and they were largely for debtors. With growing industrialism and the conditions they produced, crime increased rapidly and was treated with regimented and irrational cruelty. Uniforms were adopted both for prisoners and their warders, silence was enforced, and futile, back-breaking and demoralising labour was provided, such as the moving of cannon-balls around the prison yard, or the digging up and dumping again of piles of sand, or the inhuman treadwheel and the cranks.

The Penitentiary House of London and Middlesex, to give its full first title, was a particular dread of the criminal. On the map it looks like a pretty, ornamental star with six great pentagonal wings radiating from a central hexagonal courtyard in the middle of which the Governor's house was situated. But inside it was a dark, chilly and damp hell of unrelieved misery from where the only escape was by prison-ship to the penal settlements. This gloomy structure, all of yellow brick and in broad effect rather like a mediæval château in appearance, was conceived, strangely enough, as a humanitarian experiment in gaol design, where the convicts were expected to benefit from 'classification, employment and reform'. In some ways it may have been a slight improvement on the indescribable river hulks.

Its building began in 1813 under an architect called Harvey, but he proved to be incompetent, and another man, Hardwick, was called in. He did not like the job and backed out, and finally Smirke, who was always reliable, was asked to help the Government out of the mess.

The foundations were the main difficulty owing to the sodden soil, and the whole vast structure, covering eighteen acres and containing more than a thousand cells and three miles of corridors, was laid on foundations of solid concrete. The building was finished at last in 1821 at a cost of nearly half a million. Though in much disfavour, even by mid-century, it survived until 1890. In 1897 a more humane building took its place—the pompous Roman temple, with its Corinthian portico, of the Tate Gallery—a present to the nation by the sugar king, Sir Henry Tate, whose architect was Sidney R. J. Smith. The Gallery has been extended several times since first built and in 1919 the Tate became the national gallery of British art of all periods.

Behind the Tate Gallery and on its axis lies the Millbank Estate, built at the end of the century. Designed by R. Minton Taylor, under the LCC's architect, W. E. Riley, it is one of the earliest working-class rehousing schemes of the London County Council, which has since developed into one of the largest housing authorities in the world—and, since the war, probably the best. The Millbank Estate is in a red-brick, simplified, Norman Shaw manner and, though a trifle grim in parts, is not bad for its time.

Back on Mogg, we see a quarter of a mile north of the Penitentiary the beginning of the built-up area of Westminster, and from the approach to Lambeth Bridge up to the Houses of Parliament—that is to say where the Victoria Tower Gardens now lie—buildings run down to the river from Millbank and Abingdon Street. Then comes the Palace of Westminster, now usually called the Houses of Parliament.

❡ THE OLD PALACE IN FLAMES

Something of the ancient history of the Palace of Westminster has already been told. Now in the time of Mogg alterations to the general muddle are going on as usual. But Westminster Hall holds the jumble together because it is large, firmly rectangular and dominating—larger even than St. Stephen's Hall, which stands close to the river at right angles to it on its south. That this confusion of buildings should have been tolerated as the central visual symbol of Law and Government of a great and powerful nation is astonishing, and could perhaps only happen in England. The confusion certainly astonished a foreigner who came to London in 1805, one Benjamin Silliman, Professor of Chemistry and Natural History at Yale, who observed:

'Seen from the outside what is properly called Westminster Hall has the appearance of an ancient, time-worn, sombre, Gothic building of regular figure, viz. a parallelogram, but there are so many buildings connected with it to accommodate the various public bodies; they are in such different styles of architecture; of such different ages; so disproportionate in size but so irregularly placed, or rather jumbled in contact, that with the coffee houses and other appendages, which grow to these buildings as it were, like wens or warts, the whole has an appearance of rudeness, confusion, and incompetency to the object, which fills a stranger with astonishment, that the judicial and legislative concerns of the greatest empire which the world ever saw, should not, ere this, have been accommodated with a princely establishment, equal to the grandeur and resources of the nation. Probably a veneration for antiquity goes far towards preserving the present establishment.'

Something was done before long to improve the mess, but not much. Since Waterloo the State had become the greatest constructor of important buildings in London, and at Westminster the seven Courts of Law, clustering to the west side of the Hall, as well as the Scala Regia (the Royal Vestibule to the House of Lords), were rebuilt by Soane between 1820 and 1824. His Scala Regia was to survive for little more than a decade.

One autumn evening in 1834 the old exchequer tally-sticks were being bundled into the stove below the House of Lords. The intense heat ignited some timber panelling and before long the old, confused jumble of Westminster Palace was blazing. Soane had warned the authorities of the fire danger when he pointed out in his *Designs for Public Buildings* (1828) that 'the exterior of these old buildings is constructed chiefly with timber covered with plaster. In such an extensive assemblage of combustible materials, should a fire happen, what would become of the Painted Chamber, the House of Commons, and Westminster Hall? Where would the progress of the fire be arrested?' The answer was given six years after his book was published when, as a contemporary was to remark with heavy understatement, 'the progress of the fire afforded a *tableau vivant* of not inferior interest'.

Excited crowds, held back by three regiments of Guards, watched the spreading flames; Westminster Bridge was thronged, the river was filled

The burning of the Houses of Parliament in 1834 as seen by a contemporary from the Shot Tower by Waterloo Bridge. (A print in the Guildhall Library)

with boats and people stood for hours ankle-deep in the mud of the shore, mouths agape or else roaring a cheer as each spurt of flame and sparks arose against the night sky. Westminster Hall itself was under threat when the Prime Minister, Lord Melbourne, took charge and the firemen and civilian volunteers then concentrated all their efforts on saving the Hall. By three o'clock in the morning the fire was at last under control. The Hall, though singed, had survived, but almost everything else was a smoking ruin. It had been an enjoyable fire and regrets were few.

❲ A NEW PALACE BUILT

What was to be done to rehouse the Mother of Parliaments? There was much discussion and controversy. William IV offered Buckingham Palace, and the Green Park was considered as a possible site for a new building. But no one really wanted to leave the riverside and the historic site. Moreover the Duke of Wellington pointed out, with his usual forthright realism, that the Houses of Parliament should be so situated that they could never be entirely surrounded by a mob. So the old site was chosen. The commission which the King had appointed decided that the new building upon it must be either in the Gothic or in the Elizabethan style, partly perhaps in deference to the neighbouring Abbey and to the surviving Westminster Hall, partly because these styles were considered to be particularly British, and mainly perhaps because romantic revivalism was in vogue. An open competition was held and ninety-seven competitors sent in designs, six only in the Elizabethan manner, the rest Gothic. Those of Charles Barry were finally selected. Though forty years old he was not particularly well known and his only important job so far had been the Travellers' Club in Pall Mall, built in a columnless Renaissance style.

Barry would have preferred a classic design for the new Parliament buildings, but he did well enough in the Gothic. His design appealed to the selection committee because its plan was excellent, indeed almost of a classic regularity, and because its drawings of details were exquisite. These drawings were executed not by Barry but by a zealous and excitable young mediævalist, half-French and half-English, called Augustus W. N. Pugin, who was to be chiefly responsible throughout the construction for the immense quantity of ornamentation which covers both the outside and the inside of the whole astonishing pile. As a biographer has expressed it: 'Barry hired a ghost and found a collaborator.'

The building was started towards the close of 1837. By the spring of 1847 the House of Lords was ready for occupation; in 1852 the Commons Chamber was first occupied and then Barry was knighted. The whole structure was not completed until 1857 and even then the two towers were still building. The Victoria Tower to the south, 336 feet high, was finished in 1860, and the Clock Tower to the north, 316 feet high, somewhat earlier. This tower, which has become a symbol of London, stands almost on the same spot as the clock tower of the old palace, which possessed a great bell given by William III to the Dean of St. Paul's Cathedral. The present tower, of course, contains Big Ben, named after Sir Benjamin Hall, Commissioner of Works in 1858, when the clock and its bell were made; the bell weighs thirteen and a half tons and is cracked. We can hear it every night on the radio and then evoke in our mind's ear the ancient city of bells and of 'Paul's across the fields, bells answering bells on summer evenings long ago'. Above the Clock Tower a light burns when the House is sitting—a tradition begun in 1893.

And what of the building as a whole? It is mad in its mediævalism, though sane enough in its planning. The craftsmanship of the carving of endless figures, foliage, mouldings, crockets and finials is good, but the stone used is magnesian limestone from Yorkshire which has a troublesome tendency to turn into disintegrating Epsom Salts in the London air. Westminster Hall has been well integrated with the new building and has been very little debased, as it well might have been if Barry and Pugin had not been restrained by the authorities. The complex is huge and labyrinthine with five hundred rooms, eleven open courtyards and eighteen separate residences for officials. The amount of Pugin's ubiquitous detailing is astonishing, and one does not wonder that he died insane at an early age. The House of Lords is his finest room and a masterpiece of its eclectic kind.

Of Barry's Westminster Palace as a whole the verdict of Dr. Pevsner in his Penguin *London* must stand as reliable: 'The most imaginatively planned and the most excellently executed major secular building of the Gothic Revival anywhere in the world'.

The Commons Chamber was demolished by a bomb in the Second World War and was reconstructed in the traditional form, but with rather different proportions from the old chamber, by Sir Giles Gilbert Scott and Adrian Scott. Dr. Pevsner severely criticises their work: 'Nothing could show up more poignantly the inferiority of the twentieth century in comparison with the early nineteenth-century Gothicists'—

because, as he points out, the life has departed with the loss of faith in Gothic detailing; an honest contemporary treatment would have been far better than this half-hearted and bogus one.

Quite a lot, unfortunately, happened during the nineteenth century to the outside of Westminster Abbey across the way. Sir George Gilbert Scott and John Pearson between 1875 and 1890 were allowed to mess about with the main façade to the north, which is basically thirteenth and fourteenth century. Scott designed the porches and Pearson dealt with the details higher up. The pinnacles are nineteenth century too. The rose window in the south transept is of 1890 and so is much other detailing. The top, pierced parapet and the pinnacles above the clerestory of the Henry VII Chapel were added by Wyatt during a general restoration of 1807–22.

⟦ THE LAST OF MOGG

In 1827 there is still a large riverside garden at Whitehall; but with the exception of this and the garden of Northumberland House, all is built up between the Strand and the river; and nearly all the river's edge from there to Poplar and the West India Dock is also built up, for the wide Embankments have yet to come. The greater part of the Mogg map is shown white—that is open ground; within two generations all the whiteness will be filled in with building, mainly housing—slums in the east, and in the west those endless vistas of middle-class porticos, where, in T. S. Eliot's evocation:

> 'They are rattling breakfast plates in basement kitchens,
> And along the trampled edges of the street,
> I am aware of the damp souls of housemaids
> Sprouting despondently at area gates.'

Nor does Mogg show Battersea Park or Cremorne Gardens. The former, nearly two hundred acres in extent, was to become a public park in 1859, thanks largely to the vision of Cubitt, and it has survived down to the present time—since 1951 with a lively fair ground. The park took a long time to form, for between 1846, when the decision to create it was ratified by Parliament, and 1856, when the park was beginning to take shape, the whole marshy surface had to be raised. This was accomplished chiefly by the dumping here of the excavated earth from the Victoria Dock, then under construction. From there and from other sources no less than a million cubic yards of earth came by river to raise up the level of the land.

After Mogg came the railways, and the explosion of vast building activity. Many new bridges were built across the river, some of them for the railways, and along the riverside new brick warehouses appeared and several great terminal railway stations. And the river became for a time a stinking sewer. Now, as a poet declaimed in *Punch* in the summer of 1884:

> *'London's Thames is Trade's. Not Fashion's leisure*
>   *Flaunts on its flood; no Ranelagh now invites*
> *Wigged and brocaded devotees of pleasure,*
>   *Its stream no brick-mewed citizen delights.*
> *Its sombre bosom bears unbounded treasure*
>   *In swarth uncomely bulk; its days and nights*
> *Are toil and traffic; pageantry and sport*
>   *Are driven to Henley and to Hampton Court.'*

⟮ CREMORNE

Cremorne was the nineteenth-century equivalent of Vauxhall, and for about a decade they co-existed, for Cremorne was opened in 1843 and survived until 1877. Its riverside area is now occupied by Lots Road Power Station with its four familiar chimneys (built in 1904) at the western end of Cheyne Walk in Chelsea. Such pleasure-gardens are often believed to have been an exclusive speciality of the eighteenth century, but many were created during the nineteenth century, particularly in and around London, Cremorne being the most famous. Like the others of this sort, such as that at Walworth, they were not fashionable in the way that Vauxhall and Ranelagh had been, and they were patronised mainly by the lower-middle and working classes.   Lady Dorothy Neville tells us in the *Leaves from her Notebooks* that she sometimes went to the special fêtes of high tone at Cremorne 'when the gardens presented much the same appearance as Vauxhall in its palmy days', but, she records, at the last one to which she went, 'considerable disorder prevailed on account of a number of the usual frequenters obtaining admission and squirting ink at the ladies' dresses as a sign of their displeasure at the intrusion of another society than their own'.

Cremorne had its special charm and atmosphere, which Whistler's depictions and the beauty of the name have preserved. On the site, behind a riverside garden, had stood a house which was first built by the

N

Earl of Huntingdon in 1745 but was enlarged and altered for Viscount
Cremorne later in the century by James Wyatt. Early in the nineteenth
century the property was bought by the adventurer Charles de Béren-
ger, *alias* Baron de Beaufain, who in 1832 opened Cremorne House
grounds as the Cremorne Stadium (hence the name Stadium Street of
today), where gentlemen could be coached by the Baron in shooting,
fencing, swimming and such 'manly exercises'. There was a golf course,
and part of the grounds were allocated to the ladies. But the enterprise
was not a great success, in spite of attempts to enliven the place with
fireworks, balloon ascents and *fêtes champêtres*. The Stadium was closed
in 1843 and at once re-opened under Renton Nicholson. Not until
1846, however, did Cremorne come into its own and settle down to a
vigorous life when T. B. Simpson, a waiter, was installed as manager by
a new purchaser, James Ellis. Like his famous namesake at Vauxhall,
Simpson was a Character; he was also shrewd and competent and he ran
Cremorne for a number of years with growing success.

The gardens covered twelve acres of land between the river and the
King's Road, and by the river was a landing-stage with an elaborate
wrought-iron water gate where the penny steamers could land their passengers. A main feature in the grounds was an enormous orchestra surrounded by a dancing-floor where the stove-pipe hats and the coal-
scuttle bonnets bobbed and gyrated every evening. There was also a
Pagoda, a Circus, a Playhouse, a Banqueting Hall and a Marionette
Theatre, and many other buildings were dotted about among the trees—
kiosks, refreshment-rooms, Swiss chalets and Indian temples. Like
Vauxhall, but unlike many of its contemporary public gardens and exhibition grounds, Cremorne preserved an air of picturesque rusticity in
its rich boskage and reflecting waters, and this helped to preserve a visual
charm which was too rare in the urban England of Victoria's times.

Simpson retired in 1861 and the long-remembered E. T. Smith took
over. He began his management with the greatest spectacle in Cremorne's history—the crossing of the Thames on a tight-rope by Selina
Young, the Female Blondin. At this event, watched by a huge crowd,
the lady was well on her way across the river on her narrow path when
some scoundrel severed the guy-ropes at one end. With great presence
of mind Miss Young saved herself by clutching the rope as it subsided
and so managed to lower herself with dignity into a boat.

There were, of course, grand firework displays at regular intervals
and balloon ascents were all the rage. In 1852, for instance, Madame

The bandstand in Vauxhall Gardens sketched by Cruickshank in the reign of
William IV for *Sketches by Boz* when 'a numerous assemblage of ladies and
gentlemen, with their families, had rushed from their half-emptied stout mugs
in the supper boxes, and crowded to the spot'.

Poitevin went up seated on a heifer; and when John Baum took over from E. T. Smith in the seventies, he hired the Flying Man De Groof, who rose in a balloon but crashed to his death with his machine in Sydney Street, Chelsea, on the 9th of July 1874. Baum developed the musical and theatrical attractions of Cremorne, and Offenbach's cheerful airs were often heard floating through the gardens on soft summer nights.

Cremorne developed a naughty reputation, and as the years passed it became the recognised centre for rowdyism on special occasions such as Bank Holidays. This led to its downfall. A tailor-poet called Alfred Brandon wrote a pamphlet in 1876 on *The Horrors of Cremorne*. Baum sued and won a farthing damages, but he was now ill and debt-ridden and on the 5th of October 1877 he withdrew his application for a renewal of his licence. Cremorne closed its gates, the equipment was sold by auction, and before long the site was covered with buildings. A relic of the old gardens is still left in the form of a pair of wrought-iron gates decorated with cast lions' heads, which now give entrance to the court-yard of Watney's Wine and Spirit Department in Tetcott Road, just off the King's Road, and they are also used as a trade mark.

'Cremorne had its special charm and atmosphere.' The bandstand and open-air dance floor from a drawing of 1847.

❡ THE EMBANKMENTS AND NEW SEWERS

The Victoria Embankment from Westminster Bridge to Blackfriars was opened in 1870, the Albert Embankment on the south bank soon afterwards, and in 1874 the Chelsea Embankment. Though they have their æsthetic failings and though we have grown used to them, these Embankments at the time they were made must have seemed remarkable and exciting achievements. They impressed Dickens enormously and Carlyle, even though they killed the picturesque riverside of Cheyne Walk near which he lived, approved of them as works of 'progress'. They did certainly improve the riverside in several ways: they provided valuable new traffic arteries, they tidied up the river front, they added some riverside gardens in their reclamation of land and they afforded the pedestrian easy access to the riverside. With their generous roads, their solid granite retaining walls, their lamp standards of twining dolphins, their seats with sphinxes and camels and their rows of plane trees,* they were the creations of the engineer Sir Joseph Bazalgette, who worked for the Metropolitan Board of Works, the forerunner of the LCC. They were built at a time when other municipal improvements were being made, notably in the provision of adequate sewers; indeed the Embankments were built in conjunction with the two main outfall sewers which run on each side of the river.

Since the rebuilding of London after the Fire up to 1847, when the Metropolitan Commission of Sewers was created, no less than eight Commissions had concerned themselves with sewage disposal, but their work had always been inadequate. In 1855 sewage disposal was taken over by the Board of Works and passed to the LCC when that body was formed in 1889. Not until the sixties was an adequate system built: one which carried soil and rain-water in underground ducts on both sides of the river far away to outfall stations in the east, where the sewage was discharged into the river at ebb tide. Since then other works have been built and new purification processes have been adopted; today over two thousand miles of local sewers collect from London's houses, and these link up with four hundred miles of main sewers. These finally join up with the two main outfall lines on either side of the river, running east to the Precipitation Works and Outfall Stations at Beckton on

---

* The famous London plane-tree which thrives in the sooty air was brought to England by the Romans. Thus the Embankments of the nineteenth century have visual links, green and living, with Roman London.

the north bank and at Erith on the south. After treatment there the sludge is loaded into ships of over a thousand tons which carry it far out into the estuary and dump it in the Black Deeps. (In the long run this is probably highly unsatisfactory, for we are not putting back into the land what we take from it—the circle is broken and a long, imperceptible devitalisation of our soil and ourselves is going on.)

In the old days the sewers were merely the river's tributaries covered over, and these discharged their stinking contents into the river at low water. In 1847 cesspools were made illegal and all London's sewage was made to flow into the sewers and so into the river; within a few years some two hundred thousand cesspools were abolished. The effects on the river were appalling, for it became the main—and open—sewer of London. In 1800 salmon were still swimming up to London and beyond, but by mid-century no fish at all were to be caught in the river and even the swans could bear the foul water no more. During one hot summer the exhalations from the stinking black shore at Westminster were so overwhelming that the windows of the Houses of Parliament on the river side were hung with sacking impregnated with some strong-smelling disinfectant to make life more tolerable for the Members within. Sometimes the House would be compelled to adjourn for the day on account of the stench and there was even some talk of moving Parliament from its new buildings to Hampton Court. The pouring of tons of lime and carbolic acid into the river had no marked effect, and the protests became loud and long. A typically facetious one appeared in *The Oarsman's Guide*:

'The lunging surf of the river steamers stirs from its oozy bed, in the rear of some friendly obstruction, the sleepy sediment of the tainted Thames. A ceaseless passage of steam-craft ploughs through the sludgy compromise between the animal, the vegetable, and the mineral kingdoms. Feeble rays from a clouded sun glimmer through the murky atmosphere, and play with tarnished glister over the dingy flood. Fishes, wiser in their generation than ourselves, have forsaken in disgust a medium which in these latitudes has long ceased to be a definite element; poisoned by the impurities to which their simple natures are utterly averse, and scared by circumstances over which they feel they have no earthly control. Odours that speak aloud stalk over the face of the so-called 'waters'. The Avenues of the Fleet Ditch finds articulate echo in the Cocytus of the great Effra Sewer; and as we watch the tiny drainlet that dribbles down the shore at dead low-water, we see how it is that 'every little helps' to corrupt the stream below, and adds a fiercer zest to that satanic *Julienne* whose reek is for ever rising on the wings of Azrael, and foreshadows the terrors of a new and warmer world!'

After many committees had conferred, something began to happen at last when the Metropolitan Board of Works was entrusted with the primary duty of building new works to prevent sewage entering the Thames within the London area. But for many years yet the riverside was to be, as *Punch* declaimed in 1858:

> *'Filthy river, filthy river,*
> *Foul from London to the Nore,*
> *What art thou but one vast gutter,*
> *One tremendous common shore.'*

⟦ THE RIVER CHANGES HANDS

While the proposed Embankments and new outfall sewers were being considered, an argument had been going on between the City and the Crown concerning the rightful ownership of the bed and banks of the river within the ebb and flow of the tides. The argument lasted seventeen years. Since early times control of the Thames and of the other royal rivers had been a prerogative of the Crown; yet between 1197 and 1857 the City of London had been under the impression, and had acted accordingly, that control of the river was in its hands quite definitely up to Staines, and only vaguely so beyond. In 1197 Richard I had vested the river's care in the Mayor and Corporation of the City for a consideration of 1,500 marks (the Crusader had returned from his wars and was short of funds). Now, nearly seven centuries later, the solicitor of Her Majesty's Woods and Forests was claiming that the position of the City was not one of ownership but merely of ministry, and it was demanded that the title of the Crown to the bed and banks of the tidal river should be admitted. The City Corporation refused to do this and dug up musty documents from the Guildhall archives to prove its right to ownership. The Crown was obstinate and it is believed that the Queen herself was quite determined on the matter; so the Crown proceeded, by way of Chancery, against the Lord Mayor and Corporation. This generated some heat. The Corporation's solicitor declared himself convinced that the City's case was so strong from immemorial use that the Crown 'from a similar conviction, instead of resorting to a

A Victorian riverside idyll looking towards Waterloo Bridge and Somerset House. 'The Thames Embankment as it Might be—A Suggestive Sketch.'

(From *The Graphic* 6 August, 1881). Compare this Victorian heaven with the Victorian hell on page 183.

court of common law, have adopted this most unusual and uncon-
stitutional proceeding to gain by sinister and indirect means an advantage they could not otherwise obtain'.

The dispute simmered on while the revenue from the Thames de-
creased rapidly as the railways developed. The City, reasonably enough
under the circumstances, refused to advance any more funds for the
benefit of the navigation. The situation grew critical and in June 1847
the Corporation presented a Thames Conservancy Bill before Parliament which proposed a new river authority comprising the Lord Mayor,
the First Lord of the Treasury, the First Lord of the Admiralty, the
First Commissioner of Woods and Forests, the last Lord Mayor, the
Chairman of the Trinity Board, two aldermen, the Admiralty hydro-
grapher and eight Common Councilmen. The Woods and Forests at the
same time recommended a new river commission which would deprive
the Corporation of the conservancy control of the Thames. Finally the
City gave way and on the 18th of December 1856 the City officials
agreed to withdraw all claim to the ownership and admitted the claim
of the Crown. Litigation ended at last and early in 1857 the Crown re-
conveyed its right to a new Board of Conservancy. The Thames Commissioners were formed the same year, comprising the Lord Mayor,
two aldermen, four nominees of the Common Council, two of the Lord
High Admiral, one of the Privy Council, the Deputy Master of Trinity
House and a Trinity House nominee. And thus, as Fred Thacker writes in
his *General History of the Thames Highway* (1914), 'by *peine forte et dure*,
the City of London was at length and finally expelled from the ancient
office it had enjoyed and exercised during the larger part of seven
hundred years'.

Thacker does not add that the City was adequately represented among
the twelve new Commissioners, nor that the City's control of the river
had never been particularly efficient because too many vested interests
had been involved in the adminstration. This body of Commissioners
lasted nine years only, and under an Act of 1866 a new body was formed
called the Thames Conservancy Board, which was given control of the
whole navigable river from Cricklade down to Yantlet Creek, an unprecedented situation of overall authority which lasted until 1908. Then
the new Port of London Authority took over the tidal river between
Teddington and the sea, and the Conservancy was reconstituted to look
after the whole of the one hundred and thirty-five miles of river and its
watershed above Teddington.

PART II

LET'S TAKE A WALK

'There is only one way to enjoy what a town has to offer the eye, and that is the pedestrian's way. Moving fast along an arterial road or sitting in a traffic jam can be pleasures too, but they are fleeting pleasures which must not be allowed to interfere with the real business *of living in that area* even if "living" only consists of spending the day there.'

Gordon Cullen,
'Westminster Regained',
The Architectural Review,
November 1947

A City cherub on a gate of the bombed church of St. Dunstan's-in-the-East.

Whistler's Nocturne of Old Battersea Bridge. (Reproduced by courtesy of the Trustees of the Tate Gallery)

THE READER MUST explore by himself, or with other guides than this, such riverside walks as those through the early dockland from the Tower to Shadwell; the park, Hospital, maritime museum and the *Cutty Sark* at Greenwich (which can be reached by river bus from Westminster); the suburban stretch between Hammersmith Bridge and Chiswick Park; or along Strand-on-the-Green and across Kew Bridge to Kew Gardens (a delightful short walk where a good deal of the atmosphere of London's eighteenth-century riverside is still preserved). Other suburban reaches worth exploring are at Isleworth, where Syon House can be visited, and between Teddington and Richmond, where the chief point of interest is Ham House. In the summer months river steamers run both east and west: east from the Tower even to the Continent, and west up to Hampton Court and, for those who can spare two or three days, as far as Oxford.

Here we shall concentrate on the five miles of riverside in London itself between Chelsea and the Tower, and although we may make an occasional crossing to the south bank, we shall stick chiefly to the north bank. In this distance there is a great deal to see, and so, rather than one long walk, we shall take four short rambling and leisurely perambulations. Our point of departure lies at the south end of Beaufort Street, Chelsea, near the approach to Battersea Bridge, where the peaceful Cheyne Walk runs to east and west near the wide and restless river.

〔 OLD CHELSEA

This first walk is the most pleasant of the four, for here much of the atmosphere of eighteenth-century London persists in the settled, elegant domesticity of mellow brickwork, classical doorways and old ironwork, all set amongst trees and gardens. We have already seen something of Chelsea's past—that it possessed a church as far back as the Middle Ages, that it was hardly a place at all until Sir Thomas More built his mansion here about 1520, that it became a village of palaces and that it was separated from Westminster by a great open space of market gardens dotted with an occasional pest house, tavern or tea-garden, and haunted by the fowler and the footpad. This open space, which as late as 1810 was supplying half the vegetables sold at Covent

Garden, was swallowed up by London's expansion, but, in spite of that, Chelsea has retained its own special character and remains a more definite entity than most other London districts—an entity of which the riverside is the chief element, as it has always been.

Charles II liked the place as much as Henry VIII; he often swam in the river here, and he had a track across the open land to the north turned into his own private road, which became known as the King's Road after 1713 and only became a public thoroughfare in 1830. Chelsea has always been fashionable and it was known at one period as 'Pall Mall Afloat' or 'Hyde Park on the Thames', because here the wide reach was well suited to the grand aquatic displays of Stuart London. By the middle of the eighteenth century it was a village of small houses rather than palaces, for by then it consisted of some forty dwellings. Cheyne Row still has a few houses of Queen Anne's time, including No. 24, where the Carlyles lived for many years and which is now a literary shrine. By 1780 there were more than seven hundred houses in Chelsea and it possessed also the Royal Hospital, the famous porcelain works, the Bun House, the Physick Garden, Ranelagh Gardens, the leafy riverside parade of Cheyne Walk and its sturdy brick church. It was a suburban retreat for the upper classes and was considered to be a healthy spot. The place still holds some of its old calm felicity in spite of the heavy lorries which roar without cease along the Embankment.

In the nineteenth century writers and painters made Chelsea their own and it became the bohemian Chelsea of Rossetti, Whistler (who had in his time eight different addresses there), Whistler's protégé Walter Greaves, Carlyle, Henry James, Hall Caine and others. Old photographs still evoke the Chelsea riverside of their times before the Embankment destroyed the intimacy of Cheyne Walk.

We have been musing at the end of BEAUFORT STREET. Let us turn round and face north for an instant. Half way up the street stood More's Tudor house facing the river and surrounded by a garden and farmland. At that time and for nearly two centuries afterwards, all this area was green and open country.

Now we turn to the west to walk a short way along the riverside towards Lots Road Power Station—that is along the WESTERN END OF CHEYNE WALK. On the strand here is a London curiosity—a village of house-boats which is partly the result of post-war housing difficulties, and partly also perhaps of that urge among many people, which cannot be denied, to live in something afloat. Ahead of us, where the power station jerks up its four black chimneys, lay Cremorne Gardens. Turner lived and died at No. 119, a pleasant little house, and there we can turn back and walk steadily towards the east. Facing the river as far as Beaufort Street is an interesting and charming assortment of houses, mostly Georgian, Nos. 91–100 being among the best of their kind along the river. Nos. 95 to 100 compose LINDSEY HOUSE, the only surviving seventeenth-century house in Chelsea, being built about 1674 (some say to Wren's design) on the site of a mansion which belonged to Sir Theodore Mayerne, physician to James I and Charles I. Bertie, third Earl of Lindsey, rebuilt the place as a simple three-storey domain with a central pediment, and in 1751 it became the colony of the Moravian Brethren. In 1774 it was divided into separate dwellings; today it has been further subdivided into flats, and has been thoroughly restored, being now under the National Trust. Not much of the house can be seen from the road, but we can peep round the doorway in the high wall and across the neat paved courtyard at its façade (very white in the sunshine from the south) and the central carved doorway (an

The Village of House-Boats below the western end of Cheyne Walk.

antique but not the original). The house has had many distinguished inhabitants in its time, among them the two Brunels, Joseph Bramah, the inventor of the water-closet, John Martin, painter of vast and fabulous biblical epics, and Whistler, who lived at No. 96 for more than ten years.

Mrs. Gaskell was born at No. 93, which, like 94, is a pleasing small brick house of 1777, having a vine trailing over its first-floor balcony. No. 92, which dates from 1771, is much larger than these two and has a fine, wide doorway, well detailed in an Adam manner.

We continue now on the other side of Beaufort Street along to the Royal Albert Bridge. Here at the start much was destroyed during the Second World War, but CROSBY HALL, the first large building we meet, set behind a lawn where a few studious ladies recline in deckchairs, is still intact. This is the international hostel of the British Federation of University Women, most of which was begun in a Tudor style in 1926 and is not yet (in 1958) finished. To the north-east is a portion of the complex in stone, the south end of which is temporarily covered with a corrugated material. This part is of special interest, for it is a genuine piece of fifteenth-century architecture which was transferred here and accurately re-erected in 1910. It formed before that the

Two doorways in Cheyne Walk: No. 92, left, built early in the 1770s, has an Adam flavour.

Crosby Hall, which originated in Bishopsgate in the fifteenth century.

great hall of Crosby Place, the sumptuous mansion built at Bishopsgate in 1466 for Sir Richard Crosby, soldier, alderman, diplomat and immensely rich City merchant. It is of interest in revealing in how grand a style a prosperous wool stapler of London lived during the Middle Ages.

It was so princely a place that after Crosby died, Richard, Duke of Gloucester, used it as his London residence before he was crowned. 'There', wrote Sir Thomas More, 'he lodged himself and little by little all folks drew unto him, so that the Protector's court was crowded and King Henry's left desolate.' More himself came to own the house, though he never lived there and soon sold it to an Italian merchant when he settled in Chelsea. After that it passed through the hands of

o

many rich and noble people. In 1621 it was owned by the East India Company and after that its decline began. It served as a prison during the Civil War; it was a Presbyterian Chapel in 1672 and two years later the hall itself survived a fire which destroyed the rest of the property. In the eighteenth century the hall became a warehouse, but in the time of the Romantic Revival in the 1830s it was refurbished with respect, and at mid-century it was used by a learned society and for concerts, at several of which Mendelssohn performed.

In 1862 the hall lost caste again and became a wine store, but six years later it was converted into a restaurant where City clerks luncheoned on chops and steaks and drank ale from pewter pots. That restaurant became very popular and flourished until 1907, when the land was sold to a bank and the hall was threatened with demolition. £60,000 was subscribed for its preservation, but that was not enough, and eventually the scheme for removing it to Chelsea was adopted. The hall now stands roughly in the same relationship to its attendant buildings as it did when first built; it stands on a spot which once formed part of the grounds of the Great More House, and so it re-forms an old association. (Hence the replica of Holbein's painting of Sir Thomas and his family which was presented by the Chelsea Society in 1950 and now hangs in the hall.)

It is a fine hall, sixty-nine feet long and twenty-seven feet wide, and it still possesses the original oak roof and the oriel window above the dais, though the gallery, dormer windows, lantern and oak floor are new. It is open to the public every day, including Sunday, from 10 to 12 and 2 to 5.

The next building of interest, beyond a bombed site (affectionately tended as gardens until recently by local people and soon to become an open space under the LCC), is OLD CHELSEA CHURCH, just rebuilt at the time of writing after its war-time destruction. The walls of the nave are standing again and the same bulky form of the tower, which was so familiar a riverside landmark for nearly three centuries until a bomb reduced it to rubble on the 17th of April 1941, is now breaking the Chelsea skyline again. The new structure, since 1951 once more a living parish church in its own right (a distinction it had relinquished when St. Luke's, Sydney Street, was built in the 1820s), is a replica of the old nave and tower of the 1670s. The new red Sussex bricks will show the forms of the past, though unfortunately none of time's patina. Its completion will probably revive the debate which occurred when rebuilding

Chelsea Old Church in 1788; from a drawing by J. Malton in the Chelsea Public Library.

was being discussed, on whether the original design should be copied or a new one conceived.

Though wrong as a general principle, the decision taken in the exceptional case of Chelsea Old Church was probably the right one owing to the building's rich historical associations and its unique collection of monuments. Moreover, of the mediæval parts, some of the north chapel (Lawrence Chapel), and the chancel and almost the whole of the south chapel (More's Chapel) with its fourteenth-century roof timbers, survived the bombing and are incorporated in the new building. The tower received a wooden cupola some years after it had been built and at one time the top of the tower was castellated. Let us hope that these features will be renewed, for they were attractive and helped to lighten the heavy tower.

Two cherubs in Chelsea Old Church; left, a detail of one of the carved Holbein capitals 'with volutes, foliage, shields and tough little peeping faces'; right, one of a pair on an eighteenth-century monument in the More Chapel.

The old church was not a particularly striking piece of architecture, but a homely piece of local builder's vernacular—the sort of place that arouses growing affection rather than sudden passion. Its main part was built when Wren's City churches were being conceived, yet its character of warm brick was Tudor rather than Stuart. It was, in fact, a typical, unsophisticated English village church in having been added to and altered through the years in that improvising, practical, illogical and peculiarly English way in which so much of our environment has been formed.

In this church Henry VIII was secretly married to Jane Seymour; his daughter Elizabeth worshipped here as a girl, for she spent ten years at Chelsea Manor. More rebuilt the south chapel, though parts of it are earlier than his time. The early Renaissance capitals of the responds of the Gothic arch between his chapel and the chancel are carved with More's crest and arms and one bears the date 1528. It is almost certain that these were carved from drawings made by Hans Holbein, who was at that time staying with More in Chelsea. They are a curious pair of capitals, half-classical but very free and exuberant with volutes, foliage, shields and tough little peeping faces.

Within and without the church no fewer than one hundred and eighty-two monuments from the sixteenth century onwards existed before the bomb fell—the most remarkable and varied collection in London, if we exclude that in Westminster Abbey. By a miracle, most of these monuments were not destroyed by the bombing; then with the enthusiasm of the incumbent, the architect, the borough surveyor and the verger, most of them were salvaged and are now being replaced in the revived church more or less in their original and charming confusion.

More has his monument there, of course, but whether or not his headless body was buried beneath it is not known; it may have been interred below the simple altar tomb here, but it is more likely that it was buried at the Tower. Among the grandest monuments are those of Sir Robert Stanley and of the Dacre family. But to the writer's eye the most lovely and voluptuous carving in the church—perhaps in all London—is the white marble of Lady Jane Cheyne (1669), who reclines within a classical ædicule on the north side of the nave. The whole, made in Rome, was designed by Paolo Bernini, nephew of the famous sculptor-architect, but the figure is by Antonio Raggi, who worked from drawings of Lady Jane (a benefactress of the church) which were sent to him. The figure experienced one of those escapes from the bombing which cannot be explained, for she was hurled in all her relaxed and baroque beauty right through the outer wall of the church high into the air and was then buried deeply in rubble except for one small protrusion of white marble. It was the sight of this exposure that decided the architect and Chelsea lover, Mr. W. H. Godfrey (who designed the near-by

Lady Jane Cheyne in Chelsea Old Church, photographed before being restored to her original ædicule during rebuilding of the bombed church: 'the most lovely and voluptuous carving in the church—perhaps in all London'. (By courtesy of Messrs. Fenning and Co.)

buildings attached to Crosby Hall and has written the LCC survey volume on the old church) to dig hopefully for remains. Finding the lady quietly continuing her reading and intact except for a few missing toes, he bravely guaranteed personally to cover the cost of sifting the rest of the rubble for other remains, a risk which proved well worth while.

A new vicarage and committee rooms are being built to the north of the church in the same red brick as the church, but in a modern idiom. These attached structures will thus continue the picturesque tradition of mixing styles without self-consciousness or disharmony.

Before walking on, let us look at the monument designed by Joseph Wilton which stands on the south-east corner of the churchyard—that of an elegant pot under a canopy. This preserves the memory of SIR HANS SLOANE, who died aged ninety-two in 1753. Sloane was a wealthy man and was Lord of the Chelsea Manor for many years after William, Lord Cheyne (which means chenie or oak). From him come the names Sloane Street, Sloane Square and Hans Place. Sloane was an interesting man, a naturalist and famous physician who attended Queen Anne on her deathbed. He followed Newton as President of the Royal Society, but he is chiefly remembered as an obsessional and voracious collector, and his fame rests now mainly on his extraordinary 'knackatory' of books, antiques, curios, minerals and botanical specimens which he gathered together throughout his long life. After his death this collection formed—together with the Harleian and Cottonian libraries—the nucleus of the British Museum. Sloane did not settle in Chelsea until he was eighty-three, and then he lived at the old manor house of Henry VIII. We shall find another association with Sloane further along the bank.

Beyond the church is a hospital for children, and here the first of the two public gardens separating CHEYNE WALK from the Embankment begins. In this first one, near the end of Cheyne Row, is a monument to Carlyle of 1882, and at the corner of Cheyne Row is a homely stucco pub called the King's Head where Chelsea people gather around on Sunday mornings to sip their drinks with the latest gossip. Nos. 49 to 46 are old houses, then there is a dull block of modern flats, and at the end of this section of Cheyne Walk is a group of charming red-brick houses (Nos. 39–37) by C. R. Ashbee, built at the turn of the century with an Art Nouveau character. The first of them, built in 1894, is called the *Magpye and Stump*, the name of an old tavern which formerly

The Royal Albert Bridge, opened in 1873, 'the threat of whose demolition has produced a cry of anguish from local residents'.

stood on the same site. Then there is a tea-shop, and at the corner of Oakley Street is the Pier Hotel, a large Victorian pub. Down on the Embankment Walk here we can obtain a good view of the ROYAL AL-BERT BRIDGE of 1873, the threat of whose demolition has produced a cry of anguish from local residents—understandably enough, for this cast-iron structure has a strong personality and has settled down well into the Chelsea scene. To the east of the bridge is Cadogan Pier, where the water-buses stop.

Across Oakley Street, the rest of Cheyne Walk runs as an almost un-spoiled range of variegated old houses, mostly in red brick, set behind small gardens protected by hedges, trees and some excellent wrought ironwork. Nos. 26 to 15 are eighteenth century with alterations and on the site they occupy once stood the Manor House of Henry VIII. No. 18 is interesting in having been a Coffee House-cum-Museum—that of James Salter, nicknamed Don Saltero, an Irishman who had been a servant to Hans Sloane. Steele described him in *The Tatler* as a 'sage of thin and meagre countenance of that sect which the ancients called Gingivistae—in our language tooth-drawers'. Steele goes on: 'My love of mankind made one very benevolent to Mr. Salter; for such is the name of this eminent barber and antiquary.' Salter took over No. 18 when newly built in 1718 and his tavern became a meeting-place for the

Cheyne Walk, looking east. On the left is No. 6 with its Chinese Chippendale style of iron railings.

local celebrities and for visitors to the metropolis. Here he gathered together his whimsical collection, no doubt in imitation of his former master, and probably it contained many of the Doctor's throw-outs. The museum held such oddities as a Lignified Hog, the heads of four Evangelists carved on cherry stones, an Elf's Arrow, a piece of Solomon's Temple, idols, stuffed animals, corals, crystals, shells, a Spanish apparatus to prevent cuckoldom and in Steele's words 'Pontius Pilate's wife's chambermaid's sister's hat'. The Coffee House remained open long after the death of the jolly Gimcrack Whim Collector, but in 1799 his collection was sold for £50 and the place became a pub. So it remained until 1876. The house has been much altered since Salter's time.

No. 16 is Queen's House, the largest in the row and still retaining its original look of 1717, in spite of the added bay. This may be the work of Archer (who designed the church in Smith Square, Westminster). It has some good ironwork along the pavement in the form of railings and a gateway. The initials R. C. on the gate may give the clue to the name of the house, for they could stand for Catherina Regina (of Braganza), but in fact they stand for Richard Chapman, apothecary of St. Clement Danes, who built this house in the time of George I. It has been renovated during this century by Sir Edwin Lutyens. Rossetti lived for many years at Queen's House and in the gardens opposite is a fountain by S. P. Seddon with a bas-relief of Rossetti by Madox Brown which Holman Hunt unveiled in 1887.

Nos. 14 down to 7 are Victorian houses (11 to 7 belong to the eighties), but they harmonise fairly well with the row as a whole. Nos. 6 to 3 are genuine early Georgian of about the same time as Queen's House, No. 6 being distinguishable by its iron railing and gate in a Chinese Chippendale manner of mid-eighteenth century. To No. 6 in 1765 came Dr. Bartholomew Dominiceti, who built an annex containing medicinal baths, fumigatory stoves and four sweating bed-chambers; of those harmless, and even perhaps beneficial, contraptions Dr. Johnson sourly remarked that 'there is nothing in all his boasted system'. The 'Italian quack', as he was called, went bankrupt and after 1782 was heard of no more.

No. 5 has some good iron gates and so also has No. 4, which has a good early Georgian doorway too. Indeed many of the doorways all along Cheyne Walk are worth more than a glance. No. 3 has a good carved door hood; No. 2 has a Victorian front and No. 1 is of 1887.

Oriel windows of Old Swan House on the Chelsea Embankment designed by
Norman Shaw.

The road splits into two at the east end of Cheyne Walk: that road
going left is Royal Hospital Road and that on the right is a short arm
joining up with the CHELSEA EMBANKMENT, which is the next part of
our walk. Let us say that we are being lucky in our weather on our walks
and that the sun strikes down on us warmly now as we emerge on to the
wide embankment from beneath the cool, close shade of Cheyne Walk.
Across the river there rise the green glades of Battersea Park topped by
blue sky and the few puffy white clouds of a perfect summer day. On
the left is a row of large houses in brick, Victorian but not without merit,
and having fine views across the river to Battersea Park; they were built
soon after the Embankment was completed in 1874. Nos. 8 to 11 and
16 and 17 are by Norman Shaw, No. 17, called Old Swan House, being
a particularly good example of the work of that accomplished architect
who revived the Queen Anne style; the façade is pleasing with those
oriel windows of which Shaw was very fond. Here stood the Swan
Tavern before the Embankment came, though that was not the original

Swan Inn of Chelsea, which was higher up-river. The tavern had a garden running to the river where a floating pier projected into the river for the Penny Steamers.

Chelsea Embankment, with its broad road, granite wall and rows of plane-trees, runs straight before and behind us now, three-quarters of a mile long. No doubt it was an 'improvement', but it stole away Chelsea's pretty, Dutch-like riverside. It has, like its counterpart the Victoria Embankment further east, a rather monotonous look and it has cut off Chelsea from its old intimacy with the river.

The view across the river towards BATTERSEA PARK is pleasant enough, though the long river wall is monotonous. A tall slim tower is needed in the pleasure-ground there to act as a strong vertical foil to the long, low line of the wall and the dark green range of trees behind. London needs its own Eiffel Tower just there: *not* the timid one hundred and sixty-foot-high tower proposed by the Festival Funfair people in 1956 and eventually dropped after strong objections had been raised by Chelsea inhabitants, but a grand, uninhibited phallos at least a thousand feet high. At the time the controversy was raging a letter by the writer on the subject was printed in *The Times* and it may be worth putting on record here, for there is always a chance that the notion may be revived:

'As a Londoner who is interested in the look of his town I was delighted to hear of the proposed tower for Battersea Park. It will be a sort of folly, I suppose, London's own Eiffel Tower, costly to build and quite useless. We badly need more buildings like that and we could do especially with many more useless towers and spires to break the dreary skylines. But what does the proposed tower look like? Nobody seems to be interested in that. Yet it is the most important question. The tower might be a visual horror or a great work of art. If the design has not yet been settled, could the promotors not organise an international competition among architects and engineers so that we Londoners may acquire a new, proud, beautiful, and exciting monument? Buildings are symbols and need not always be dull utilities. Anyway, ideas on what is useful in life vary a good deal.'

Perhaps we shall yet have something by the river here even better than the Eiffel Tower—a structure which was reviled by Paris æsthetes at the time it was built and whose threatened demolition not long ago was violently opposed by æsthetes of a later generation.

The Botanic Garden, bestowed in 1728 by Sir Hans Sloane on the Society of Apothecaries and now run by the Imperial College of Science. This is the view through a gate in Swan Walk towards the statue of Sloane by Rysbrach.

But we must turn around now, for we have missed an interesting garden on our side of the river. It breaks the line of the row of houses we have described and stretches back to the Royal Hospital Road to the north. This is the BOTANIC GARDEN (once known as the Apothecaries, or the Physick, Garden). Sir Hans Sloane in 1728 bestowed it in perpetuity upon the Society of Apothecaries, whose emblem, the rhinoceros, decorates the garden gates.

The garden became world renowned and has been important in history. Linnaeus visited the place in 1736 and took away specimens, and it is said that three-quarters of the world's cotton crops are descended from cotton seeds grown here.

Botanic Garden carries on its old tradition of practical horticulture to this day, under the control of the Imperial College of Science. Unfortunately the garden is locked against the public and special permission must be obtained to explore it. But we can glimpse most of it through the railings along the Embankment pavement or through the gate on the east side along Swan Walk. In the centre, down a dappled walk and suitably elevated upon a pedestal, stands Sir Hans Sloane in the form of a weather-worn statue by Rysbrach.

Our Chelsea pilgrimage is near its end and concludes with the grand, harmonious climax of CHELSEA HOSPITAL, framed by trees and grass. We can enter the grounds from the Embankment side and walk up the axis, past Cockerell's obelisk of 1849, erected in memory of the Battle of Chillianwallah, to the great courtyard where the statue of Charles II stands facing the central portico. We can stroll freely about the place among the old veterans in their scarlet uniforms which show links with the uniforms of Marlborough's time. We must not miss the Chapel or the simple, functional brickwork stables added by Soane which lie to the north-west. And afterwards we can walk to the east of the building and into Ranelagh Gardens, there to imagine among the thick foliage and municipal gravel the great rotunda of pleasure which was once part of the fabric of another London.

The courtyard of Chelsea Hospital.

8 | By Pimlico to Westminster

THIS WALK CONTAINS the Tate Gallery and its treasures and, at the end, the Abbey and the Palace of Westminster to provide a climax.

We begin at CHELSEA BRIDGE, quite a pleasing, honest but too heavy suspension bridge of 1934 designed by Topham Forrest and E. P. Wheeler, in strong contrast to the old iron Albert Bridge to the west, though only three-quarters of a mile and sixty years separates them. It replaced an earlier and highly ornate suspension bridge of 1858 which (at least in the old prints) had a period charm in spite of its gross stone piers.

The approach road running to Chelsea Bridge beside Ranelagh Gardens marks the boundary line between Chelsea and Westminster, so that we shall now be walking along the edge of Westminster by Grosvenor Road, the riverside embankment here which, built in 1857, is a continuation of Chelsea Embankment. Battersea, on the south of the river, continues beyond Chelsea Bridge as far as Vauxhall Bridge.

Beyond Chelsea Bridge, Grosvenor Road crosses a waterway which can be seen receding northwards down a valley of warehouses; it is all that now remains of the old GROSVENOR CANAL (previously part of the Chelsea Waterworks) which ended in a large basin on the site where Victoria Station now stands. The remnant is used today by the Westminster Cleansing and Disinfecting Station, and if we arrive at the right moment we shall see below us a string of barges, loaded with human spoor, locking through and moving with slow dignity into the river where it will hitch on to a tug and be towed down-river for dumping on the Essex marshes.

Beyond the canal on the left is a small structure with arched windows and French architectural effects built in 1875 and having an ugly square tower of yellow brick behind it. This is the WESTERN PUMPING STATION of the LCC's main drainage scheme and it provides a contrasting foil to the huge, functional brick pile of Sir Giles Gilbert Scott's BATTERSEA POWER STATION on the other side of the river here, which, as Dr. Pevsner points out in his Penguin *London*, is the first example in England of frankly contemporary industrial architecture. (Visits taking two hours under a guide can be arranged through the London Division of the Central Electricity Authority.) The VICTORIA RAILWAY BRIDGE of 1863, formerly the property of the Southern Railway, which we now pass beneath, was designed by Sir John Fowler, who with Sir Benjamin Baker, created the Forth Bridge.

Beyond the bridge the great new housing estate of CHURCHILL GARDENS begins, built since the war by the Westminster City Council and, at the time of writing, barely complete. It contains some two thousand dwellings in thirty-six blocks of flats and maisonettes, together with amenities such as a row of shops along Lupus Street on the north boundary. Some of the blocks are eleven storeys high. To live in cells like this may not be part of the Good Life, but if we accept without question the conditions of existence in a big city today and the social-economic values on which it is based, this new housing estate is admirable—a great advance both in standards and in appearance on most municipal housing of the past. The design, honest, imaginative and 'contemporary' is the result of an open competition held in 1946 and

A corner of Churchill Gardens, the vast housing estate built by the Westminster City Council which contains some two thousand dwellings. On the right is the *Balmoral Castle*, a Victorian pub which has been retained as a foil to the modern buildings.

won by two young architects, Powell and Moya, who had then only just completed their training.

A prominent feature on the riverside is a strange, tall, polygonal tower of steel framework faced with panels of obscured glass. This is a heat accumulator for storing hot water for the whole estate, and below it is a pumping-house which brings hot water to the tower by pipes running under the river from Battersea Power Station. This pumping-house is a small building in the true functional tradition and an excellent piece of architecture, though as yet few people may regard it as such; 'architecture' is still too closely associated in the public mind with eclectic stylism like that displayed on the LCC pumping-house we have passed. The base of the glass tower is composed of granite setts which once paved the quay of the old Belgrave Dock which ran in here from the river before it was filled in.

On the river side of Churchill Gardens a row of pleasant early nineteenth-century terrace houses with decorative iron balcony railings still survives, and so also does a typical Victorian pub called *The Balmoral Castle*, set back a short way from Grosvenor Road. Let us hope that these will be allowed to remain, for they serve as valuable foils to the modern buildings, and help to preserve that continuity with the past which adds charm and interest to any urban scene.

Beyond Churchill Gardens, and covering the site of the former Army Clothing Factory, is the huge pseudo-Georgian brick block of DOLPHIN SQUARE—'luxury' flats completed in 1937. With its gloomy central courtyard it covers over seven acres and contains 1,200 flats to house some four thousand souls. It was at one time the largest self-contained block of flats in Europe, but architecturally it is a failure, and adds no æsthetic pleasure to our walk.

From a point opposite Dolphin Square, right along to Vauxhall Bridge and for a short distance beyond the bridge, is a range of wharves and low structures of undistinguished appearance which cut off the view to the river from Grosvenor Road. The County of London Plan rightly advises that these buildings should be removed so that the small public garden, which breaks the range of buildings opposite St. George's Square, could be extended in both directions. As it is, this square patch of green, called PIMLICO GARDENS, is dull and gives little chance for imaginative landscaping. The view from its river wall is also dull, if not to say squalid, for it looks across the river to a jumble of industrialism in the district called Nine Elms. There are no trees there now and the nine elms disappeared long ago; so also did the old Cumberland tea-gardens which once graced this part of the south bank.

A dignified man in a white Roman toga stands brooding over Pimlico Gardens. This is a statue of 1836 which, in the classical manner of the period, represents the figure of William Huskisson, M.P. (1770–1830), a railway pioneer who died tragically at the opening ceremony of the Liverpool and Manchester Railway when he was struck down by 'The Rocket' while shaking hands with the Duke of Wellington.

We come now to an open space on our left where a Victorian Gothic church stood until destroyed by a bomb in the Second World War. Then we cross Vauxhall Bridge Road, glancing right towards the wide bridge built by the LCC in 1906. If we care to walk up to it we shall see a group of trees near its southern head on the Surrey side; they mark the spot where Vauxhall Gardens once lay—'those green retreats where fair Vauxhall bedecks her sylvan seats'.

Grosvenor Road continues beyond the bridgehead as MILLBANK. The first building of importance there is the TATE GALLERY, which occupies part of the site of the huge Penitentiary which was pulled down in 1890. Behind the Gallery, as we have recorded, lies an early and good example of LCC housing.

Beyond the Gallery is the Queen Alexandra Military Hospital, of no architectural merit, and after that some quite pleasant houses built several decades ago. These are—at time of writing—to be pulled down soon, to make way for a gigantic tower thirty storeys high with out-buildings to serve as offices for the Vickers group. From the drawings one can gather that the design will be a good deal better than those vast and bogus imperial blocks which are its neighbours to the east.

Before passing them, let us glance across the river, where we can see a whole range of enormous new buildings. They stand behind the ALBERT EMBANKMENT (completed in 1868) which is a traffic artery here but runs as a riverside footway further east between the bridges of Lambeth and Westminster. The best of the big buildings are the latest, which lie to the west—Frederick Gibberd's National Dock Labour Board headquarters, and just east of it, a general office block by T. P. Bennett and Son, both completed in 1956. Then comes the new National Coal Board offices by Leslie Norton and after it the Decca building by Grace and Farmer, the LCC Fire Service headquarters in brick of 1936, the premises of W. H. Smith and Son, Messrs. Doulton's new block and finally at the corner, where Lambeth Bridge joins the

P

Albert Embankment, a huge sombre affair occupied by the Ministry of
Works. The whole uncoordinated range fills one—even in the sunshine
—with a gloomy sense of foreboding and futility. If this is civilisation,
let us return rapidly to the Dark Ages and try again.

On the north bank now we pass two great Roman office blocks faced
with stone, separated by HORSEFERRY ROAD. They are the work of
Sir Frank Baines and came in the late twenties to wreck the riverside
scene here with their overbearing, insensitive, false and sterile pomposity. They house the Imperial Chemical Industries and, in the one
called Thames House, the Board of Trade. LAMBETH BRIDGE is a
work of 1932 by the LCC engineer helped by Sir Reginald Blomfield
who stuck on the 'architectural' bits.

Beyond the bridge on the riverside lies a pleasant frondiferous garden
which runs up to the foot of the Houses of Parliament and its Victoria
Tower. This public oasis of green is, indeed, called VICTORIA TOWER
GARDENS. Mrs. Pankhurst, the Suffragette leader, stands therein de-
claiming without end; and there also is to be found Rodin's group of
the Burghers of Calais, a work of 1895, erected here in 1915, though recently reset with great advantage on a low pedestal and re-sited. If we
enter the garden and walk to the wall we can see across the river the
worn old LAMBETH PALACE rising among a thrust of trees, and to its
west the tower of ST. MARY'S, the parish church of Lambeth. This
church is mentioned in the Domesday Book, but it was rebuilt in the
fifteenth century, and of that building only the tower now remains. The
rest is mainly a nineteenth-century reconstruction in the Gothic style,
except for a chapel on the south side called the Leigh Chapel, which
dates from 1552, and there are some old and interesting monuments
both inside and out. No less than six archbishops have been buried in
the church.

LAMBETH PALACE is still used by the Archbishop of Canterbury as
his London inn, as it has been for seven centuries, and part of it now
serves also as a hostel for visiting Anglican bishops from the provinces
and overseas. One of the Archbishops, called Morton, who once lived
there, built the sturdy brick gateway towards the end of the fifteenth
century, and that still stands. Another archbishop, called Juxon, rebuilt the Great Hall in 1663 with a fine hammer-beam roof, and that
hall now houses part of the famous library of Lambeth Palace, which
contains among other things a magnificent collection of 1500 mediæval
manuscripts dating from the ninth century. (The library is open to the

Rodin's *Burghers of Calais* in the Victoria Tower Gardens seen against the Gothic Revival background of the Houses of Parliament.

public between 10 and 5. Parties may visit the Palace as a whole on Saturday afternoons by arrangement with the Domestic Chaplain.)

To the east of the Palace is a medical school, followed by the seven ugly pavilions of St. Thomas's Hospital, several of them ruined by bombs. The hospital has plans for rebuilding—one day.

Back in Millbank we can turn down the short Dean Stanley Street and into SMITH SQUARE to inspect for a moment the shell of Archer's curious square Baroque church of St. John's. Millbank now becomes the short ABINGDON STREET, which leads into the open space west of the Houses of Parliament called Old Palace Yard, where Richard Lionheart waves his sword in a romantic gesture. Only a few of the Georgian houses are left in Abingdon Street, which is a pity, because they formed a good foil to the scale and style of the elaborately carved walls of the Houses of Parliament opposite. A good stone-faced Georgian house survives in the corner of Old Palace Yard, and near it stands the statue of George v unveiled in 1948.

More or less opposite the Victoria Tower is a small building which is
open to the public. This is the JEWEL TOWER, the last surviving
domestic part of the mediæval Palace of Westminster. It was built in
1365 to house the jewels and precious plate of Edward III and was still
doing a job five hundred years later when in 1869 it was occupied by the
Weights and Measures Testing Department. A bomb damaged the roof
in 1941, but now it is in good order again and the original moat has been
reformed.

The elaborate pinnacles and carved panels of the HOUSES OF PARLIA-
MENT continue on our right, and the simple shape of the ancient Westminster Hall is clearly visible now. Opposite is Westminster Abbey's
east end in the form of the splendid late-Gothic chapel of Henry VII.

We shall explore the inside of WESTMINSTER ABBEY, of course, but
to tell its whole story would be impossible here. Enough to say that the
main things to look at are: the whole dim vastness of the soaring interior, the elaborate fan vaulting of Henry VII's Chapel, the octagonal
Chapter House (1250) with its wall-paintings and its central column
and radiating vaulting, the soothing main cloisters, the intimate little
cloisters and all the wonderful monuments. In the words of Oliver
Wendell Holmes this is a 'great museum of gigantic funereal bric-à-
brac'. The remarkable wax effigies in the Abbey Museum should also be
seen; they form a kind of miniature Madame Tussaud's, and a fascinat-

Lambeth Palace with its Great Hall of 1663 which houses part of the famous
library; to the right is Lambeth Parish Church. (An early Victorian print)

The vaulted roof and central column of Westminster Abbey's Chapter House.

ing one, because the faces and costumes are original and authentic. Queen Elizabeth, for instance, almost certainly looked like her image here, for the face was probably taken from a death-mask. Here too is Charles II in a costume of his time, William and Mary are together in a case, the pale face of Queen Anne is here and so is Lord Nelson wearing his own, original clothes (except the coat).

On the left the old parish church of ST. MARGARET'S lies, small and unadorned in the shadow of the Abbey. Apparently small, that is, for it seats 1,000, which is half the seating capacity of the Abbey. The exterior has a simple Portland-stone facing of 1735 but the fine interior is of the Perpendicular Gothic period.

From Old Palace Yard the short thoroughfare of St. Margaret Street leads into PARLIAMENT SQUARE, first planned by Barry, but altered a few years ago. It is a square lawn without trees and rather boring, around which the traffic flows. Many statues of statesmen stand about here in solemn meditation, though the recent controversial figure of Smuts by Epstein strides eagerly forward. We leave them to their lonely thoughts and turn east into Bridge Street, automatically glancing up at the time on the Big Ben tower. Ahead is Page's undistinguished WEST-MINSTER BRIDGE, which replaced Labelye's noble one in 1862.

Henry VII's Chapel at the east end of Westminster Abbey.

THIS WALK TAKES us along the sweep of the King's Reach below the Strand, where once a range of prelates' palaces stood as the link between Westminster and the City. We begin at the corner of the Victoria Embankment and Westminster Bridge amidst a bustle of people, which thickens down by the pier where the river buses come and go. QUEEN BOADICEA (or more correctly Boudicca), attended by two daughters who are driving her along in a chariot drawn by two spirited horses, raises a spear in an operatic gesture. It is a bronze work by Thomas Thornycroft of the 1850s, set up here in 1902. Though a pretentious piece, it does form a useful focal point and an articulation at an important place on the riverside right at the start of the Victoria Embankment. It also marks the beginning of a reach of the river extending to London Bridge which had no special name until it was designated King's Reach on the Silver Jubilee of King George V in 1935.

This reach, which runs round in a splendid curve from Westminster to Blackfriars, where the river proceeds due east again, is firmly lined by the VICTORIA EMBANKMENT. This is the most imposing of Bazalgette's great riverside works: built between 1864 and 1870, it runs for one and a third miles as far as Blackfriars Bridge and the City's edge. When built it reclaimed some thirty-seven acres of muddy riverside wasteland, about half of which is now occupied by public gardens and some buildings and the other half by the wide road and pavements. The construction of the Victoria Embankment required no less than six hundred and fifty thousand cubic feet of granite, eighty thousand cubic feet of brickwork, one hundred and forty thousand cubic feet of concrete and one million cubic yards of earth filling.

Across the river to the east of Westminster Bridge is a large, classical, stone-faced building—the offices of the London County Council called COUNTY HALL. The site was acquired in 1906 and an architectural competition was held which was won by an unknown young man called Ralph Knott. His design, carried out with the help of the Council's own architect, W. E. Riley, was not fully completed until 1933, when Knott had been dead four years. Indeed the additions behind are still going on, though these are by other architects. The building—a piece of Edwardian 'Beaux Arts' brio with a huge central colonnade and heavy rustications—makes a remarkable contrast with the LCC's new concert

Victoria Embankment fauna. Above, one of Boudicca's energetic horses. Near right, a camel seat of cast iron. Far right, a dolphin lamp-post.

hall of 1951, which stands a little way down-river on the same bank. The two conceptions are separated by only one generation and two world wars; yet they belong to different worlds.

Along on our left is NEW SCOTLAND YARD, the Metropolitan Police headquarters which preserves the name of one of the old Strand palaces —the one where the Kings of Scotland lived when in London. This strong Scottish Baronial pile was designed by Norman Shaw (his head is on the building as a bas relief) and it is partly of brick and partly of granite quarried by convicts on Dartmoor. The north part was built in 1890 and the south block in 1912. Before this, however, a scheme had been launched to erect an opera-house on this site, and the foundation stone had actually been laid in 1875 (still to be seen in the cellars of the police headquarters) when funds ran out. Then a company bought the land for flats and offices, but this project also failed, and finally the site was acquired for the police premises. The annex to the north is a modern building of 1930 faced with stone which is very dull but has at least the virtue of serving as a flat contrast to Shaw's vigorous fortress. So also have the equally dull new government buildings which follow and which obscure the back of Inigo Jones' Banqueting Hall.

We cross the bottom of Horseguards' Avenue and there find a strip of garden behind which rises WHITEHALL COURT, designed by Archer and Green and completed in 1887 as a block of flats—a great, eight-storey 'palace' which breaks the sky with a series of pavilions and helps to create that superb, romantic and quite unpremeditated landscape that can

be enjoyed to the full on a quiet summer evening in St. James's Park. When floodlit at the 1951 Festival of Britain, Whitehall Court helped to create an equally wonderful, fairy-tale landscape when seen from the concourse of the South Bank Exhibition. (Why cannot such scenes be made permanent?)

The attached annex to the north is the NATIONAL LIBERAL CLUB, of the same date, designed by Sir Alfred Waterhouse, who among other things created those alarming monstrosities—the Natural History Museum at South Kensington and St. Paul's School, Hammersmith.

Northumberland Avenue comes down to the Embankment now, and on the Embankment wall here is a mural tablet in memory of SIR JOSEPH BAZALGETTE, here immortalised in a bas-relief, with a magnificent moustache. We pass below CHARING CROSS RAILWAY BRIDGE, and on our left we see the entrance to the Underground. The main station, a terminus, behind it, was built by the engineer John Hawkshaw in 1863 on the site of Hungerford Market. The bridge was built at the same time to take the extension of the South Eastern Railway across the river to the terminus. It replaced Brunel's short-lived suspension footbridge of 1836, though Brunel's brick piers are still in use here and the name of Brunel's small structure, HUNGERFORD BRIDGE, has been handed on to the footbridge which is attached to the north side of the railway bridge. The whole structure will probably be demolished before long, and that will be no great loss. The view from the footbridge towards the City, however, is magnificent especially at night, in spite of the coarse and elephantine structures which rise above the Embankment Gardens on the left.

This is one of the few grand views in the whole of London. As we stand on the footbridge we can see below us on the left another waterbus pier. A short way beyond it Cleopatra's Needle makes an exclamation mark along the curve of the Embankment wall, and right ahead are the five, low, white arches of the new Waterloo Bridge. Above it, far off, the dome of St. Paul's dominates the skyline; while to the left of it rises the lead spire of St. Martin's on Ludgate Hill, and slightly further to the left the white Portland-stone spire, tapering gracefully and pierced with arched openings, of another Wren church, St. Bride's, in Fleet Street.

WATERLOO BRIDGE, which replaced Rennie's fine structure, was built during the war years 1939 to 1945. It is the first concrete bridge to cross London's river and the most notable contribution to the river scene

A view of the Shot Tower and the Royal Festival Hall from Hungerford Footbridge. On the left is an arch of Waterloo Bridge and in the distance is St. Paul's Cathedral.

of our century. Happily, owing to the austerity of the times, it was not embellished with 'architectural' decorations and so it preserves a clean and honest look. The engineers were Rendel, Palmer and Tritton in association with Sir Peirson Frank, the LCC's chief engineer, and the architect was Sir Giles Gilbert Scott. Its wide flat arches, each spanning two hundred and forty feet, are in fact not arches in the strict sense, but monolithic beams running continuously over the piers and projecting over the central span as cantilevers meeting in the middle. The facing is of Portland stone slabs and they still gleam with white elegance above the dark river. An arch on the south bank now contains the National Film Theatre.

Raising our eyes again to the skyline we see to the right of St. Bride's, and behind it, the dome of the Old Bailey, surmounted by its blind-folded statue of Justice. On the south bank to our right rises the square tower of Oxo, then to its right the old round SHOT TOWER of 1826 in yellow brickwork, two hundred feet high and looking like a fat chimney.* During the 1951 Festival of Britain it was incorporated in the exhibition and served as a kind of lighthouse topped with a rotating radio telescope. Next to it stood the old Lion Brewery, which was demolished when the exhibition was built.

On our extreme right, approached by Hungerford Footbridge, is the ROYAL FESTIVAL HALL, built by the LCC in 1951 to the designs of the official architects, Dr. (now Sir) John Martin and Robert Matthew, as a permanent concert hall among the temporary exhibition buildings—sadly temporary, for the exhibition was an exciting architectural *tour de force*. The concert hall must be hailed as one of the first large public buildings in London to be designed in a truly modern style. It will form part of a new South Bank area which has hitherto been badly neglected, and in time developments along the river will extend to Southwark Cathedral and London Bridge. The concert hall, though heavy and clumsy in its riverside façade, is a brilliant work, notably in the imaginative way in which the interior space has been handled, particularly in the large concourse below the main hall and in the circulation areas. (We can, if we wish, take tea, a snack or a full meal here in the restaurant or the café facing the river.) The whole is a commendable attempt to bring a touch of civilisation to the bleak brick desert of south London.

In 1953 the LCC produced an excellent plan for developing the area around the Festival Hall as a cultural centre with pleasant riverside gardens, but this scheme has fallen rather flat and the Oil Power has butted in again. We are to be treated with a monstrous tower, lumpish, heavy and domineering, which is now growing up between the Festival Hall and the County Hall to serve as offices for the Shell Petroleum Company. It is to be twenty storeys high (only two feet lower than the Victoria Tower of the Houses of Parliament) and has been well described in the *Architects' Journal* as 'South Bank's Vertical Failure'. It will be one more huge, depressing lump of cultural impotence beside the river; a magnificent architectural opportunity will have been thrown away. What a pity that the LCC has let this site go and disappointed Londoners' hopes of a new riverside centre for leisure instead of toil. Why cannot big businesses now build their offices below the ground and install automatic machines to do their work?

---

* A shot tower works thus: at the top there is a floor with a hole in the middle over which a sieve is placed; molten lead is poured over the sieve and the drops congeal as they fall to the water tank at the bottom.

A view from the roof of Festival Hall with part of the Shot Tower on the right, Waterloo Bridge and Somerset House in the distance. The miniature 'Crystal Palace' in the foreground is a remnant of the 1951 Festival of Britain exhibition— unfortunately soon to be removed.

Back to the Embankment and into the VICTORIA EMBANKMENT GARDENS, which since the end of the war have become the liveliest of all London's small public gardens—a gay and colourful area with a new bandstand, an open-air café, well-designed lamp-standards and other furnishings, well-shaved lawns of brilliant green and flower-beds care-fully cultivated by the uniformed gardeners of the LCC, many of them now women. A number of statues of British worthies stand in the gar-dens, though none is of special interest as sculpture. Less than a cen-tury ago this area was a muddy shore stinking with sewage; three cen-turies and more ago it was clean and above it lay the gardens of the Strand palaces with their parterres, river gates and stairs. As we have seen, the palaces ran all the way from Whitehall Palace as far as the Temple and their names are preserved in the street names of the district —Northumberland, Buckingham, York, Durham House, Savoy, Lan-caster, Norfolk, Arundel, Essex and, of course, Whitehall.

At the back of the Embankment Gardens to the west is an interesting small relic of the old days preserved by the LCC—all that now remains of York House. This is the YORK WATER GATE, erected in 1626 as the riverside exit and entrance to the grounds of the mansion built by George Villiers, first Duke of Buckingham. Some, including the writer of the inscription placed near the little monument, say that the designer was Inigo Jones, but there is no evidence for this. It may have been designed by the mason who built it, one Nicholas Stone, but John Summerson in his Penguin *Architecture in Britain 1530–1830* writes that it is very nearly certain that Gerbier designed the water-gate as part of his work at York House and that it is a direct and rather feeble imita-tion of the Fontaine des Médicis at the Luxembourg in Paris. If we have not been to the Luxembourg, the water-gate may seem to us to be a pleasing little piece with its half-columns with rusticated bands, its broken pediment and its pair of crouching lions. It must, of course, have looked much better standing beside the water.

York House was demolished in 1673 and on the site were formed George Street, Villiers Street, Duke Street, Of Alley, Buckingham Street—names which were intended to preserve the full memory of the Second Duke. The house which stood on the site before the Duke's mansion was built was occupied at one time by the Archbishops of York and for a period by the Lord Keepers of the Great Seal, one of whom was Francis Bacon.

Behind the gardens rises, first, the large ADELPHI office block of 1938 which replaced the Adelphi terrace houses of the Adam brothers. It is thirteen storeys high and brutish. Beyond it is the oil-power block of SHELL-MEX HOUSE of 1931, whose coarse white clock-tower, known as Big Benzine, dominates the scene in these parts. It occupies the site of the former Cecil Hotel, named after Robert Cecil, Earl of Salisbury, Lord High Treasurer to James I, who owned the former Salisbury House which stood here. On the north-east of Big Benzine is the SAVOY HOTEL on the site of the old Savoy Palace, completed in 1889, with a comparatively unobtrusive and functional façade, though it now lacks its original balconies.

Now we brave the embankment traffic again and cross to the river wall to inspect the famous CLEOPATRA'S NEEDLE. It has nothing to do with the Egyptian queen, but was originally one of a pair of obelisks erected at Heliopolis about B.C. 1450 by Thothmes III in front of a temple to the sun. Then in B.C. 23 Augustus Cæsar had them transported to Alexandria to adorn his palace there, and it may be because Cleopatra had died in the palace seven years before that her name became attached to the obelisks. After the Battle of the Nile some patriots considered bringing one of them home as a trophy; they managed to move it a few feet and then abandoned the idea. On his accession in 1820, George IV was offered the thing as a gift by Mehemet Ali, Egypt's ruler, but the gift was not accepted. Ali renewed his offer to William IV, promising free delivery CIF; again the offer was declined. In 1849 the Government wanted it brought to London, but the Opposition objected. Several other proposals followed, one being made by the Sydenham Palace Company, who considered erecting it in the Egyptian Court of the re-sited Crystal Palace. The land on which the Needle lay was then sold and it seemed doomed to destruction by the breakers when General Alexander went out to inspect it and obtained enough support back home, notably from the surgeon, Sir Erasmus Wilson, to have it shipped to London; meanwhile the Metropolitan Board of Works offered the Embankment site. A special cylindrical iron barge was made to carry the obelisk, the designer of this eccentric craft being Benjamin Baker, one of the two partners who were later to build the Forth Bridge. So in 1877 the tug *Olga*, with the cylinder in tow, steamed out of Alexandria harbour. She ran into a storm and to save the lives of the crew the cylinder was cast off. Later it was found by another steamer and towed into Vigo; in time it reached London and was at last erected in 1878 where we now see it. A year later the companion obelisk was transported to New York.

Cleopatra's Needle, over sixty-eight feet high, is a monolith of pink granite, a pleasing, textured object of abstract geometrical form which makes a good focal point on the Embankment. It stands on a pedestal

A Victorian stone building in the Tudor style opposite Temple Stairs, until recently the Hall of the Incorporated Accountants. 'Not all late Victorian architecture was bad.'

and is flanked by two fine sphinxes sculpted by Vulliamy; apparently they were placed by the contractor facing the wrong way, that is, towards the obelisk. One of the inscriptions on the pedestal reads:

'The obelisk prostrate for centuries on the sands of Alexandria was presented to the British Nation A.D. 1819 by Mahommed Ali, Viceroy of Egypt, a worthy memorial of our distinguished countrymen Nelson and Abercromby.'

Within the pedestal are two large jars containing a strange collection of odds and ends, including a standard foot and a standard pound, a complete set of British coins of the period of erection, a parchment copy of a translation of the obelisk's hieroglyphics, several Bibles in different languages, a case of cigars, a box of hairpins, a dozen photographs of attractive English women of the time, a copy of *The Times* for the day the obelisk was raised, specimens of submarine cables, Bradshaw's Railway Guide and a portrait of Queen Victoria.

Savoy Hill runs down to the Embankment just before we pass under the dark and echoing canopy of Waterloo Bridge, and a little way up the hill stands the SAVOY CHAPEL. Notice a relic of the old bridge under the arch and notice too the dramatic perspective view below the bridge towards the south. Beyond the bridge on our left lies SOMERSET HOUSE, which, as in the case of the York Water Gate, we must imagine as it was intended to be seen before the Embankment was built, rising straight out of the river. The central water-gate is particularly fine. It seems a pity that the broad flat roof above the riverside podium has not been converted into a public garden and promenade with a lively *al fresco* café.

A river-police station and pier lies on the east side of Waterloo Bridge, and a little further on is moored Scott's ship H.M.S. DISCOVERY with its wooden sides two feet thick to resist the pressure of the Antarctic ice. Then comes H.M.S. WELLINGTON, the only floating Hall of a City Company, that of the Honourable Company of Master Mariners. After that is H.M.S. PRESIDENT, the training ship of the London Division of the Royal Naval Volunteer Reserve, escorted by H.M.S. CHRYSANTHEMUM. DISCOVERY was a Scout headquarters not long ago, but it has now been taken over as another escort ship to PRESIDENT. These vessels make a pleasant contribution to the riverside scene and take the eye away from the confused assembly of buildings on the far side of the river.

There is a bold great archway on the river front here, giving entrance to TEMPLE STAIRS, a detail of Bazalgette's Embankment which is strong and impressive.

On the other side of the Embankment is a small garden broken by the entrance to the Temple Underground Station. In the garden are more statues, including one on the south corner of BRUNEL by Marochetti. (London's outdoor statues and monuments are on the whole remarkable only for their mediocrity; a rapid mental survey conveys to me only five good ones: Le Sueur's bronze of Charles I on horseback at the top of Whitehall, Westmacott's Achilles in the Park near Hyde Park Corner [virtually a copy of a Roman piece], Epstein's Madonna and Child facing Cavendish Square, Rodin's Burghers in Victoria Tower Gardens and Grinling Gibbons's figure of James II outside the National Gallery.)

Set back to the east end of the gardens, opposite Temple Stairs, is a Victorian stone building of two storeys in the Tudor style, originally the home of the first Lord Astor but until lately the HALL OF THE INCORPORATED ACCOUNTANTS. It was built in 1895, the architect

Q

being J. L. Pearson, and it indicates that not all late Victorian architecture was bad, even if it was usually eclectic. For its time, this is a fine piece of pastiche. Above it on a vane a gleaming galleon bounds along.

Now the TEMPLE GARDENS begin; they are in two parts, separated by Middle Temple Lane—delightful green spaces surrounded by buildings which are mostly Georgian or post-war reconstructions. In the past the river flowed along the garden's edge.

Between the Temple Gardens and Blackfriars Bridge stand a number of fairly large buildings of little architectural worth: they include the pompous climax of this walk, UNILEVER HOUSE built in 1931. Here is the site of Bridewell Palace and, long after its demise, of the Royal Hotel, an exclusive centre of late Victorian years.

On the right is BLACKFRIARS BRIDGE, built in 1869, below whose abutment from a small culvert the old Fleet Ditch flows into the river at times when the outfall sewer requires release from floodwater. We have now reached the edge of the ancient City.

The Fleet Sewer below Ludgate Circus looking towards the emergency storm gates into the river. This was once the open Fleet River.

10 | Along Thames Street to the Tower

OUR LAST WALK is along Thames Street, which runs fairly close to the river as far as the Tower of London: along the full distance of the old river wall of Roman days and the original busy wharfing and mercantile line of London from its birth up to the nineteenth century. Now the docks have moved downstream, the Second World War has left its wounds and we shall walk through an area which, though lively still in parts, is often like a ruined and deserted city. Nothing much has been done to rebuild the street since the war ended because a plan is afoot to widen the whole street as a City by-pass for heavy traffic. At one time this was a street, not only of warehouses, but also of churches, for in the Middle Ages two dozen stood along it or nearby. Now five only remain, all by Wren.

The street is forlorn and shabby now with damage, neglect and age, but it is fascinating to traverse, for it still retains many interesting structures and many relics of its long and lively waterside life of nearly twenty centuries.

From Blackfriars Underground Station we turn east for a short way up Queen Victoria Street, crossing the spot where the Black Friars Monastery once stood, now recalled by Ye (ornate and not very ancient) Black Friar pub, below the railway bridge. A few fragments of the monastery still exist hereabouts. Here also was the south-west corner of the old City Wall, at the spot where Queen Victoria Street and Upper Thames Street converge in a row of bolasters. On the left lie the unimposing offices of the world's most imposing newspaper, *The Times*, and close to it is Play House Yard recalling the theatre built here in Shakespeare's time.

On the right PUDDLE DOCK forms a short arm of the river and there within the walls of a bombed warehouse is now arising (1958) the parabolic arch of the City's new theatre—the MERMAID—which will have its own restaurant overlooking the river. An attempt was made back in 1616 to build a theatre on this same site, but then the City authorities frustrated it, fearing that the players, in their easy way, might be tempted to rob the royal wardrobe which was accommodated close by. Since then the Stage has become respectable, and on the 17th October 1956 the Lord Mayor of London himself, in the person of Sir Cuthbert Ackroyd, laid together as a symbolic foundation of the new theatre two

243

bricks—one from a bombed London dock, the other taken from the bedroom in which Mozart was born in Salzburg—thus confirming the goodwill of the City Corporation towards this venture. The charter read out by the Lord Mayor at this ceremony had a suitably Elizabethan ring: 'We, the Lord Mayor and Aldermen and Commonalty of the City of London, at the contemplation of the letters of Bernard Miles, and other poor players of London, and having regard to the fact that her Majesty sometimes takes delight in such pastimes, do welcome the said Bernard Miles and his Mermaid Theatre Company to use the exercise of playing at Puddle Dock and nowhere else within this City, providing they play not upon the Sabbath Day, nor play any matter tending to the dishonour of Almighty God, or to the displeasure of her Majesty, nor to the quiet peace and government of this City.'

A short way beyond Puddle Dock on the right is a commercial Victorian building (Nos. 12 and 13) standing on a part of the site of BAYNARD'S CASTLE, first erected here in 1100 but rebuilt in 1428 and virtually destroyed in the Great Fire. After that two turrets were reconstructed and survived as dwellings for a time. In 1540 Anne of Cleeves was living there and both Queen Elizabeth and Charles II supped there. A model of the castle can be seen at the London Museum.

Beyond Paul's Pier Wharf on Nos. 24–25 is a plaque reading: 'On a House on this site lived Hugh Herland, Chief Carpenter to Edward III, Richard II, Henry IV, Designer of Westminster Hall roof.'

We soon reach the first of the surviving Wren churches in the street—that of ST. BENET'S, facing Paul's Pier Wharf. A church stood here at least as early as 1181, and in 1260 it was called St. Benedict Wudewharf, being near 'High Timber Street or Hithe, so called from the timber or boards there taken up and wharfed' (Stow). After the Fire Wren designed a new church, and this was completed, as we now see it, in 1685, a charming Dutch-like square piece with red brick walls, stone quoins, carved swags over the round-headed windows, and a square tower surmounted by a lead dome and spire. This church was one of those scheduled for demolition during the last century, but luckily it was saved by being taken over by the Welsh Episcopalians in 1878.

The church inside has two small galleries at the north and west sides and there is much good carving, a fine Royal coat of arms and other details worth seeing. In the church which stood here before the Fire the body of Inigo Jones was laid in 1652, beside those of his parents, beneath a small monument for the making of which the King's Architect

St. Benet's Church by Wren.
(From Godwin's *Churches of
London*, 1839)

had left the sum of £100; this was to be 'in memorie of mee, to be made
of white marble and set up in the church aforesaid'. But that monument was destroyed with the old church, and now a small tablet on the
east wall, placed there by a descendant in 1878, recalls the association.*

We can stroll down the alley of PAUL'S PIER WHARF to the sudden
wide space of river and sky: behind us is the distant vista of Paul's dome
framed by close, grimy walls. On the river a police boat called *Winston*
swims by, followed in mid-stream by a huge, long, squat boat of the
South Eastern Gas Board, and then a small river bus. Near us some
steel lighters are moored and, in the swell of the passing gas-boat, they
boom a deep syncopation with the chiming bells of the Cathedral behind
us. We are gazing across the river now at BANKSIDE and only records,

---

* Most of the City churches are unfortunately open only at certain times, and
enthusiasts who wish to see the insides of them will no doubt either find out
what those times are or else manage to borrow keys from the vergers.

A glimpse of St. Paul's from the waterside up Paul's Pier Wharf. A corner
of St. Benet's Church can be seen in the distance.

books and old illustrations can recreate the area as it was when Bankside was London's leafy playground.

On the south bank the new power station by Gilbert Scott dominates
the medley of industrial buildings; then slightly to the left we can spot
a little white house with a red door. If we had a powerful telescope we
should be able to read an inscription on its wall: 'Here lived Sir Christopher Wren during the building of St. Paul's Cathedral. Here also in
1502, Catherine, Infanta of Castile and Arragon, afterwards first queen
of Henry VIII, took shelter on her first landing in London.'

That is a false statement in every way but the house is a pleasing little
one of the formal period of the early eighteenth century. Near it stand
others of the same age, undistinguished by any myths and all in a pitiful
state of neglect.

A little to the west are the premises of the London Hydraulic Power
Company, on which is an inscription stating that on the site stood until
1906 a house from where Sir Christopher Wren watched the building
of St. Paul's Cathedral—a story which in this case may be true. When
the Cathedral and all the City churches were completed, the view from
there across the river which Wren obtained must have been superb.
The dome of St. Paul's still rises above the present waterside confusion,
but the scene from the south bank is now spoiled, especially since the
erection of Faraday House in Queen Victoria Street.

Back in Thames Street, we find opposite No. 26 a little green retreat
containing some shrubs, a clump of hollyhocks, a few worn gravestones
and a ragged individualist asleep on a bench. A tablet on the wall close
by reads: 'Before Y' late Dreadful Fire This was Y' Parish Church of
St. Peters Pauls Wharf Demolished September 1666 and New Erected
For a Church Yarde Anno Domini 1675. This Stone was new faced and
lettered the wall and iron Pallisados erected—Mr. Boxes Traver, Mr.
William Norner, Church Wardens, Anno Domini 1770.'

Next on our left opposite Broken Wharf is a lonely square tower of
Portland stone crowned with a thicket of four pyramids and four pedes-
tals with pots, all that remains of Wren's ST. MARY SOMERSET
CHURCH, for the body was pulled down in 1872. From hereabouts we
can, in this year 1958, obtain a grand view across the weedy wilderness of
bombed sites of Paul's great dome and its round belly below.

Beyond Stew Lane and Darkhouse Lane we are in the furriers' district above Queenhithe. Strange tongues are spoken here and the names
on the doorways read Wolosker, Elishahoff, Nagioff, Klemin. . . .

To the north is the private staff garden of the Hudson Bay Company, and to the south an open roadway embellished with sturdy bollards of sculptural worth. We can walk down here to the old bay of QUEENHITHE, still in use as a river port, as we can see by the lighters which are moored there beneath the brick warehouses. At the south-east corner of Queenhithe we can once again catch a glimpse of the dome of St. Paul's through a gap between walls—one of those fascinating glimpses you get all over the City.

Back once more in Upper Thames Street we come to the churchyard of ST. MICHAEL QUEENHITHE. A church was here early in the twelfth century and was rebuilt by Wren, but this was pulled down in 1876. The tower, one hundred and thirty-five feet high, had a gilded ship in sail at the top, and this survives on a building on Huggin Hill just here. In Little Trinity Lane is the quiet and bedraggled churchyard of HOLY TRINITY THE LESS, redolent of amorous city cats on starry nights.

After this, a little way up Garlick Hill, stands Wren's ST. JAMES'S GARLICKHITHE, completed in 1687 but having a history going back to 1170. Says Stow: 'Of old time, on the bank of the river Thames, near to this Church, garlick was usually sold.' A square tower with a fine projecting clock of 1682 rises on the west side, and the keystone above the arched doorway is a charming cherub's head—one of a host of Thames-side cherubim. The inside contains some good wood carving, an organ of 1697, and some splendid wrought-iron sword rests and hatstands. Above the altar is a picture of the Ascension by Andrew Geddes, A.R.A., presented to the church in 1815; also a well-preserved mummy with a noble, hairless head which was found below the chancel in 1839 —perhaps one of the six Lord Mayors who were buried in the church. A warning quatrain reads:

> *'Stop, stranger, stop as you pass by.*
> *As you are now so once was I.*
> *As I am now you soon will be.*
> *So pray prepare to follow me.'*

The figure is now in a glass case, but in former days it was not imprisoned, and occasionally cavorting choristers would carry Jimmy Garlick around for a run with that sardonic humour frequently generated by small boys in a gang.

On the right of Thames Street now lies VINTNERS HALL, an Edwardian-looking stone building outside, bearing on its side down Vintners'

Clink Wharf by Bankside where the twelfth-century Palace of the Bishops of Winchester stood for five centuries.

Place a figure of a charity boy made of Coade stone in 1840. The hall was built in 1671, the architect being Edward Jarman, but the building has been altered a good deal since his time and was largely restored in 1948. Inside is a masterly carved staircase in its original seventeenth-century state.

Next comes the churchyard of ST. MARTIN VINTRY, at the corner of Queen Street; the church was not rebuilt after the Great Fire. Then a wide space of bombed sites and up on our right lies SOUTHWARK

BRIDGE, rebuilt in 1921, and no beauty. To the left we can see the
church of ST. MICHAEL PATERNOSTER ROYAL, with entrance in College Street beside the site of Dick Whittington's house. The church
was rebuilt by Wren between 1686 and 1694 and has a steeple of 1713
as graceful as that of St. James's Garlickhithe. The church was rather
badly hurt in the Blitz, but it is to be restored. On its south wall
can be seen five round-headed windows with chubby cherub heads as
keystones. Whittington, four times Lord Mayor, was buried in 1423 in
the pre-Fire church which he built here.

Some good eighteenth-century houses stand near the church in College Hill; and in College Street, near the great yellow brick wall of
Cannon Street Station which looms ahead, stands a red brick building—
the INNHOLDERS' HALL, which has a good seventeenth-century door.
It was damaged in both World Wars, but has been well restored.

Now let us look at CANNON STREET STATION rising ahead of us like
a cliff. It is a noble work of Victorian engineering completed in 1866

Looking east below London Bridge towards Tower Bridge, 'the last of the
Thames bridges before the sea . . . an imposing river gateway to London'.

for the South Eastern Railway by John Hawkshaw and J. W. Barry: six hundred and eighty-seven feet long, two hundred and two feet wide, one hundred and twenty feet high and composed of 27,000,000 bricks.

The great segmental roof of iron lost nearly an acre of glass during the Blitz which has not been replaced. The station is to be modernised, and if, as may happen, its curving roof and the two towers at the river end are removed, London's riverside will lose a dramatic piece of architecture. Let us hope that they may still be preserved. The station stands on the site of the old Steelyard, once the property of the Hansa merchants. Down on its south-west corner is Dowgate Dock, a small indentation for barges, and beside it is a riverside club. The ancient Walbrook trickles into the river here beside the station wall.

We now plunge right under the centre of the station through a dark archway and emerge into the short final stretch of Upper Thames Street; ahead runs the raised approach to London Bridge. Along here lie two more sad and unkempt little churchyards—those of ALL HALLOWS THE LESS and ALL HALLOWS THE GREAT. Here churches existed in the thirteenth century. Wren rebuilt the Great, but that was demolished in 1893. The Less was destroyed in the Great Fire and never rebuilt.

We reach another open, bombed area and there we can walk to the riverside again to gaze across at the row of warehouses belonging to the Hay's Wharf Company which now stretches from Tower Bridge up to Southwark Bridge. On our left LONDON BRIDGE runs across the river, and below one of the arches we can see the gateway to London's river— the distant Tower Bridge. At the southern end of London Bridge the square tower of SOUTHWARK CATHEDRAL (formerly St. Saviour's and before that St. Mary Overy) rises above the warehouse roofs. We can, if we wish, visit the place quite quickly by crossing the bridge, and we shall find that the nave is a nineteenth-century reconstruction in the Gothic style but that some old parts and several interesting monuments still survive; a few old fragments in the north transept, indeed, date back to Norman times, the east ambulatory is thirteenth century and the south transept is all fourteenth century, except for the Victorian south window. The square tower is also old, the lower part being fourteenth century and the upper fifteenth. In the south chancel can be seen the tessellated pavement of the Roman villa which once stood on the site. Within the building is the Harvard Memorial Chapel, with decorations of 1907, dedicated to the memory of the founder of the American

university, who was sired in Borough High Street by a local butcher, one
of a number of parishioners who in 1614 bought the church from James I
for £800.

Up on London Bridge we can look back and see on the immediate
right hand the 1833 FISHMONGERS' HALL, the only City Hall to have a
good riverside position. The stone building is a dignified one in a
Greek Revival style with a row of six Ionic columns on its river façade
and a balustraded terrace in front. It was designed by Henry Roberts,
his chief assistant at the time of building being George Gilbert Scott,
who was to become a ruthless restorer of many a mediæval church.
The grand banqueting hall with ceiling, curved, coffered and gilded,
is worth seeing here (though permission to enter will have to be obtained).

On the right of the bridge approach rises the vast Egyptian-type office
block called ADELAIDE HOUSE, built in the twenties by Sir John Burnet
and Tait.

We step down to the level of Lower Thames Street and find on the
right a church of 1676 hiding behind the high back of Adelaide House:
ST. MAGNUS MARTYR, one of Wren's most delightful churches. On its
south lies a small, dark courtyard with a tree, part of which once formed
the footway to Old London Bridge after the houses on the bridge had
gone and the whole bridge had been reconstructed. The filling walls in
the north and south arches of the tower were removed in 1768, and the
footway then ran below the tower.

> *'O City, city, I can sometimes hear*
> *Beside a public bar in Lower Thames Street,*
> *The pleasant whining of a mandolin*
> *And a clatter and a chatter from within*
> *Where fishmen lounge at noon: where the walls*
> *Of Magnus Martyr hold*
> *Inexplicable splendour of Ionian white and gold.'*

So wrote T. S. Eliot in one of his nostalgic London moods. Once the
beautiful tower of 1706 dominated the picture here and not the great,
bleak commercial temple of Adelaide House. But the fishmen of
Billingsgate near by no doubt look and behave and swear in much the
same way today as they have for generations past. Their strange billy-
cock hats are said to be descended from the helmets of the bowmen of
Agincourt, but why and how I cannot say.

A clock projecting from the tower of St. Magnus, made in 1709, overhung the road to the old bridge for many years. It is still there, but the original gilded figures which once decorated it have gone. The wonderful tower is square below, with Ionic pilasters above that, then a stone lantern, then a lead cupola and finally a lead lantern and spire, all crowned by a finial and weathervane. At one hundred and eighty-five feet it is only seventeen feet less in height than the Monument. In two senses, therefore, St. Magnus is the highest church in the City.

Inside is the 'inexplicable splendour' with tunnel-vaulted nave and side aisles separated from it by elegant Ionic columns. There is much masterly detailing, especially of carved woodwork, and there is a sweet smell of incense. Outside again, under the porch, we can see some curios—a piece of piling of Old London Bridge from the year 1176, and a piece of wood from a wharf of Roman London found below Fish Street Hill in 1931, while in the courtyard is a stone from the first arch of the old bridge uncovered in 1920.

Fish Street runs northward from St. Magnus and up there stands the MONUMENT, on the site of the parish church of St. Margaret, which was destroyed in the Fire. The parish was then joined to that of St. Magnus, whose Rector to this day receives a ground rent from the Monument. The last incumbent of St. Margaret's before the Fire was Geoffrey Wren, uncle to Christopher. As we have seen, the Monument once lay on the approach axis to Old London Bridge. It is two hundred and two feet high, which is the exact distance it stands away from the former bakery in Pudding Lane where the Great Fire, which it commemorates, began. We can climb to the top for the sake of the view.

Along Thames Street on our right lies BILLINGSGATE MARKET, an undistinguished building. For centuries Billingsgate has been a fish port, though today most of the fish sold here comes not by river as formerly but by road and rail, and it is now served by its own underground railway connections. The name probably comes from the Roman Belinus, who built Stane Street, which runs from London Bridge and passes through Billingshurst in Sussex. The present structure of yellow brick, Portland stone and ironwork replaced an earlier one of 1852 and was built for the City Corporation in 1877 to designs by Horace Jones, the City Architect, who, with J. W. Barry, the engineer, was also responsible for Tower Bridge.

Opposite the fish market at the corner of Thames Street and St. Mary-at-Hill is the COAL EXCHANGE, by J. B. Bunning, opened in

The roof of the Coal Exchange built in 1849, 'a very poor man's Pantheon'.

1849. This was an advanced building for its time, being very light in its iron-rib structure. It is entered below a round tower and within lies a wide circular hall, sixty feet in diameter, top-lit and having around it three tiers of galleries made of ornamental wrought ironwork.* On its site once stood a tavern where collier captains conducted their business with the coal merchants. Here too once stood a ROMAN BUILDING, parts of which can still be seen below the Coal Exchange, consisting of a small room with walls of flat bricks and a pillared hypocaust (warm-air sub-floor heating system). These Roman remains have often been regarded as part of a bathing establishment, but it is as likely that they were part of a villa or possibly the office premises of a merchant.

* Professor Henry Russell Hitchcock, who knows about Victorian architecture, thinks the Coal Exchange is a monument for the ages. Mr. J. H. V. Davies has remarked on the radio that it is merely 'shoddy-ornate, a very poor man's Pantheon'. The truth lies in between. The detailing is unexceptional but the advanced structure and the pure and simple geometry of its forms make this a remarkable building, especially inside. The interior now has a neglected air and it certainly deserves to be treated respectfully with fresh paint, good light fittings and an interesting new floor to take the place of the original mariner's compass of inlaid woods which was destroyed during the war.

Let us stroll a short way up the narrow lane of St. Mary-at-Hill to inspect two interesting buildings there, noting as we go the pleasing street vista ahead of us. The first building on our left is the stone-faced little City Hall, built in 1786, of the WATERMEN'S AND LIGHTER-MEN'S COMPANY, a sadly depleted body since the arrival of steam. The Company's Hall formerly stood just south of the churchyard of All Hallows the Great, facing the river off Upper Thames Street. The façade of the present Hall is a formal and carefully designed one with Ionic pilasters, a generous window in three parts with the centre part arched and fanlit, and some pleasing carved decorations. Inside hangs the portrait of the Company's most worthy member—John Taylor, the Literary Bargee and watermen's champion. Among his creative achieve-ments was the planning of the river pageantry for the wedding of Lady Elizabeth, daughter of James I, with Prince Frederick, the Elector Palatine. His considerable volume of doggerel may be no more than a literary curiosity, but it has vigour and is of some interest to the social historian. Taylor died in 1653 and was buried, like others of his calling, in the churchyard of St. Martin-in-the-Fields.

Beyond the Hall stands the church of ST. MARY-AT-HILL, the foun-dation of which goes back at least to the twelfth century. Most of the old church was burnt in the Fire, though the tower and some of the walling survived. Wren reconstructed it in the 1670s, but the tower was rebuilt in 1780 and the west wall in Love Lane in yellow brickwork

'Guns from old ships of the line derated to a peaceful, landlubberly job.'

was rebuilt by George Gwilt in the 1780s. Inside, the aisles are separated from the nave by four Doric columns and there is an arched ceiling with a central cupola. There is a good west gallery and an interesting organ of Charles II's time built by Father Smith, who made the organs for St. Paul's Cathedral and Westminster Abbey. The church was redecorated in 1849 and the wood carving, of excellent quality and design, was executed by W. Gibbs Rogers at that period. Alone of the Wren churches, St. Mary-at-Hill retains its old box pews. By the north door is an old carved Resurrection stone preserved from the old building, and to the north of the church lies a little secret churchyard.

Back in Thames Street we pass the CUSTOMS HOUSE, a simple classical building of 1817 partly damaged by bombing. On the riverside here to the east we can find a broad quay in front of the building decorated with a few trees and there by the river steps we can sit for a while and watch the river life go by.

On the hill to the north of the Customs House rises the strange and beautiful Gothic-style spire, with flying buttresses, of ST. DUNSTAN'S-IN-THE-EAST. The rest is a bombed ruin, though parts of the outer walls still stand upon the raised area above the narrow road which curves gracefully around its base. The church has a Saxon foundation and was almost destroyed in the Great Fire, though the outer walls were then preserved. Wren reconstructed it with nave and aisles divided by Tuscan columns and he designed anew the Gothic tower with its steeple which still stands intact to prove that the Gothic revival did not begin in the nineteenth century. In 1810 the walls of the church were found to be out of the perpendicular and between 1817 and 1821 it was rebuilt in the Gothic manner by David Laing.

Along Thames Street again we come on our right to the TOWER PIER of the Port of London Authority from where river trips run to Greenwich and where every twenty-five minutes water buses depart for Westminster. From here also run the Eagle steamers to Southend and Margate and No Passport trips to the Continent. Some old bollards lounge around here— guns from old ships of the line derated to a peaceful, landlubberly job.

And at last we reach the grand climax—Tower Hill and the TOWER OF LONDON. Being a Londoner born and bred, I have, of course, never been inside the place. Let us therefore buy a guide-book at the kiosk and explore it together under official guidance. My own chance to discover London's most venerable monument has come at last.

PART III

CONCLUSION

'While the city comes into existence for the sake of
life, it continues to exist for the good life.'

Aristotle

A keystone in Chelsea Old Church

R

WE HAVE WATCHED London's riverside changing through the centuries and we have seen it from Chelsea to the Tower fixed and still in the moment that is today. How will it change in the future?

Perhaps it will all vanish soon in an explosion so hot that the river will boil from Teddington down to the Nore. Frank Lloyd Wright, the American architect, has said that an atomic bomb is the only adequate solution of London's problems—but then he is a perfectionist. Let us take the view that life and London will go on for many centuries yet and let us consider, in that hope, what could happen for the best in the future to the riverside of the greatest city the world has known.

Many schemes have been proposed from time to time for its improvement which have come to nothing. As we have seen, there was that idea which nearly came off after the Fire for a 'fair key or wharf on all the river side' along the edge of the City. During the dock-building days of the early nineteenth century many grand plans for new bridges and docks were projected but never executed, such as Willey Revelley's 1795 schemes for the Isle of Dogs. The younger Dance produced a monumental layout between two bridges which were to replace the old London Bridge (pp. 264–5); but Telford's single-arch bridge of iron was among the most famous of these bridge projects: it was a magnificent structure of six hundred feet span which failed to materialise mainly on account of the difficulties of the high approaches and the effect these would have on local land values. The nineteenth century produced many schemes for the Thames, especially in the way of patent bridges. John Martin, the epic painter, who was interested in sewage schemes as well as in depicting the Fall of Babylon, designed a riverside project with long colonnades, like those he painted on his huge canvases, which ran along both sides of the river to take railways and pedestrian ways from Hungerford Bridge to the Tower and from Vauxhall to Deptford.

⟦ POST-WAR PLANS

Since the war produced clearances by fire and explosion many ideas for improvements have been put forward, most of them dealing with some specific local problem, such as the provision of fly-over and fly-under approaches to some of the busier bridges, the gradual development of the South Bank with embankments and gardens, the rebuilding of

258

Thames Street as a wide arterial by-pass to the City, the construction of a huge Autosilo, or multi-storey garage, near the north approach to Southwark Bridge, the clearing of the site south of Westminster Abbey to form a public garden, the creation of the area around Westminster Abbey as a quiet pedestrian precinct, the construction of a great double-decked pier at Westminster as a restaurant and dance-hall overhanging the river—to mention only a few.

The Forshaw–Abercrombie Plan for the LCC of 1943 provided some strong recommendations for the river banks, mainly concerned with clearing unsightly and semi-derelict warehouses, the building of roads and open spaces on the south from County Hall to Southwark Cathedral, the removal of all the railway bridges across the river, the building of two new road bridges at Charing Cross and the Temple, and the running of all railway lines in tunnels under the river. The general zoning tendency of the plan is to reduce the amount of industry along the riverside, to reduce wharfing above London Bridge, where its existence is less justified today than it was at one time, and to increase there the number of residential, public and business buildings. It rightly advocates 'multiple use' of the river as an industrial artery, a place of recreation and an architecturally dignified element in London as a whole. In general the plan would open up, and tidy up, the present overbuilt squalor of the river banks, 90% of whose length has been closed in. The plan aims to open up a third of their length. It also aims to break down the isolation and cultural sterility of the area south of the river. Within its limitations this is a good and practicable plan for the immediate future.

There have been other post-war plans, such as that prepared by the Royal Academy and another by the Royal Institute of British Architects. The RA Plan was superficial and was concerned mainly with street lay-out and the provision of pompous, formal vistas. Other post-war ideas included one for extending the Embankment from Chelsea to Putney Bridge on the west and from Blackfriars to the Tower on the east, thus providing a riverside drive eight miles long which would be very monotonous.

[THE CITY'S OWN PLAN

As for the City itself, a special official plan was published in 1951 by C. H. Holden and William Holford which had some excellent and imaginative proposals, including those for visual satisfaction. The authors think that the seventeenth-century scale of the City should be preserved and that the great Cathedral should remain the dominant focus. And they suggest that the Cathedral should have a new approach from the river so that 'the King's barge would again be able to moor at St. Paul's steps and a terrace would be provided where not only the King but his subjects could stand and watch the multifarious activities of the most fascinating river in the world'. From that terrace one could walk up to the south portico of St. Paul's, passing the College of Arms on the left and emerging into a new open space on the south side of the cathedral. To quote again :

'Water buses would no doubt call at the new landing in summer and it would be one of the most popular approaches to the Cathedral for sightseers. If there were a pedestrian walk along the river the new approach would become more than occasional or processional; and a host of City workers would be able to see the sights of the river in the lunch hour, or on the way from Blackfriars Station, and then see St. Paul's revealed by stages as they mounted from level to level.'

The authors also propose a radical, long-term reconstruction of Thames Street as a two-level artery having a road for fast traffic above and a broad road for warehouse traffic below; opportunities for pedestrian access to the river would be provided and the upper road could serve as a shelter for a pedestrian way below; here and there the lower road would connect with open spaces—for instance, near St. Dunstan's-in-the-East. New offices might displace some of the old warehouses and occasionally a restaurant or pub could be built overlooking the river. Another suggestion is that the new buildings along Thames Street could be warehouses below and offices above, the offices being set back to provide a pedestrian walk overlooking the river—possibly one with a distinctly maritime character. 'A riverside pedestrian walk from Blackfriars to St. Paul's Steps or even to Southwark Bridge would be one of the sights of London.'

⟦ THE THAMES BARRAGE

Not forming an integral part of any of these post-war plans is the big idea of the Thames Barrage. The Thames below Teddington is not, strictly speaking, a river at all in the sense of a stream which flows constantly in one direction; it is an estuary where the water flows up and down twice a day with the tides. A barrage, built say at Woolwich,

The riverside walk below Upper Thames Street with a maritime character as proposed in the Holden and Holford post-war reconstruction plan for the City. (A drawing by Gordon Cullen from *The City of London: A Record of Destruction and Survival—with a Report of Reconstruction*, Architectural Press.)

would stop this flow of the tides and would make the Thames as it ran through London a true river.

This idea of a dam built across the river below London has been propagated by a number of enthusiasts for some time. As long ago as 1858 a Mr. Robinson proposed a dam at London Bridge to create a tideless river for docking upstream, but, as we have described, the river was then like an open sewer and the tides were needed to clear it. So nothing came of that. Then between 1904 and 1907 Mr. Thomas W. Barber, civil engineer, began to propound his scheme for a barrage at Gravesend through his Thames Barrage Association. This aroused considerable interest, but was eventually turned down by the authorities; the PLA was about to be born and more urgent matters then needed attention.

In 1935 a second Thames Barrage Association was formed to advo-
cate the building of a barrage at Woolwich, its chairman being Lieut.-
Col. Lionel Beaumont-Thomas, M.C., until 1942, when he was killed in
action. A great deal of research and planning went into the scheme, and
in 1938 it looked as though the PLA was going to notice it, but again
nothing happened, this time because war was in the offing and a barrage
in wartime would inevitably be bombed.

Two designs for the dam were made by the TBA, the second and
improved one in 1938. This latter consisted of a roadway passing across
the river over a series of sluices; at either end locks would raise and
lower fairly small vessels, such as barges, while on the south a short
ship canal, five hundred feet wide, and having three locks at its eastern
end, would lift and lower the larger sea-going vessels. Running off this
canal to the south would lie a row of non-tidal berths. The whole dam
would cross the river just above the entrances to the Royal group of
docks and well above London's main sewage outlets. The whole river
above the barrage would thus become tideless and the river would flow
down continuously in one direction through London at an average speed
of about three-quarters of a mile an hour.

The advantages of the barrier would be several. Freedom for shipping from the time restrictions of the tides, and continuous access to
every dock and wharf above Woolwich would be possible. A cleaner
river would result and no unsavoury and unsightly mud banks would
be revealed, as they are now at low tide. Shipping above barrage would
always be water-borne and thus free from the present hull strains on
mud-berths at low tide, while tidal scour on all river walls, bridge
foundations and camp-shedding would be eliminated, with a consequent
reduction of upkeep costs and river dredging. Water sports of all kinds
would again become possible—regattas, sailing, swimming, rowing and
perhaps in time fishing, as of old. Passenger transport could be greatly
increased on the river, and a final advantage would be an additional
bridge or causeway on top of the barrage at Woolwich.

Prosperity would return to the river with the return of craft of all
kinds and the whole riverside would be revivified and become as alive
again as it was when it served as London's high street. The river would
flow between its embankments with slow, clean dignity and would
never again reveal its sordid bed twice daily.

Little has been heard of the Thames Barrage scheme in recent years,
but no doubt we shall hear about it again before long.

❨ PRINCIPLES FOR THE FUTURE

Like other specialists who often fail to see the wood for the trees, architects and town-planners tend to work on the assumption that the present social-economic structure and its confused purposes are Acts of God and will go on for ever in the same old unsatisfactory way. But obviously the social and economic conditions which mould our culture and its visual expression in the environment are changing all the time: at some periods imperceptibly, at other periods, as now, with revolutionary speed.

One of the main objectives of modern society is to provide everyone with toil; this is called Full Employment. It is an absurd objective based on a moralistic, anachronistic philosophy of rewards and punishments which we have inherited as part of our tradition of patristic and punitive puritanism. The financial system with its needless debts and taxes is a big part of that tradition and some of its results are Subtopia and the spreading of an environment which is beginning to look like a vast labour camp.

Let us now imagine London's riverside of the future in a new light, in the light not of the boring, compulsive and depressing Workhouse State, but of the gay and genial Leisure State. It will be a state in which modern technology with its immense sources of physical power and its automatic factories are rapidly taking over most of the toiling and moiling which people have formerly been forced to do: a society in which the objective is no longer Full Employment, but Full Enjoyment. Under such conditions—prohibited today not by physical realities but only by false values and, deep down, by a self-immolating impulse generated by unconscious and needless guilt—the whole of our environment, including that of our riverside, will undergo a rapid and agreeable transformation. We shall at last come to realise the existence of that virtue in ourselves which the Dane, Steen Rasmussen, has clearly seen and expressed in his *London: the Unique City:* 'In English culture idleness has been the root of all good.'

Under conditions of leisure and free from financial anxiety and compulsive toil, people will have time to educate themselves in the things that matter to a culture—in that visual sensibility, for instance, which is now growing atrophied. With leisurely living, competitive and aggressive commercial values may not die at once, but gradually new co-operative and æsthetic values will develop and take their place as the

main formative force in life. London will then become as much a cultural centre of enjoyment as a mercantile and distributive centre—'not only commodious and serious, but merry and sportful'. The deep human impulse to create beauty will return. To quote Bernard Shaw: 'It all comes back to fellow feeling and appetite for fruitful activity and a high quality of life.'

The visual principles for the new world—especially in the art of townscaping—have been nowhere better expressed and clarified than in that remarkable monthly magazine, the *Architectural Review*. It propagates the human English tradition of the Picturesque, the tradition of making pictures of the environment wherever you happen to be standing and looking—the tradition of unity in variety, of coaxing past and present, the old and the new, into a fascinating and viable whole. As Joshua Reynolds put it: 'Variety and intricacy is a beauty and excellence in every other of the arts which address the imagination; and why not in architecture?' And what splendid visual possibilities the London riverside provides for variety and intricacy. There will be pleasures of every sort, especially for the pedestrian, in a quieter, calmer world than the tense, neurotic, despairing and exhausted one we know, having many quiet places and precincts away from the ceaseless, grinding traffic: places where one can stroll about in relaxed mood and enjoy the

An imposing project for twin bridges by George Dance the Younger, one of
the many schemes of the period for improving the Port of London, depicted
in an aquatint of 1800 by William Daniell. In the semi-circular place on the
left the Monument stands, while on the right is a new obelisk to commemorate
the recent naval victories; Fishmongers Hall and the churches of St. Magnus
and St. Olave have been pulled down. The steeple of St. Dunstan's-in-the-
East and the Tower of London can be seen in the distance.

urban scenes, where one can sit and dream and converse and watch life
going on; places where one can stand high up on a hanging garden
above the river in the sunlight and watch some brilliant river pageant,
ending as night falls in a flash of fireworks showering down into the
river at Westminster.

Night lighting will then be important as an art in itself. And so will
tree planting, for architecture comes alive only when it associates with
trees. That neglected element, the floorscape, will be consciously considered in its colour, texture and variety. Important also will be the
furnishing of small repeated utilities such as lamp-standards, seats, litter
bins, gutter gratings and river steps. And then the skyline, now ignored,
will need careful thought; in this we shall require many more vertical
features along the river, even if these serve no more useful purpose
than look-out towers or follies.

In the future many more dwellings will face the river, having generous, flower-filled balconies like small gardens or open-air rooms, and more buildings for music, drama and the arts, all 'buylded after gorgious and gallante sorte'; more restaurants, more dancing-places for the Dancing English, more pleasure-boat stations and riverside gardens too, both as large parks and as small, enclosed and intimate retreats.

The river will be fishful once more and as pure as the air above it. Like the wires, the power stations and the automatic offices, all the railways will have gone underground and some of the road traffic too, so that the pedestrian will be safe and free again.

Yet in the end, principles of æsthetics and technique will not by themselves make our civilisation beautiful. For that, a new approach to living in this age of technology is needed. The time has come to connect creative ideas in every sphere. Once we begin to do that the riverside, like the rest of the environment, will improve as if by magic, the true architects will come into their own at last, and the poets will once again be able to sing as Wordsworth could:

> *'Glide gently, thus for ever glide,*
> *O Thames! that other bards may see*
> *As lovely visions by thy side*
> *As now fair river! come to me.'*

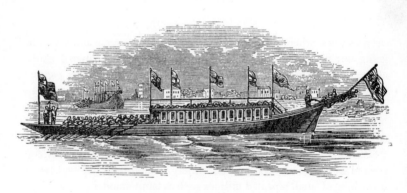

The old Lord Mayor's Barge from a
Victorian print.

SELECTED BIBLIOGRAPHY

GENERAL

Ormsby, H. *London on the Thames: A Study of the Natural Conditions that Influenced the Birth and Growth of a Great City.* 1924.

Belloc, Hilaire. *The Historic Thames.* 1907.

Belloc, Hilaire. *The River of London.* 1912.

Thacker, Fred. S. *The Thames Highway: General History.* 1914.

Kent, Wm. (Editor). *An Encyclopaedia of London.* 1951.

Linney, A. G. *Lure and Lore of London's River.* c. 1933.

Timbs, John. *Curiosities of London.* 1867.

Pevsner, N. *London: The Cities of London and Westminster.* 1957.

Pevsner, N. *London: Except the Cities of London and Westminster.* 1952.

Young, Elizabeth and Wayland. *Old London Churches.* 1956.

Stanley, Louis T. *The Old Inns of London.* 1957.

Maré, Eric de. *The Bridges of Britain.* 1954.

Jenkinson, W. *Royal and Bishop's Palaces in Old London.* 1921.

Head, G. *The Buried Rivers of London.* Trans. Auc. Inst., 1907.

Foord, A. S. *Springs, Streams and Spas of London.* 1910.

Humphreys, Geo. *The Main Drainage of London.* 1930.

Humpherus, Henry. *History of the Origin and Progress of the Company of Watermen and Lightermen of the River Thames.* 2 vols. 1887.

Mitchell, R. J. and Leys, M. D. R. *A History of London Life.* 1958.

THE PORT OF LONDON

Broodbank, Joseph. *History of the Port of London.* 2 vols. 1921.

Bird, James. *The Geography of the Port of London.* 1957.

Stewart, Bertram. *The Library and the Picture Collection of the Port of London Authority.* 1955.

Barrett, C. R. B. *The Trinity House of Deptford Strond.* 1893.

ROMAN LONDON

Royal Commission on Historic Monuments. *Roman London.* 1928.

Lethaby, W. R. *Londinium: Architecture and the Crafts.* 1923.

London Museum Catalogue. *London in Roman Times.* 1946.

Home, Gordon. *Roman London: A.D. 43–457.* 1948.

MEDIAEVAL LONDON

Riley, Henry T. *Memorials of London and London Life in the Thirteenth, Fourteenth and Fifteenth Centuries.* 1868.

TUDOR LONDON

Stow, John. *A Survey of London.* First published 1598.

STUART LONDON

Pepys, Samuel. *Diary.*

Evelyn, John. *Diary.*

Brett-James, Norman G. *The Growth of Stuart London.* 1935.

Hind, A. M. *Wenceslaus Hollar and His Views of London and Windsor in the Seventeenth Century.* 1922.

Howell, James. *Londinopolis.* 1657.

Bell, W. G. *The Great Plague in London.* 1924.

Bell, W. G. *The Great Fire of London.* 1920.

Reddaway, G. F. *The Rebuilding of London after the Great Fire.* 1940.

GEORGIAN LONDON

Summerson, John. *Georgian London.* 1945.

Strype, J. *Stow's Survey of London Brought Down to the Present Time.* 2 vols. 1720 and later editions.

Wroth, Warwick. *The London Pleasure Gardens of the Eighteenth Century.* 1896.

NINETEENTH CENTURY

Jerrold, W. B., illustrated by Doré, G. *London.* 1872.

Smiles, Samuel. *Lives of the Engineers.* 1861.

Beamish, R. *Memoir of the Life of Sir Marc Isambard Brunel.* 1862.

Rolt, L. T. C. *Isambard Kingdom Brunel.* 1957.

Welch, Charles. *History of the Tower Bridge.* 1894.

CHELSEA

Beaver, Alfred. *Memorials of Old Chelsea.* 1892.

Gaunt, Wm. *Chelsea.* 1954.

Kroyer, Peter. *The Story of Lindsey House, Chelsea.* 1956.

Davies, Randall. *Chelsea Old Church.* 1904.

267

Dean, C. G. T. *The Royal Hospital, Chelsea.* 1950.

WESTMINSTER AND WHITEHALL

Royal Commission on Historic Monuments. *Westminster Abbey.* 1924.

Besant, Walter. *Westminster.* 1907.

Russell, A. L. N. *Westminster Abbey: A Guide to the Buildings and the Monuments.* 1946.

Saunders, H. St. G. *Westminster Hall.* 1951.

Hastings, Maurice. *The House of Commons.* Architectural Review, Sept. 1950.

Palme, Per. *Triumph of Peace: a Study of the Whitehall Banqueting House.* 1957.

Westlake, H. F. *St. Margaret's, Westminster.* 1914.

THE STRAND

Chancellor, E. Beresford. *Annals of the Strand.* 1912.

Pendrill, C. *The Adelphi.* 1934.

Needham, R. and Webster, A. *Somerset House, Past and Present.* 1905.

Williamson, J. Bruce. *The History of the Temple.* 1924.

Ashton, John. *The Fleet: Its River, Prison and Marriages.* 1889.

LAMBETH

Ducarel, Dr. *The History and Antiquities of the Palace of Lambeth.* 1785.

Dodwell, Dr. C. R. *Lambeth Palace.* 1958.

SOUTH BANK AND SOUTHWARK

Rendle, W. *Old Southwark.* 1878.

Golden, Grace. *Old Bankside.* 1951.

Myers, S. P. *London South of the River.* 1949.

The South Bank Exhibition. Special issue of the Architectural Review, Aug. 1951.

Royal Festival Hall: Its Design and Construction. Official Record, 1951.

THE CITY

Royal Commission on Historic Monuments. *The City.* 1929.

Rogers, M. *Down Thames Street: A Pilgrimage among its Remaining Churches.* 1921.

Home, Gordon. *Old London Bridge.* 1931.

The Tower of London. The Ministry of Works Official Guide, 1954.

GREENWICH

Richardson, H. S. *Greenwich: Its History, Antiquities, Improvements and Public Buildings.* 1834.

EAST LONDON

Royal Commission on Historic Monuments. *East London.* 1930.

Sinclair, Robert. *East London.* 1950.

PROJECTS

London Town Planning Schemes in 1666. Journal of the Royal Institute of British Architects, Dec. 1919.

Trench, Lt.-Col. *Thames Embankment from Westminster Bridge to London Bridge with Proposed Quay.* 1827.

Forshaw, J. H. and Abercrombie, A. P. *The County of London Plan.* 1943.

Holden, C. H. and Holford, W. G. *The City of London: A Record of Destruction and Survival with a Report on Reconstruction by the Planning Consultants.* 1947.

Bunge, J. H. O. *Tideless Thames in Future London.* 1944.

MAPS

Wyngaerde, Antony van den, panorama, *c.* 1543–1550.

Hoefnagel, Braun and Hogenburg's *Civitates Orbis Terrarum, c.* 1572.

Agas, Ralph, *c.* 1575.

Norden, John, London and Westminster in *Speculum Britanniae,* 1593.

Visscher's panorama, 1616.

Hollar's panorama and drawings before and after the Great Fire.

Ogilby, John, 1677.

Rocque, John, 1746.

Dance, G., a Survey of the River between London Bridge and Blackfriars Bridge, 1799.

Laurie and Whittle, 1809.

Mogg, Howard, 1827 and later.

Stanford, 1862 and later.

Ordnance Survey maps of London, modern.

Mitton, G. E. (editor). *Maps of Old London.* 1908.

Gomme, Lawrence. *The Story of London Maps.* Geographical Journal, 1908.

INDEX

Bold numbers indicate illustrations

11